UNDERSTANDING THE
HOLOCAUST

Betty Merti

WALCH PUBLISHING

1   2   3   4   5   6   7   8   9   10

ISBN 0-8251-2708-4

Copyright © 1982, 1995
J. Weston Walch, Publisher
P. O. Box 658 • Portland, Maine 04104-0658

Printed in the United States of America

Contents

Acknowledgments

A special word of appreciation is due to the many Holocaust survivors who consented to being interviewed and to having their testimonies included in this book.

I am grateful to the University of Pittsburgh and to Jonathan Flint, coordinator of educational programs there, for allowing me to use the institution's fine libraries and other facilities during my research and preparation of this book.

I extend my gratitude to Dr. Alexander Orbach, assistant professor in the department of religious studies at the University of Pittsburgh, for his informative lectures on the history of the Holocaust and the Jewish people.

My thanks go to my colleague James D. Wehs, M.A. in Germanics, for his helpful advice concerning German history and politics.

Thanks are also due to Holt, Rinehart and Winston, publishers, for permission to reprint the chart "Estimated Number of Jews Killed in the Final Solution" from *The War Against the Jews*, by Lucy Dawidowicz, on page 149 in this text.

Finally, special thanks are in order for my family, my friends, and my students at Dorseyville Junior High School in the Fox Chapel Area School District. This book could not have been completed without the understanding and support of my husband, Edward, and my children, Val and Greg; without the encouragement of my friends Sandy, Marlene, Eunice, and George; and without the burning curiosity and enthusiasm of my students, who have eagerly undertaken this study of the Holocaust for the past ten years and have continually inspired me with motivation and sense of purpose.

Introduction

Adolf Hitler, The Creator of the Holocaust

Adolf Hitler, leader of the Nazi party, has been called the most evil man in history. In his quest for power, becoming dictator of Germany in 1933 was not enough. He strove to rule the world and to make all conquered peoples the slaves of the German "master race." And because anti-Semitism, or hatred of Jews, consumed his mind like a dreadful disease, he also wanted to make the entire Jewish people extinct.

Hitler came very close to accomplishing all his goals. Over 45 million people died in the world war he started. Before the Allied powers could bring his armies to defeat in 1945, his Nazis had, within six years, conquered and occupied most of Europe, enslaved millions of Europeans in Nazi mines and factories, and murdered 6 million of the 9 million Jews living in continental Europe. The Nazis also murdered 5 million non-Jewish people, among them Catholics, Lutherans, Gypsies, and many who opposed the Nazi regime.

The term **Holocaust**, which literally means "a fire that causes total destruction," has been used to describe the mass killing by the Nazis because it was like a great fire burning everything and everyone in its path.

No one before Hitler had ever tried to murder an entire group of people. For this reason, his crime has provided our dictionaries with a new word, **genocide**, meaning "the planned killing of an entire cultural or racial group of people."

However, Adolf Hitler did not invent anti-Semitism. Hateful feelings and actions against Jews had persisted throughout Europe for centuries before this Nazi leader came on the scene. In fact, many Nazi anti-Jewish laws were the same restrictions that other Europeans had imposed against Jews hundreds of years before.

Perhaps without this long European tradition of resentment toward Jews, the Holocaust might never have happened. In any case, the Holocaust was not an isolated incident that occurred during World War II. Its roots date back hundreds of years. That's why the study of it must also include an examination of the past.

Discussion Question: How is the Holocaust of the twentieth century related to ancient European history?

What Is Anti-Semitism All About?

The word **anti-Semitism** was first used by a Jew-hating German named Wilhelm Marr in 1879, ten years before Hitler's birth. Marr used the word to mean "opposed to Jews" whom he classified as the "Jewish race." Actually, Marr misused the word. There is no "Jewish race." Moreover, **Semitic** refers not to a group of people but to a group of languages. Hebrew, the ancient language of Jews still in use today, is just one of the many Semitic languages. A few others are Syrian, Arabic, and Ethiopic. Therefore, a Semite can be an Arab, an Ethiopian, a Syrian, or anyone else who speaks a Semitic language.

What Marr was actually saying when he called himself an anti-Semite was that he was opposed to anyone who spoke a Semitic language. Nevertheless, Marr's inaccurate definition has remained ever since. Anti-Semitism has come to mean prejudice against Jews, including hateful feelings, attitudes, and actions.

Anti-Semitism has also been defined as "dislike of the unlike." This definition partly explains why anti-Jewish feelings have persisted over 2,000 years. From ancient times, because Jews were exiled from their homeland in Palestine, they scattered far and wide. They settled in many lands among peoples whose customs and beliefs differed from their own. Cultural differences not only singled the Jews out from their neighbors but also often triggered suspicion and hostility.

Up until the end of the Middle Ages, Jews were persecuted for their religious beliefs. Judaism, the Jewish religion, is not only based on the belief of one God in heaven (monotheism), but is also a way of life. A code of religious laws governs what observant Jews eat, how they behave, even how they think.

No matter where Jews migrated or what people they lived under, the story was the same. They were always a minority religious group. Roman and Greek pagans, Christians, and Muslims alike frowned on Judaism's "strange" behaviors and beliefs. First they tried to persuade, then to force Jews to accept their God or gods and goddesses.

Jews rejected the deities of all others: the idols of pagans; Jesus, the Messiah of Christians; and Muhammad, the prophet of the Muslims. Believing they had a special covenant with God, Jews held fast to their own beliefs. This was how the trouble always started.

The so-called "Jewish Question" arose in many lands. "What should we do about this Jewish minority among us?" asked the angry and shocked natives. Superstition and fear soon took hold. People viewed Jews as aliens, or foreigners, living among them. They began to call them wicked and evil. They used them as scapegoats for every disaster that came along, including floods and earthquakes. They began to punish them. Finally, the passage of discriminatory laws made the mistreatment of Jews an acceptable practice in many communities.

Jews became social outcasts. Anti-Jewish laws stripped them of all rights including the privileges of owning land or of engaging in any profession to support their families. Jewish breadwinners were forced into occupations shunned by non-Jews: often trading and moneylending.

Their small numbers made them easy targets for abuse. As a result, religious persecution kept them on the move for centuries. Eventually, the diaspora, or Jewish settlements in countries other than Palestine (Israel), became worldwide.

Western Europe—especially the countries of Germany, France, and Spain—was the center of Jewish life during the Middle Ages. However, harsh persecutions between the eleventh and fifteenth centuries forced most Jews to migrate to Eastern Europe. There remained the heartland of European Jewish life until well into the twentieth century.

In the meantime, despite the increasing religious tolerance of the modern world, anti-Semitism did not disappear. It seemed the pattern of resentment and nonacceptance had too long been set.

As the medieval feudal economy gave way to industrialization and the growth of cities, Jews, with their long experience in trade and moneylending, joined with non-Jews and became involved in business and banking. Their participation in these areas helped to bring about economic progress in Europe. They also took part in the struggle for equal rights that had swept over Europe during the eighteenth and nineteenth centuries and eventually won their emancipation, or freedom. However, they remained the whipping boy for many problems. Whenever economic crisis or political revolution struck, people in need of an explanation still cried, "The Jews caused it, of course!"

Soon overly ambitious and unscrupulous politicians began to beat the drums of anti-Jewish prejudice to gain votes, power, and wealth. Anti-Semitism became a political weapon.

Adolf Hitler capitalized on anti-Jewish feelings among the masses, too, in order to gain votes. However, his anti-Semitism had nothing to do with religious beliefs. He and his Nazis cared less about religion than anything else.

The Nazis were racists; that is, they believed there were superior and inferior races of people based on their physical, mental, moral, and cultural characteristics. According to Hitler, Germans belonged to a superior Aryan or Nordic race while all non-Aryans—especially Jews—were inferior. Jews he labeled as the lowest form of human life. "Subhumans," he called them. Thus, Nazi anti-Semitism was pure **racism**.

None of these Nazi racial theories had any scientific basis whatsoever. In fact, Adolf Hitler, like Wilhelm Marr, was confused about the difference between language families and races of people. There is no such thing as an Aryan race. **Aryan** is really the name of a family of languages often referred to as the **Indo-European**. Not only Germans but nearly half the world's population speaks a language belonging to this group. Besides German, the Aryan family includes English, Dutch, Armenian, Lithuanian, Greek, Czech, Polish, Irish, Hindustani, French, Italian, and many, many other languages.

Readers of this book, then, should keep in mind that the Nazi usage of the word **Aryan** was actually a misnomer. It is being employed in this text only because it was the term in use during the Holocaust era.

Discussion Question: Why are people generally suspicious or critical of others with different manners or dress?

Why Study the Holocaust?

No words can make us truly see and feel and understand the Holocaust. Even the most brilliant writer would find it difficult to make up a tale like it. It is a real horror story. The events are not only sickening, they are beyond human understanding. The mind really cannot deal with 6 million murders. Nor is it easy to understand why and how human beings could have carried out this crime.

So why study about so much tragedy and pain? Why not forget about it and concentrate on more pleasant things? The philosopher George Santayana once said, "Those who cannot remember the past are condemned to repeat it." Many other scholars also believe that history repeats itself because people continue to make the same mistakes.

All the ingredients that made the Holocaust are alive today. For example, many countries in the world are experiencing political and economic problems such as Germany had before World War II. Totalitarianism, or total control of the government and citizens by one party and a dictator, also exists in many countries and threatens to take over in others. And people everywhere still harbor hostile feelings toward Jews and other minority groups. Remember, too, those Nazi killers were ordinary people like you and me.

Could such a thing happen again? What you are about to read should convince you that it can.

Discussion Question: Do you think we can improve our own behavior by studying the mistakes of others?

A Review of the Introduction

REVIEWING KEY POINTS

Exercise 1

1. What were Hitler's three goals? How did he almost accomplish all of them?

2. Explain how anti-Jewish feelings originated and why they became so widespread.

3. How did Jews come to have an "evil" image? Explain how this image led others to use them as scapegoats.

4. Name the three types of anti-Semitism and explain the nature of each.

CHECKING YOURSELF

Exercise 2
Matching Terms with Definitions

Directions: On your paper, make two columns of numbers from 1–10. For both Part A and Part B, match each word or phrase in Column I with a phrase from Column II that defines it. Your answers will be letters. (All the terms used here have appeared in the preceding pages.)

PART A

I—TERMS	II—DEFINITIONS
1. diaspora	A. The religion and culture of the Jewish people.
2. anti-Semitism	B. Except for Israel, the countries of the world that made up the Jewish home.
3. Holocaust	C. Term used for the Nazi massacre of Jews during World War II.
4. religious anti-Semitism	D. A religion based on the belief in one God.

5. genocide   E. How Jews were viewed because their customs and beliefs differed from the widely accepted pattern.

6. Judaism   F. The killing of an entire cultural or racial group.

7. Wilhelm Marr   G. Coined the word anti-Semitism.

8. monotheism   H. Hateful feelings, attitudes, and actions toward Jews.

9. Hebrew   I. Ancient language of Jews still in use today.

10. aliens   J. The earliest kind of anti-Jewish feeling.

PART B

I—TERMS

II—DEFINITIONS

1. Western Europe   A. Because Jews refused to change their ways, angry non-Jews wondered what they should do about them.

2. Eastern Europe   B. Nazi hatred of Jews based on the idea they were an inferior race.

3. emancipation   C. Heartland of European Jewish life in the twentieth century.

4. political anti-Semitism   D. Someone on whom to heap the blame for others' problems or mistakes.

5. racist anti-Semitism   E. Freedom

6. discrimination   F. Center of European Jewish life during the Middle Ages.

7. scapegoat   G. Mistreatment because of bias.

8. Palestine   H. Absolute control of all citizens and government by a one-party system led by a dictator.

9. totalitarianism   I. Using prejudice toward Jews to gain votes.

10. the "Jewish Question"   J. Ancient homeland of the Jewish people.

GIVING REPORTS

Topics to Research

1. The word **genocide.** What is the derivation of the word, who coined it, what year did it come into being, and why was it not used before that year?

2. The word **scapegoat.** Tell its derivation, give the meaning once used by ancient Jewish high priests, explain how that meaning is related to the current use of the word.

3. The word **holocaust.** Give its derivation, its literal meaning, and the reason it is used to describe the mass killing of Jews in World War II.

4. What is a Jew? Give a definition. Good sources: *What Is a Jew?*, by Morris Kertzer; encyclopedias.

5. Investigate the causes and effects of racism.

6. Areas of the world where there has been a resurgence of anti-Semitism (good source: the Anti-Defamation League).

7. Modern-day holocausts (post World War II) and the reaction of the world to them.

8. Statistics and literature concerning Holocaust denial and the reasons for and consequences of such thought.

9. Analyze the purpose and effectiveness of the national Holocaust Memorial Museum in Washington, DC. Why are such memorials important?

Books to Review

1. *Man's Most Dangerous Myth: The Fallacy of Race*, by Ashley Montagu.

2. *The Anti-Semite and the Jew*, by Jean-Paul Sartre.

3. *Bigotry*, by Kathlyn Gay, a look at the history of bigotry and racism in American society.

BULLETIN BOARD SUGGESTIONS

1. Illustrate three Nazi solutions to the "Jewish Question." Make use of colors: red, black, and white (Nazis); and yellow (star worn by Jews), blue and white (shirts worn by Jewish prisoners).

2. Show that the Holocaust is today's news too. Use current newspaper articles dealing with the Nazi era, the Holocaust, anti-Semitism, and so on.

AUDIOVISUAL AID SUGGESTIONS

1. Display a set of twenty "Posters of the Holocaust, 1933–1945" during this entire unit of study. **ADL**

2. Display actual photographs "The Nazi Holocaust, Series I and II," by Photo-Aids. **SSSS**

3. Present the color filmstrip *Understanding Prejudice* for a better understanding of scapegoating, stereotyping, and the myth of racial superiority. **ADL**

4. Show the color and black-and-white film *You've Got to Be Taught to Hate* as a discussion stimulator concerning prejudice as transmitted to children and adolescents. **ADL**

5. Present *Beyond Hate*, a 90-minute color video in which Bill Moyers, through interviews and meetings with others, examines the historical, philosophical, and psychological roots of hatred. **PBS**

NOTE: A list of audiovisual aid distributors and their addresses appears on pages 225 and 226 of this book.

Religious Anti-Semitism

ANTI-JEWISH FEELINGS DURING ANCIENT TIMES (to the Mid-Fourth Century)

Pagan Resentment

The writings of the Greeks and Romans tell us that anti-Jewish feelings existed in those ancient civilizations. As pagans, or idol worshippers, most early peoples held polytheistic beliefs that included the worship of not only many gods and goddesses but also of emperors who claimed to be "divine."

Judaism, in contrast, is based on the belief in one spiritual God in heaven, whom Jews serve in part by honoring many laws governing behavior. Trouble and hard feelings arose between Jews and their neighbors whenever these laws prevented Jews from participating in community activities such as bowing down to pay homage to emperors or idols, eating certain foods during festivals, or working on the Jewish sabbath. Occasionally, proud emperors punished them. Their Roman and Greek neighbors frequently called the Jews atheists, or complained that they were lazy, superstitious, and unfriendly.

However, except for this type of occasional rumble, Jews got along fairly well with their ancient neighbors. Outright attacks on Jews rarely occurred. Many leading statesmen who cared little about their subjects' religious practices gave Jews permission to practice their Judaism. Some Roman nobles. in fact, accepted the Jewish faith themselves. And as of A.D. 212, Jews were fully qualified Roman citizens. Many even held public office.

Early Christians and Jews

While some emperors granted Jews privileges, early Christians did not fare as well.

The first Christians had been practicing Jews. Jesus Christ and his twelve apostles were Jews. The Old Testament, too, was written by Jews. Judaism, however, had split into two groups. One group came to believe that Christ was the Messiah, or savior. They became Christians, or the followers of Christ.

The other group refused to accept Christ as the Messiah. These Jews who rejected Christianity are the persecuted group who have clung to their Judaism to this day.

When Christianity became a distinct, separate religion from Judaism, the Romans began to persecute the Christians as heretics, or believers in an unacceptable faith. For three centuries Christians suffered horrible punishments. Romans accused them of blasphemy, or contempt for God. They blamed Christians for causing droughts and famines and other calamities. To punish them, Roman authorities destroyed churches and holy books. Many Christians were killed—some by being thrown to the lions in the Roman sports arenas.

Despite pressure from Roman authorities,

Christianity began to take hold and eventually spread to many parts of the Roman Empire. Then in A.D. 312 the tables were turned for Christians and Jews. From that point on, Judaism, not Christianity, was out of favor with the Roman authorities.

Discussion Question:	Explain how Judaism is the "parent" religion of Christianity.

CHRISTIAN PERSECUTIONS DURING THE MIDDLE AGES IN WESTERN AND CENTRAL EUROPE (to A.D. 1500)

Introduction

In 312, Emperor Constantine the Great made Christianity the official religion of the Holy Roman Empire. This now meant the government was responsible for carrying out Church affairs. Even after the Roman Empire fell in the late 400's, Church and government remained tied together for the next 1,200 years. For Jews, as well as for other nonbelievers, this spelled trouble.

Attempts to Convert Jews

In the newly Christianized Roman Empire, Church and state authorities expected all citizens to accept Christianity. Church leaders who took over the responsibility of converting Jews did so in earnest, for they believed Christianity to be the only true faith.

Conflict soon arose, for few Jews were willing to give up their own religion. Angry Church leaders began to regard Jews as evil people.

At the end of the fourth century, a new charge blackened the Jews' "evil" image even further. They were blamed for having caused the crucifixion of Christ. This charge was to create much suffering for Jews throughout the Middle Ages, for now the name of "Christ-killer" followed them wherever they went.

Throughout the medieval period, Christians continued to pressure Jews to convert. In some cases, Jews were even forced to be baptized, or to undergo the rite of admission to the Christian Church. Once baptized, whether by force or consent, a Jew was fully accepted into the Christian community. However, state and Church law strictly prohibited a baptized Jew from ever returning to his original faith of Judaism. If he did, he was condemned and tried in court as a heretic. Heresy, or opposition to Church teachings, was a major crime against Church and state. The penalty was death.

In the sixth century, Pope Gregory I (590–604) forbade the practice of forced baptism. He urged Christians to use peaceful means to convert Jews. Many Christians followed his advice. They constantly exposed Jews to Christian teachings but at the same time protected them from harm. On the other hand, there were Christians who believed Jews should be made to live in shame as punishment for their stubbornness. And in some places, the forced baptisms continued.

Laws Against Jews

Some Church leaders became anxious that Jews might sway Christians against Church beliefs. They urged Christians to stay away from Jews. Finally, to segregate both groups, both Church and state passed anti-Jewish laws. Another reason for the laws was that the authorities hoped the restrictions would make Jews so uncomfortable that they would change their minds about becoming Christians.

These discriminatory laws made Jews second-class citizens. They were not allowed to hold public office, to be in the army, to own land, to engage in any craft or profession, or to marry Christians. No Jew could testify in court against a Christian, but the reverse was not true.

Furthermore, Jews were forbidden to own Christian slaves. Since agriculture was the leading occupation of these times, and everyone routinely used slaves as the main source of labor, this law put Jews, many of whom were important farmers, right out of business. In addition, all Jewish property was taken and given away to others. And Jews had to pay taxes just for being Jewish!

Jewish religious activities were curtailed, too. The celebration of the festival of Purim was outlawed, and Passover had to be postponed until after Easter. The building of new synagogues was also forbidden. Furthermore, any Jew caught trying to convert a Christian to Judaism received the death penalty.

Jews soon became social outcasts. Denied of all rights to own property and to earn a living, they went off by themselves to live in separate communities called **ghettos**. There they engaged in many crafts to support themselves. But in the outside world, they had no choice of jobs.

They turned to trading. At first, they dealt only with other Jewish communities in widely scattered areas. Later, they developed and expanded trade routes across Europe to Asia and North Africa and peddled their wares between medieval cities. Because cities were the places where Jews earned their livelihood, they became urban rather than rural residents.

In spite of the harsh anti-Jewish laws, there was not too much hostility between Jews and most Christians during the so-called Dark Ages (500–1000) of the medieval period. Although they were outsiders, Jewish traders fulfilled a need in the Christian community, for they were the only ones who dared foreign trade routes. Business dealings created much interaction between the two groups. Moreover, in some medieval cities, Christians and Jews still lived side by side.

The strongest anti-Jewish feelings came mainly from the higher-ups, the Church and state authorities. Yet they too recognized the positive effect Jewish trading had on the economies in their lands.

Discussion Question: Even though the Jewish trader had business dealings with the Christian community, how was he still an outsider?

The Crusades Lead to Pogroms

Eventually anti-Semitism began to infect the masses. By 1096, the relatively calm relationship that Jews had enjoyed with the general population had broken down completely. This was not only the year of the first Crusade but also the real beginning of the pogroms, or violent attacks on Jews by angry mobs of non-Jews.

The Crusades, a series of wars waged by Christian leaders between 1096 and 1271 to reclaim the Holy Land of Jerusalem from the Muslims, became a nightmare of persecution for Jews.

Christians thought that Muslims, as infidels or nonbelievers in the "true faith," had no right to occupy the Holy Land, the birthplace of Christianity. In 1096, as European knights from France and Germany set out to recapture it, great throngs of people—monks, nobles, commoners—joined them. Some were inspired by the holy cause. But the greater number of Crusaders were peasants looking not only for an excuse to break away from their feudal landlords but also for a chance to adventure and plunder.

The Crusaders began a mass march down the Rhine River Valley in France and Germany, through Bohemia (now the Czech Republic), and across the continent. An important trade route, the Rhine Valley was the center of the Western European Jewish community.

All along the way, troublemakers and fanatics whipped up the mobs to a religious frenzy. "Why wait to get to Jerusalem to kill the Muslim infidels? What about the Jewish infidels in our midst? Hep! Hep! Death to the Jews!" the

Crusaders shouted. The unruly mobs began a wave of attacks. The synagogue, or Jewish temple, which always stood at the center of Jewish communities, made Jews easy to find.

Jews tried to battle the mobs but were overpowered. Church and government leaders also tried to protect them. Local bishops worked out "protection contracts" promising to send out their militias. They hid Jews in their castles. Kindhearted town leaders and townspeople also opened their homes up as shelters. Often these friendly gestures saved lives. In other instances, however, the frightened bishops' militias deserted Jews whenever the mobs became too great. Then the crowds massacred the Jews.

Sometimes the mobs gave the Jews an ultimatum: baptism or death. But most Jews remained steadfast to their faith. Some even committed suicide to avoid baptism.

Thousands were massacred. Synagogues were burned down, homes were looted, and entire Jewish communities were destroyed. Within a six-month period during the first Crusade alone, the Crusaders wiped out nearly one fourth of the Jewish population living in Germany and France—approximately 12,000 lives. The wildest massacres occurred in cities such as Speier, Worms, Cologne, Metz, Ratisborn, Treves, and Prague.

Surviving Jews reacted to the bitter experience of the Crusades in two ways: (1) Thousands left German lands and headed toward Central and Eastern Europe. Many made new homes in Poland, where King Casimir, eager for the expansion of trade and commerce in his domain, had invited them to settle. (2) Those who stayed behind sought greater protection from future pogroms. Realizing the protection contracts with the bishops' militias had been ineffective, they turned to kings and noblemen whose authority and stronger armies offered greater security.

The price was high. Before long, the royalty began to drain as much "protection" money out of Jews as they could. Some Jews became the "private purses of kings." It became common for a king to give "his Jews" to his creditors as a way of paying off his debts!

Discussion Questions: 1. Even in the face of persecution, why do you think some Jews decided to remain at home?
2. How would those who fled to the East also face many hazards?

Libels Lead to More Pogroms

During the twelfth century Jews also became victims of hideous libels, or false charges. These myths grew out of the ignorance, folklore, and superstition common to the Middle Ages, a time of witchcraft, demons, and spells.

One charge, which began in England and spread to Germany and France, accused Jews of ritual murder. This "ceremony" supposedly involved the kidnapping of a Christian child in order to drain him of his blood. This Christian blood was reportedly used as a wine substitute and for baking **matzo**, or unleavened bread, for Jewish Passover services. The blood was also said to remove a foul body odor from Jews. This rumor spread panic among gullible people, who reacted by drawing their blinds and keeping their children under lock and key during Passover time each year.

Another libel originating in Germany charged Jews with host desecration: stealing the wafer that is used to represent the body of Christ in the communion service of Christian churches, and then stabbing or puncturing it. There were rumors that the host bled, or became whole again, or caused the Jew who stabbed it to convert to Christianity.

As non-Christians, Jews also were accused of being devils or devils' agents out to destroy and take over the Christian world. In Vienna during the twelfth century, Jews were compelled to wear hats with horns. Medieval paintings actually show Jews with horns growing out of their heads and long pointed tails trailing behind them.

Of course, all these charges were barbaric and ridiculous. Many popes and government leaders urged the masses to ignore the myths. Nevertheless, superstitious people didn't listen. Now viewed as child-killers, devils, and religious enemies, Jewish communities came under attack every time a child was missing in a community or other disasters occurred. Jews were dragged off to secret trials and tortured until they "confessed." The torturers used the confessions to keep the myths alive. Then violent pogroms wiped out more thousands of innocent lives.

These libels forced many fearful Jews to leave their homes in Western Europe and seek refuge elsewhere. Many joined the trek to Central and Eastern Europe.

Discussion Question: How do all the libels reflect religious bias?

Moneylending, Another Black Mark Against Jews

After the eleventh century, Jews lost their important role as traders. Non-Jews, motivated by the new trade routes and new markets the Crusades had created, took over. The medieval economy was also changing. New markets had stimulated industry. Growing cities were replacing the old feudal manors. And money was becoming the most important ingredient in the newer economy.

With no choice of jobs open to him, the Jewish trader turned to an occupation no one else wanted—moneylending. Condemned by the Church as wicked and immoral because it did not represent an honest day's work or the sweat of a man's brow, usury, or collecting interest on loans, was considered an "un-Christian" practice.

In spite of this attitude, more and more people began to need and to borrow money. This increased demand only made money more

scarce. Everyone began to approach the Jewish moneylender for loans: merchants who needed capital, peasants whose crops had failed, kings who needed funds to pay mercenary soldiers, and even churchmen who wanted to build large cathedrals. Soon many people were in the Jewish banker's debt.

The Jewish banker was no longer an outsider. He was a very important part of an ever-growing money economy. However, this new "inside" role worked against him. Envious people began to look upon him as a competitor. He had what everyone else wanted—money.

Selfish kings and noblemen added to the moneylenders' problems. They not only demanded a percentage of the Jews' profits earned on interest but also continually pressed them for money for big loans, money for "Jewish taxes," and money for protection. To meet these demands, Jews were forced to charge higher and higher interest rates. Then outraged borrowers complained that Jews were greedy and money-hungry.

Kings and noblemen used Jews to cover up their own greed in yet another way. They raised taxes. And they assigned the unpopular role of tax collector to the Jewish financiers. Now anger about high taxes fell not on the upper classes who were the real villains, but on the unfortunate Jewish bill collectors.

All this activity put the Jew into a vicious money-circle. The rich grew richer, the poor grew poorer, and resentment toward the Jew as the middleman grew stronger and stronger. Oftentimes moneylenders were not even paid back. Some Crusaders who joined the movement to the Holy Land did so simply to get out of debt, for leaders of the Crusades had used the cancellation of all debts to Jews as an incentive to get people to join the cause. Borrowers or tax-weary subjects sometimes went to extremes. They even killed Jewish moneymen.

By the end of the thirteenth century, kings in debt, with an eye on Jewish wealth, used a new anti-Semitic weapon: total expulsion of Jews from their countries. All Jews were expelled from England in 1290, from France in 1306 and 1394, from some parts of Germany in the fourteenth and fifteenth centuries, and from Spain and Portugal in the fifteenth century. By doing this, the monarchs had simply erased their debts and had filled their royal treasuries with Jewish monies.

With expulsion, anti-Semitism took on a new dimension. Jews were now persecuted not just for religious reasons, but for their economic position as well.

Jews did not return to France and England until the seventeenth century. Not until the late eighteenth and early nineteenth centuries did they begin to migrate back to Spain and Portugal. By this time, non-Jews had long since taken over banking.

Discussion Question:	If the Jewish moneylender rendered a valuable service, why did he become unpopular in the Christian community?

The Black Plague, "A Jewish Conspiracy"

Early in the fourteenth century, a folktale that took root in France accused the Jewish people of conspiring to subvert and take over the Christian world. One rumor had it that Jews had appointed lepers to poison all the wells of Europe. Another story depicted the Muslim King of Spain as the villain who persuaded Jews to poison the wells.

When the black plague struck Europe in 1347, it killed one of every three Europeans. Now the world conspiracy myth exploded again. Fearful, superstitious people pinned the blame for the black death on "Jewish well-poisoners."

"Hep! Hep! Death to the Jews!" again rang out in the streets. Jews were dragged off to questioners who used vile tortures to make them "confess." The "confessions" supposedly revealed that Spanish Jews had worked with other European Jews to poison all the wells in order to exterminate the entire Christian community. The poison? A typical witch's brew of frogs, lizards, spiders, pieces of human hearts and, believe it or not, sacred host wafers.

For two long years, a violent wave of pogroms swept over Europe. The mobs used the popular execution method of the time: death by fire or hanging. Hundreds of communities in France and Germany were wiped out. Tens of thousands of Jews were killed.

And all for nothing. The truth was that (1) many Jews had died of the plague themselves, and that (2) the plague is not a waterborne disease but one carried by rat fleas.

As before, Church and government authorities had tried very hard to put a stop to the persecutions. Yet once again their words had gone unheeded.

The Jewish Badge Singles Out the Jew

The idea of marking the Jew with a badge or special piece of clothing began in medieval Europe in 1215 with Church law. For religious reasons, authorities wanted to prevent contact between Christians and Jews. By identifying the Jews with a symbol, Christians were more easily able to avoid them.

The use of a Jewish marker spread across Europe, varying in color, shape, and form from place to place. In France and Germany, where it was worn first, it was a yellow circle of felt—representing a gold coin, the symbol of Jewish involvement with money. In some areas, Jewish men were required to grow beards. Other identifying articles included a belt, a pointed hat, a black wide-brimmed hat, a long black cloak, a yellow star, a green or white patch, or other things, depending upon the place.

All Jews—men, women, and children—were compelled to wear the distinguishing badge or article of clothing. If caught not wearing it, a

Jew was heavily fined. In Sicily, even Jewish shops were marked with a circle.

Wearing the badges created many problems for Jews. No longer could they roam the countryside as free men. They became easy targets for abuse. The only others to wear such markings in the medieval communities were heretics and prostitutes. This badge was a wedge that drove Christians and Jews further and further apart.

The Ghetto Segregates Jews

By the fifteenth century, most Jewish communities in Western Europe had vanished. Pressured by the Crusades, libels, pogroms, and badges, many Jews had fled to lands east of the Rhine River. Kings had also expelled them from England, France, Spain, Portugal, and some German lands.

The reason Jews were not expelled from German lands altogether was that at this time there was no German nation as such. Germany was a group of "little Germanies," a widely scattered patchwork of German lands each inhabited by German-speaking peoples and ruled over by a king or noble. While some German kings expelled Jews from certain sections, others allowed many to remain or to resettle in their neighboring lands.

From the twelfth century on, the Church law forbidding Christians and Jews to dwell together had not been strictly observed. However, starting in 1555 this old law requiring separate living quarters was again enforced. A Church decree from Rome forced Jews living in the Papal States, or Church-controlled areas around Rome, to be confined to ghettos—Jewish sections of cities. The ghetto idea then spread to Jews in German lands. Eventually it affected Jews living in other Christian lands, too.

In some ways, ghettos were like prisons. Many were surrounded by high walls. Only two gates were permitted and both were guarded by Christian sentries. No Jew was allowed past the gates during the daytime except for business dealings in the Christian communities, and never without a Jewish badge. At night and always during Christian holidays, the ghetto gates were tightly locked. After curfew, any Jew caught in the city was severely punished.

In some cities, the ghetto consisted of only a few streets barred by gates. Most others, however, were small towns within the larger cities. Inside the ghetto walls lay homes, shops, a hospital, the school, and the synagogue. Synagogues were never permitted to be built higher than the surrounding churches of the outer city. But the houses of the ghetto were another matter.

The ghetto was never allowed to expand. Over the centuries, the Jewish population increased many times over, of course. To compensate for lack of space, Jews were forced to build upward, often adding as many as ten stories per building. Thus, from the Jewish ghetto arose Europe's first skyscrapers. But the overcrowding led to many problems. The ghettos became firetraps. Raging infernos often took many lives. So did improperly supported buildings that collapsed from too much weight and strain. Diseases spread into epidemics.

How did Jews in ghettos earn a living? Forbidden to trade, to lend large sums of money, or to enter any of the professions, some Jews became usurers for the poor of the Christian cities. Others became hucksters and peddlers who left the ghetto gates each day to call out and sell their wares in city streets. A Jewish huckster was permitted to sell only secondhand goods, never anything new.

Within the ghetto walls, however, Jews went about their daily routines. They participated in many trades and professions to fulfill their own needs. Denied education in Christian schools, they created their own schools within the ghetto, for the Jewish love of learning was a most important value. And although still forced to attend Christian services from time to time, they were able to practice their Judaism without interference.

Contact with the outside world remained open for business purposes, but at times it became unfriendly. Pogroms and expulsions still occasionally took place. Fanatics, roused by libelous rumors or during religious holidays such as Easter, led mobs to attack the ghettos. And Jews continued to be taxed severely. They had to pay not only overly high rents for living in ghetto homes, but also taxes for entering and leaving Christian cities, taxes to get married, taxes for the birth of every child, and taxes to bury their dead. Money still remained the Jewish ticket to life.

In the beginning, some Jews looked upon enforced ghetto life with relief. The walls and guarded gates offered at least some protection from attackers. As time went on, however, life in the ghettos became stifling, monotonous, and dreary. Many Jews, especially young ones eager for life's experiences, became bitter about being penned up. This bitterness was, of course, directed at the Christian world that kept them there.

As the Middle Ages drew to a close, the rift between Jews and Christians had become complete. Jews were to remain shut out from the mainstream of European life for several generations. This sad period between the sixteenth and the eighteenth centuries is sometimes referred to as the Dark Ages of European Jewish history.

Discussion Question: Imagine yourself as a Jew living in a medieval ghetto. Describe your feelings.

A Look Backward

We've come to the end of the Middle Ages. We've taken a very brief look at more than a thousand years of Jewish life under Christian rule in Western Europe. It is a sad story of separation. What began as a religious separation ended up as a wide separation of two peoples. Jews were on one side, Christians on the other.

After so long a time of so little contact, neither group was able to judge the other as real flesh and blood people. The thinking of the times had a lot to do with this tragic gap. Superstition, fear, and emotions ruled people's minds. Reason, common sense, and toleration had not yet entered the scene.

The Negative Stereotype of the Jew

Years of religious prejudice had produced a negative stereotype of the Jew in most Christian minds. No consideration was given to individual differences; all Jews supposedly had the following characteristics:

1. *Not a part of the regular community, Jews were strange outsiders, wanderers, without allegiance to any land. They couldn't be trusted.*

2. *Jews were devils or devils' agents who had rejected Christianity and crucified Christ. God had therefore condemned them to wander homeless all over the world and to suffer. They deserved all the punishment coming to them.*

3. *Evil Jews were out to take over the Christian world. That was why they spread out and developed "connections" everywhere. They were well-poisoners, child-killers, religious enemies.*

4. *All Jews cared about was money. They cheated and grabbed all they could get. They did not work for a living.*

Jewish Response to Christians

Naturally, Jews developed negative attitudes toward Christians, too. Memories from past pogroms made them wary, fearful, and suspicious of Christians. They clung together because they viewed the Christian world as cruel and hostile. They also came to believe that the only time Christians showed them any kindness whatsoever was when money was involved. In short, they viewed Christians as enemies.

RELIGIOUS ANTI-SEMITISM SLOWLY FADES IN THE MODERN WESTERN WORLD (from A.D. 1500 on)

Introduction

With the discovery of America in 1492, the world "opened up." Great changes that began to affect mankind drew the dark Middle Ages to a close. And while life for Jews in the ghettos remained frozen until the nineteenth century, the changes in the outside world gradually affected them, too. Religious anti-Semitism slowly slipped by the wayside. The ghettos opened up. However, among German-speaking peoples, all these changes occurred slowly. Consequently, religious anti-Semitism there was not only slower to die but also quicker to grow in a new form.

Great Changes Affect People's Thinking

The agricultural feudal system, with its landlords and peasants, had broken up in most of Western Europe by 1500. Cities had grown. Trade and travel were expanding. And the number of factory workers and middle-class merchants was ever increasing.

The monarchs of Spain, France, and England had united their feudal lands to form nation-states. Their subjects now showed loyalty to one king and one nation. Nationalism, or a feeling of pride in one's country and cultural traditions, began to take hold among the peoples in these new nations.

The Renaissance, or a renewed interest in learning and books, spread beyond the educated clergy and nobility to the common man. Startling scientific discoveries and new inventions began to usher in a Machine Age and an Industrial Revolution. The fear, ignorance, and superstition of the medieval period began to fade.

The Power of the Church Is Weakened

Industrialization brought about a newer mercantile economy in which the power of the new nation-states became totally dependent on wealth, gold, land, trading, commerce, and productivity. As this happened, kings soon decided that the business of the state should be not the saving of souls but the gathering of money. This thinking led to a conflict of Church and state interests.

There was dissention within the Church, too. A German priest named Martin Luther (1483–1546) bickered with the Church over certain practices. By the sixteenth century, most of the German part of the Holy Roman Empire had broken away from the control of the Roman Catholic Church in Rome.

Soon other reformers within the Church began to question Church practices. At this point, the unity of the Church was shattered. These religious arguments led to the Reformation, the period during which Christianity split into the Protestant and Catholic churches.

The Reformation Leads to Religious Tolerance

A separation of Church and state affairs followed. The Reformation was plagued by over one hundred years of terrible religious wars waged between Catholic and Protestant monarchs. Jews played no part in these religious struggles. However, after the Thirty Years' War

(1618–1648), kings granted a handful of Jews the privilege of living outside the ghettos. These lucky Jews had been financiers whom the monarchs had turned to for funds to pay their mercenary soldiers. Every king and nobleman kept one privileged Jew in his court to help him handle his personal financial matters. These Jews were called Court Jews.

By the time a hundred years of bloody religious war had passed, Europeans had come to realize that tolerance was a better way to handle differences. Some countries remained Roman Catholic while their neighboring countries were Protestant.

Efforts to convert Jews to Christianity slowly stopped. In Protestant countries like Holland and England, Christians began to show some tolerance toward Jews and Judaism.

But this was not true in Protestant German lands. Martin Luther had shown Jews compassion at first. He was confident he could convert them to Protestantism. When they resisted his efforts, he became violently angry. He expelled them from many Germanic lands and wrote and distributed many anti-Semitic papers that called for punishments of Jews. (Some four hundred years later, Adolf Hitler's Nazis would reprint and recirculate Luther's papers.)

Discussion Questions:
1. How did the ghetto begin to break up during the Reformation?
2. Why were Protestants the first to show religious tolerance?

Jews Become Involved Economically Again

In the meantime, Jews in England, France, and Holland were enjoying newfound tolerance for economic reasons. Since the power of the states rested on wealth, Jewish skills were valued again. People argued that Jews were a productive people whose knowledge of banking and merchandising could only contribute to the wealth of their nations.

Thus, when Jews began to return to England and France during the seventeenth century, they were permitted to become economically involved. By the eighteenth century, English and French Jews were fairly well accepted in the Christian communities.

This was not true for Jews still locked up in the Italian and German ghettos. Living a poor existence, they remained sealed off from the outside world. Frederick the Great (1740–1786), ruler of the Germanic land of Prussia, exemplified the negative attitude toward Jews still prevalent in this area. On one hand, he encouraged certain Jews to build up industry and commerce. Yet he denied them the privilege of religious freedom that he had freely extended to both Catholics and Protestants living in his realm.

French Revolution Heralds Jewish Emancipation

By the sixteenth century, a class conflict—a power struggle between the old ruling classes and the common man—had finally emerged. Having already spread through the New World and into England, "enlightened" ideas about the rights of man were now taking hold in France. "Were not all men created equal in the eyes of God?" people asked. This notion questioned the "divine rights" of kings to rule the masses.

In July 1789, issuing the "Declaration of the Rights of Man," which affirmed liberty, equality, and fraternity for all people, the French people cried out for democracy. They rebelled against their king. By the time their revolution was over, they had beheaded their king and queen and proclaimed France a republic. The French were no longer subjects of the king's whims but citizens with equal rights. A decree in 1791 made French Jews free and equal citizens, too.

Napoleon's Armies Free Jews from Ghettos

In the early nineteenth century, a French general named Napoleon Bonaparte had a dream: to conquer and unify Europe. As his conquering armies invaded Europe, they carried their ideas of freedom with them. By 1810 most of Europe, including Italian and German lands, was under French rule. For Jews in the dreary ghettos, this meant emancipation and full citizenship at last. In fact, French soldiers had literally ripped the Roman ghetto gates from their hinges to set Jews free.

Enjoying their first taste of freedom, Jews put their hearts and souls into the new world opened up to them. Since those in German lands faced greater adjustments in the Christian communities, many went out of their way to be accepted. Some became baptized. Others, who could not in good conscience change their religion, called for reforms in their Jewish worship. Eager to mix as much as possible, they crowded into schools and universities newly opened to them. Jewish peddlers put their carts aside and built bona fide business establishments.

Discussion Question: Why did Jews face greater adjustments in Germany?

Germans and Austrians Reject Jewish Emancipation

Unfortunately, Jewish freedom—especially in German and Austrian lands—was to be short-lived. The countries of Europe rose up against French rule. Combining their strength, they defeated Napoleon by 1815. Loyal to their homelands, many Jewish soldiers had also joined in the fighting to bring down the French ruler.

But Jews in German and Austrian lands were not to be rewarded for their efforts. After the Napoleonic Wars, when victorious European rulers got together at the Congress of Vienna in 1815 to work out a peace settlement, they also discussed the issue of Jewish emancipation. Austrian and German rulers, who had long regarded the French as archrivals, complained, "After all, Jewish emancipation was a French idea, not ours!" And in their domains, many of the old restrictions again oppressed Jews. In some German cities, the old cry of "Hep! Hep!" rang out and instigated open attacks on Jews. Even in France, much time was to pass before Jews were actually on an equal footing with their neighbors. Age-old prejudices had not disappeared.

Jewish Freedom Comes with Popular Rule

The desire of kings to rule the masses also died slowly. The next century of European history was to be marred by many revolutions. Not only had the French nobles again risen to attack the new French republic, but all of Europe was to witness similar revolts between reigning monarchs and rebels who screamed for democracy. In many places, Jews became a part of this political struggle for freedom and civil rights.

By the end of the nineteenth century, most of the royal families of Western Europe were forced to accept that popular rule and equal privileges for all men were facts of life. Consequently, by 1880 most European countries had passed laws granting Jews full rights as equal citizens—even Germany and Austria where the ideal of democracy was just beginning to take hold.

The ghetto was now a memory.

JEWS IN THE MODERN WESTERN WORLD

Religious Anti-Semitism Dies

By the late nineteenth century, Jews were making great strides forward. Their progress and contributions in a wide variety of fields were remarkable.

The old stereotype of Jews had faded. By now, they had assimilated or adopted many of the habits of their Western neighbors. Walking along a modern city street without their pointed hat or yellow badge, they looked like anyone else. They had even changed their religious practices, which still adhered to traditional laws but did not set them apart from the rest of the community. New, modernized Reform Judaism and the somewhat less modified Conservative Judaism had come into being.

Although some people had strong religious prejudices, they no longer viewed Jewish people as dangerous religious enemies. Jews, too, had dropped their defenses against Christians. Intermarriages and intermingling at social events were commonplace. In this busy modern Western world where people worked for more and more material comforts, few really cared what anyone else did in church or synagogue on the Sabbath.

For the most part, religious anti-Semitism had died.

Nationalism Gives Rise to New Secular (Nonreligious) Anti-Jewish Feelings

Unfortunately, anti-Jewish feelings did not disappear completely in the modern Western world. Nationalism had prompted many Europeans not only to look upon their own language, traditions, and culture with pride but also to look down their noses at people who were different. Many began to question whether the Jewish citizens in their nations truly belonged. "With their ties to Judaism and their ancient roots in Palestine, are the Jews really one of us?" they asked.

And in the newly formed nation of Germany, where nationalism was at a peak, and among Austrians, who were now yearning to form their own nation-state, feelings of intense German nationalism began building up to a new and wicked form of nonreligious anti-Jewish feelings: racist anti-Semitism.

Chapter One Review

REVIEWING KEY POINTS

Exercise 1

1. Name some of the restrictions that Roman laws placed on Jews, and tell how they segregated Jews from Christians.

2. To escape Christian persecution, Jews did have an alternative to running away. What was it?

3. How did the Crusades lead to mob attacks on Jewish communities?

4. Explain why Jews had to resort to jobs like trading, tax collecting, moneylending, and peddling.

5. Why did Jews have no place in the old feudal agricultural economy? Why did they become an important part of the newer mercantile economy?

6. Give several reasons why most Jews had left Western Europe by the end of the fifteenth century.

7. Why did kings expel Jews from France, England, Spain, Portugal, and some German lands? Why did many Jews still remain in German lands?

8. Tell how the following events helped to break down religious bias toward Jews: the Renaissance, the separation of Church and state affairs, the Reformation, the French Revolution.

9. Why did German and Austrian rulers reject Jewish emancipation in their countries?

10. Why did emancipated German Jews try so hard to blend into the Christian community?

CHECKING YOURSELF

Exercise 2
Matching Terms with Definitions

Directions: Number your paper from 1–15. Provide the correct answer for each definition by using a word from the list below. Each word can be used only once.

I—TERMS	II—DEFINITIONS
1. pagan	A. A person who held a belief contrary to Church teachings.
2. polytheistic	B. Wars waged by Christians to seize the Holy Land of Jerusalem from the Muslims.
3. atheist	C. A ceremony that admits a person into the Christian Church.
4. Muslim	D. A religion based on the teachings of Christ and His followers.
5. blasphemy	E. Contempt for God and sacred things.
6. Judaism	F. A person who does not believe in God.
7. Christianity	G. The Jewish religion, based on the belief in one God.
8. heretic	H. A person who does not accept a particular religion.
9. baptism	I. An idol worshipper.
10. Crusades	J. A religion based on the worship of many gods.
11. infidel	K. FoMuhammadllower of a religion founded by Muhammad.
12. stereotype	L. To label an entire group of people with a set of fixed characteristics without giving thought to individual differences.
13. ghetto	M. A section of a medieval city where Jews had to live.
14. synagogue	N. Mob attacks on Jewish communities.
15. pogroms	O. A Jewish temple.

Exercise 3
Finding Reasons

Directions: Religious anti-Semitism in Germany died a slower death than in other Western European countries for many reasons. Some are explained here. In Part A are incomplete
statements relating to German-Jewish history up to the mid-nineteenth century. Part B
has reasons to complete the statements. Number your paper from 1–5. Write the letter
of the reason that best completes each incomplete statement.

PART A—Incomplete Statements

1. Anti-Jewish feelings had a longer life span in Germany because

2. German Jews never had a breathing spell from anti-Semitism because

3. Frederick the Great kept up the old line of resentment toward Jews because

4. Martin Luther did little to promote tolerance toward Jews because

5. The German ghettos, dating back to the sixteenth century, helped to maintain an
   attitude of intolerance because

PART B—Reasons

a. they had remained in some German lands for a thousand years.

b. they served as a constant reminder of the separateness of Jews and Christians.

c. all the great social, economic, and political changes that had brought tolerance to
   other lands were much later in coming to Germany.

d. he refused to grant Jews the same privilege of religious freedom that he had willingly extended to German Catholics and Protestants.

e. he called for their punishment whenever they refused to convert to Protestantism.

GIVING REPORTS

Topics to Research

1. The good and pleasant side of Jewish life in the ghettos. Good source: *Jewish Life in the Middle Ages*, by Israel Abrahams.

2. The trial of Captain Alfred Dreyfus in France in 1894. Good source: *The Dreyfus Affair: A National Scandal*, by Betty Schecter.

3. Jews in Christian Spain during the Middle Ages. Include the following terms in your report: marranos, New Christians, Holy Inquisition, Thomas de Torquenada, autos-de-fe. Good sources: *A History of the Jews in Christian Spain*, by Yitzhak Baer; *The Chosen One*, by Harry Simonhoff (a novel).

4. The differences between Orthodox, Reform, and Conservative Judaism.

5. Jewish orthodox customs concerning one of the following: weddings, funerals, dietary laws.

6. Byzantine Emperor Justinian the Great (A.D. 482–565) and his treatment of Jews and laws against them (the Justinian Code).

7. The historical and religious significance of the Star of David.

8. Napoleon's code of laws.

9. Moses Mendelssohn, great German-Jewish philosopher.

10. Jewish financiers. Good sources: *The Story of Samson Wertheimen, The Court Factor*, by Alfred Apsler; *The Rothschilds*, by Frederick Morton; *Don Isaac Abravanel*, by Benzion Netanyahu.

11. One of the better-known Jewish holidays, such as Rosh Hashanah, Yom Kippur, Purim, Passover, or Hanukkah (origin, significance, and traditions).

12. The fundamental beliefs of Judaism.

13. Famous Jews from ancient times to the twentieth century and their contributions to society.

14. The pogroms in Eastern Europe in the early twentieth century and resulting emigrations.

15. Jews in the Renaissance.

Books to Review

1. *The Star and the Sword*, by Pamela Melnikoff, a novel about two Jewish children during the Crusades and the pogroms of twelfth-century England.

2. The excellent novel *The Fixer*, by Bernard Malamud, based on an actual blood libel trial in pre-World War I Russia.

3. The novel *The King's Persons*, by Joanne Greenberg, concerns the massacre of the Jews of York in 1190.

4. The excellent historical novel *Last of the Just*, by Andre Schwarz-Bart, begins with Jewish persecution in medieval England and ends with the gas chambers in Nazi Germany.

5. The novel *My Glorious Brothers*, by Howard Fast, reveals the struggle of Jews under Syrian-Greek oppression during the second century.

6. *Heritage: Civilization and the Jews*, by Abba Eban, based on the PBS television series.

7. *Anti-Semitism: The Road to the Holocaust and Beyond*, a look at anti-Semitism from ancient and medieval times through the Holocaust and to modern times.

MAKING PROJECTS

Poster and Artwork Ideas

(You may need to research the information for many of the projects.)

1. Find out what the Shema, a Jewish prayer, is. Locate it written in Hebrew. Print it in large three-inch Hebrew letters, and below it in parentheses print the English translation.

2. Draw a large picture (bird's-eye view) of a walled ghetto within a large city. Label your picture.

3. Make a map of the Crusade routes. Label the Rhine Valley, where most pogroms took place.

4. Using large, colorful pictures of food from magazines, make one side of your poster show foods Orthodox Jews are permitted to eat; on the other side, picture foods forbidden to them. (Locate this information under **Judaism** in the encyclopedia.)

5. Picture an Orthodox Jewish wedding ceremony. Label it.

6. Using the *World Almanac* or the *American Jewish Yearbook*, find the ten countries of the world with the largest Jewish populations. Make a chart of the countries and population figures.

7. Using the same sources mentioned in Exercise 6, make a chart listing the major cities of the United States or major world cities with the largest Jewish populations.

8. Draw a large picture of an Orthodox rabbi wearing a prayer shawl and skullcap.

9. List Jewish holidays and explain the significance of each.

Model Ideas

Directions: Use a large piece of material such as masonite, firm cardboard, or wood as the base of your project. Firmly glue all parts of your project together. Paint it with spray or brush. Place a 3" x 5" card on your model to identify it.

1. Construct a menorah, a candelabra with varying numbers of candlesticks used mostly in Jewish religious services. To make one for the Jewish holiday of Hanukkah, use nine empty spools of thread, nine candles, and at least four firm pieces of wood. Use wood glue to stick the parts together. The finished product should look like the drawing below. (The elevated candlestick in the middle is called the **shamash**. It is used to light the other eight candles, one to be lit on each of the eight days of the Hanukkah celebration.)

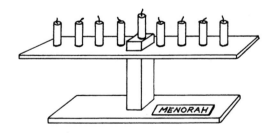

2. Construct a synagogue. Synagogues can be various shapes. Look for pictures of them in books. Pick a style, fashion it with milk cartons, small boxes, building blocks, cardboard, wood. (Some students have even shingled the roof and made stained glass windows.)

3. Make a model of a ghetto. Show it as a part of a larger city. Make the synagogue a lower structure than the surrounding churches. Show tumbledown skyscrapers. Surround your ghetto with a wall of Lego™ blocks, sugar cubes, or even marshmallows glued together.

4. Make a model of a Jewish star from wood, cardboard, or other firm material. Cut out two equilateral triangles. Paint or color them yellow. Glue them together to form a six-pointed star. Mount on a firm base.

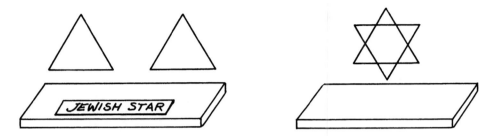

AUDIOVISUAL SUGGESTIONS FOR CHAPTER ONE

1. Rent the 60-minute black-and-white film *The Jew in the Middle Ages: Evolution of a Stereotype*. **ADL**

2. Show the filmstrip *The Sad Centuries*, depicting Jewish community life in medieval Europe up to the eighteenth century. **BJE**

3. Rent the 60-minute black-and-white film *The Jewish Stereotype in English Literature: Shylock and Fagin*. **ADL**

CHAPTER TWO

Adolf Hitler, the Failure

GRANDSON OF A JEWISH GRANDFATHER?

Adolf Hitler was not German but Austrian. He was born in Austria on April 20, 1889, in the small village of Braunau on the River Inn near the German border. His father, Alois, was fifty-two years old at the time, while his mother was in her twenties.

Adolf Hitler was not part Jewish, as many people believe. This idea originated because the real identity of Hitler's paternal grandfather has never been proven. Hitler's father was born to an unmarried woman named Marianne Schickelgruber. A few people have tried to prove that the father of Alois was the Jewish homeowner who had hired Marianne as a maid. However, there is little, if any, evidence to support this theory. Most historians dismiss it as false rumor. Even when Hitler himself had the Gestapo, or Nazi secret police, investigate the matter in 1942, they were unable to prove anything.

One amusing fact does remain, though. Adolf almost had the last name of Schickelgruber instead of Hitler. Hitler's father kept his mother's family name of Schickelgruber until he was forty years old. Then just twelve years before his son Adolf was born, he changed it to Hitler. Just imagine if he hadn't. Excited German crowds would have been saluting and shouting in their booming voices, "Heil, Schickelgruber!"

The Constant Failure

Two words describe Adolf Hitler during the first thirty years of his life: **big failure**. A school dropout, this future leader of Germany and world conqueror never received a diploma from any school. Poor grades and constant failure forced him to quit school at sixteen.

All his life Adolf Hitler needed a scapegoat for his failures. He blamed his lack of interest in school on his father and his teachers. He said he deliberately failed his studies to get even with his father, whom he hated. He called teachers boring and stupid. The truth was that Hitler was a spoiled child. Because his mother pampered and overprotected him, he revolted against his stern father, his teachers, and every other authority figure.

Young Hitler frequently suffered from hallucinations. His favorite boyhood fantasy was to tear down and rebuild the entire Austrian city of Linz. To prepare for this, he used to wander about the city with notebook in hand studying the layout of the city and making sketches of changes to be made. Once he was even seen giving a loud, passionate speech in the middle of an open field.

Laziness was another of Hitler's lifelong traits. In fact, Adolf Hitler never held a regular job until he became dictator of Germany. After his father died, his mother was forced to support him and his sister on a small pension because he flatly refused to get a job. He moved to Vienna at the age of eighteen, insisted that his mother send him an allowance to live on, and then proceeded to live in high style. He dressed in fine clothes, attended the opera several times a week, and had visions of being a great artist or architect.

When Hitler tried to enter the Academy of Fine Arts, however, he twice flunked the entrance test and was told he had no artistic talent. Authorities at a school of architecture also refused to admit him without a high school diploma. As usual, Hitler shifted the blame for his failures to the "stupid professors."

Hitler's allowance stopped when his mother died, but he still couldn't be bothered with working. For the next five years he became a tramp. In good weather he slept on park benches. When it turned cold, he joined other tramps in Austria's flophouses for the poor.

Hitler's condition had deteriorated so much by the end of this period that he was once judged unfit company for other tramps. The director of a home for hobos took one look at this filthy, lice-infested man and ordered him to leave immediately.

By this time, Hitler's mind was already harboring some very extreme ideas about people and politics. The thinking of this failure and tramp would emerge as official Nazi policy sixteen years later.

Discussion Question: Why would you expect a person like Hitler to be an extremist?

THE MIND OF ADOLF HITLER

Events in Austria Affect His Thinking

Hitler always referred to Vienna, the capital of Austria, as his school of life and politics. Many events were occurring in Austria at this time that helped to distort Hitler's thinking.

For one thing, the Austrian empire—then a vast union of countries called Austria-Hungary—was a hotbed of social unrest. Conditions that had long existed in most of Western Europe were only beginning to take effect in Austria-Hungary in the late nineteenth century.

By this time, the countries of Europe had risen against French rule and defeated Napoleon. In the wake of that defeat, a wave of nationalism had spread. People of each nation had said, "We are not French. We have our own language, traditions, and culture. And we are proud of it!"

Italian- and Germanic-speaking peoples decided the time had finally come to form their own nations, for they had lagged behind Spain, France, and England in the nation-building process by hundreds of years. By 1870, the new state of Italy came into being. And at long last, the widely scattered lands that housed German-speaking people came together to form the powerful new nation of Germany in 1871.

Nationalism was sweeping through Austria-Hungary, too. But instead of being a unifying force, it had the empire on the verge of splintering up. A dual monarchy existed, composed of two supposedly independent states but dominated by Austrians and ruled by Austrian King Franz Joseph, a member of the royal Hapsburg family. This empire also held many Eastern Europeans: Poles, Slovaks, Czechs, Serbs, Croats, Slovenes.

Conflict had arisen within this empire. The Austrians, who spoke German and considered themselves true Germans, wanted to unite with the new German nation to form one powerful Germanic state. At the same time, the Eastern Europeans in the empire were overwhelmed with their own nationalistic feelings. They wanted independence and the right to rule themselves.

Hitler Becomes a Radical German Nationalist and Racist

The center of all these nationalistic arguments was Vienna, home of Adolf Hitler. Caught up in the fervor, Hitler agreed with other Austrians that Austria should become a part of Germany. But he became more radical than most. An intense German nationalist, he felt Austria was "polluted with foreigners." He even favored the German Kaiser Wilhelm, a member of the royal Hohenzollern family, over his own king, Franz Joseph.

The false but very popular European notion at this time—that nationalities comprised separate "races" of people—also made a deep impression on Hitler. Already an extremist, he soon became a radical racist. He believed that certain races were mentally and physically superior to others.

Germans, in his opinion, were the most intelligent, the best-looking, the strongest, and the most skilled "race" on earth. He despised Eastern Europeans. "Rule themselves? Utterly ridiculous! Those inferior races are fit to live only as slaves of the German master race! And Jews are the lowest form of human life. They should be banished from Europe altogether!" he preached to anyone who would listen.

Hitler Develops Extreme Ideas About Politics

In Vienna, Hitler witnessed the rise of socialism—the workers' movement to take the ownership of industry out of the hands of a few wealthy capitalists. Socialists wanted to have some control of industry themselves, in order to improve inadequate salaries and poor working conditions. They complained that the people had little say in their government. To gain political power, the socialists had formed their own party, the Social Democrats. This party, based on the communist teachings of Karl Marx, was demanding the right to vote, the right to form labor unions, and the right to strike. Other workers had united under the banner of communism. Communism was a more extreme form of socialism, without the democratic ideals of the Social Democrats.

Hitler hated capitalism, socialism, communism, and democracy. He said all these movements were backed by Jews trying to gain power in any way they could. In his opinion, only one strong leader was needed to run any country. He called pure nonsense any democratic system that gave the "ignorant masses" the right to govern.

Discussion Question: When Hitler blamed Jews for communism and democracy and capitalism and socialism, how was he contradicting himself? Why, according to Hitler, did Jews "back" all these movements?

HITLER BECOMES A FANATICAL JEW-HATER

He Learns Jew-Hating from Others

Hate controlled all of Hitler's thinking, but his hatred of Jews knew no limits. Vienna became the spawning ground for his anti-Semitism, for as a child in Linz, he had known only one Jewish classmate. Ironically, his family had admired and respected his mother's Jewish doctor.

Hitler probably learned his racist anti-Jewish feelings from two Viennese Jew-haters. One was Georg von Schonerer, a politician who headed a political party called the Pan Germans. Like Hitler, the Pan Germans were German nationalists who wanted to create an all-German **reich**, or state, including Austrians. A violent anti-Semite, von Schonerer even called for Germans to reject Christianity on the basis of its Jewish origin. (Hitler would later use this notion as official Nazi policy.)

The other Austrian who filled Hitler's mind with racist nonsense was a writer named Lanz von Liebenfels. This man published a regular series of anti-Semitic pamphlets that always pictured Jews as apelike men. Von Liebenfels also used the swastika symbol to represent the superiority and purity of the blond, blue-eyed German race. Hitler was a regular reader and collector of von Liebenfels's materials.

From observing Karl Lueger, the mayor of Vienna, Hitler probably learned how anti-Semitism could be used to get votes. Lueger took stands opposing Jewish emancipation and Jewish influence in Austrian life as unjust and undesirable. These ideas gained many votes for him and his Christian Social party.

He Develops His Own Grudges Against Jews

No doubt Hitler catalogued in his mind all these and other anti-Semitic ideas of the society around him. However, he developed some personal grudges, too.

He witnessed in the early twentieth century a large number of Eastern European Jews who had fled to Vienna to escape violent pogroms in Poland and Russia. Unlike the modern, assimilated urban Jews of Vienna, these Jewish immigrants had kept their old customs and style of dress. They wore long black caftans, or robes, tall hats, and long beards. Their unusual appearance angered Hitler. He hated all "foreigners" in his country, but after looking at these traditional Jews, he became more convinced than ever that Jews could never be Germans.

As a penniless, uneducated, unskilled vagabond, Hitler also envied the lifestyle of many well-to-do Viennese Jews. It was easy for this art-school reject to be jealous of successful and talented Jews in the fine arts. As a passionate opera lover who had once gone back to see a favorite performance thirty times (while his mother was still paying the bills), he smarted at the large number of Jews in opera audiences.

And although it was Jewish charity that kept Hitler alive during his five lean years in Vienna, he resented accepting free food from Jews at the soup kitchens they operated for the poor.

Hitler resented, too, the look of pity in the eyes of Jewish art dealers who agreed to buy the second-rate picture postcards he had painted to earn a few pennies. "Why should these inferior Jews have more than I, a member of the master race?" he thought.

Jews Become Hitler's Universal Scapegoat

It was not long before Hitler began to use Jews as scapegoats for his failures. He once stormed back to the Vienna Art Academy, demanded the names of all persons on the admissions committee, and discovered one Jew among many non-Jews in the group. That was enough for Hitler to vow, "The Jews will pay for this!" Obsessed with hatred, he even came to believe that not cancer but the family's Jewish doctor had caused his mother's death.

Hitler's unbalanced mind carried his hatred of Jews one giant step further: He blamed world Jewry for all the evils on earth. He screamed:

They have invaded all countries on earth for one reason only—to grab all the money and power. And they almost have succeeded. Jewish writers control the presses. Jewish bankers control all the money. Jewish capitalists control big business. And the trade unions, communism, and democracy are all backed by power-hungry Jews trying to seize power in every way they can. Jews are contaminating the world. They are poisoners! Bloodsuckers! Parasites! It is up to the German master race to get rid of this poison. We, not Jews, are the rightful leaders of the world!

These ideas became a ruling passion in Hitler's mind. In fact, this whole philosophy of anti-Semitism became the core of Nazism.

Discussion Question:	Go back to Chapter One. Locate the summary of medieval attitudes about Jews. Compare them to Hitler's prejudices.

HITLER, THE WORLD WAR I SOLDIER

Hitler, the Draft Dodger

In 1913, armed with these extremist notions and determined to avoid being drafted into the Austrian army that he considered "contaminated with Jews, Eastern Europeans, and other mongrels," Hitler left Vienna and headed for his beloved Fatherland, Germany. He settled in Munich.

Although the Austrian police later tracked him down and arrested him for draft dodging, Hitler, an expert liar, was able to convince them that as a poor and homeless struggling artist he had simply kept on the move to find work and keep alive. His wasted physical condition also worked in his favor. The examining Austrian army doctor rejected him as unfit to bear arms. So off again to Munich he happily went.

Hitler, the German Soldier

In 1914 World War I broke out. To Adolf Hitler, serving in the Reichswehr, or German army, was the greatest of all honors. In fact, he got down on his knees and thanked God for giving him the opportunity to show his love for the Fatherland. Immediately he joined up and was assigned to the 16th Bavarian Infantry Regiment. For the next four years, he served as a dispatch runner on the Western Front in France.

At last Adolf Hitler had met his calling—war! He loved everything about it. He volunteered for the most dangerous missions. When his comrades complained about the muddy, rat-filled trenches, he went into rages about their disloyalty to the Fatherland. Once when he was shot in the leg, he begged not to be shipped to a hospital and away from the front—even though he had been in battle for two years without leave.

Twice wounded and the winner of four medals for bravery including the Iron Cross, Hitler never was promoted beyond the rank of corporal. His superior officer thought him too unstable. Like his old classmates at Linz, his fellow soldiers also shied away from this oddball who would sit silently in a corner for hours on end and then suddenly burst into wild screaming fits.

His Vision As the German Messiah

Hitler's hallucinations also continued. Several narrow escapes from death on the battlefield had created a fantastic vision in this strange man's mind. He became convinced that God had put him on earth for some divine mission.

According to Hitler this mission became clear on November 10, 1918, as he lay in an army hospital, temporarily blinded from a gas attack. A priest suddenly burst in with some shocking news: Germany had lost the war. The Fatherland was in a state of revolution. The monarchy had toppled, and Kaiser Wilhelm had fled to Holland. The new revolutionary German government was a democracy! For the first time in its history, Germany was a republic!

Hearing this, Adolf Hitler buried his head in his pillow and sobbed uncontrollably. His mind exploded with hate and suspicion. "How could Germany have lost the war? The Reichswehr was winning! It must be traitors in the revolutionary government! They forced the German army to give up so that they could take over the country. It's the Jews! They're behind it all. They stabbed Germany in the back!"

Then according to Hitler, "voices" began calling out his divine mission to him. He was to become Germany's savior, who would rescue the Fatherland from a Jewish takeover!

To accomplish his mission, Adolf Hitler decided then and there to go into politics. That he was thirty years old, uneducated, unskilled, penniless, and without a friend in the world bothered Hitler not at all. He was determined to find a way to fulfill his destiny.

Discussion Question: In view of Hitler's army record, why is it unusual that he never rose above the rank of corporal?

HITLER, THE ARMY SPY

The New German Republic Comes Under Attack

After the war, Hitler was posted in Munich, the capital of the German state of Bavaria and then the center of much political unrest and bloody revolution. Hitler soon became involved.

Many plots were under way to overthrow the newly established German republic and to seize the government. The German communists were the main instigators of the revolution. They hated the democracy. They wanted to make Germany a communist state just as the Bolsheviks (Russian communists) had done in the Soviet Union the year before. To defend the new republic, the new German President Friedrich Ebert had to send for the support of regular army troops. These troops along with Free Corps, or hired groups of ex-servicemen who had returned home from the war, now battled the communists in the streets of Munich.

In the meantime, the defeated German army generals had no love for the new German democracy, either. They wanted the abdicated Kaiser Wilhelm to return and rule Germany again, for under the old monarchy, the military had always helped the kaiser rule the Fatherland. Needless to say, the old generals also wanted the communists out of the way. While promising President Ebert that their army troops would defend his new government, they really sent their troops to crush the communists for their own selfish reasons. They were merely biding their time until they could eliminate the democracy themselves and restore the German monarchy.

The high command of the German army, Field Marshall Paul von Hindenburg and General Erich von Ludendorff, had been unwilling to admit defeat in the war. Like Hitler, they claimed victory in the battlefield and told the German people that politicians in the homeland had stopped the war and "stabbed the German army in the back." They and other high-ranking officers planned a military comeback in which Germany would rise to become a leading military power again.

Besides the communists, dozens of other political groups also sprang up and attacked the German government. The army generals wanted to keep tabs on all of them. They also needed to weed out their own ranks, for many German soldiers, especially of low rank, had begun to side with the communists.

Hitler Spies on Political Groups in Germany

Adolf Hitler agreed to spy on his fellow soldiers for his army officers. He lived among the men in the barracks, deliberately talked politics to draw out their opinions, and then informed on communist sympathizers. He also took the witness stand to testify against the men he accused. The condemned communists were then shot before firing squads. Hitler enjoyed this first taste of power.

The officers also sent Hitler, dressed in civilian clothes, to sit in on many different political meetings throughout Munich to see what the groups' intentions were. By attending one of these meetings, Hitler finally slipped into active politics.

Discussion Question: In your opinion, why was the new German democracy weak?

He Becomes the Seventh Member of the German Workers' Party

On September 12, 1919, on army orders, Hitler sat in on his first German Workers' party meeting, held in a back room of a Munich beer hall. This group had been meeting for eighteen months but still had only six official members and less than two dollars in the treasury. The group had no organized program, only complaints about the government and the poor wages and working conditions of the working classes.

During the meeting, Hitler stood up and gave a wild speech about the greatness of Germany. Everyone listened in amazement: Hitler really had a way with words. Impressed by Hitler's speaking ability, the six members later asked him to join their party. Hitler became their seventh member.

Chapter Two Review

REVIEWING KEY POINTS

Exercise 1

1. Discuss aspects of Hitler's early life that are contrary to what you'd expect to find in a potential world leader.

2. Why was late nineteenth-century Austria the center of many nationalistic arguments?

3. Hitler wanted Austria to become a part of what nation? Why?

4. How did Hitler evaluate Germans compared to other nationalities? Eastern Europeans? Jews?

5. How did Hitler explain the German defeat in the war? Who else promoted this untruth?

6. Which two groups were the strongest enemies of the new republic before the Nazis came to power?

7. Why did the German army officers want a monarchy restored to Germany?

8. Discuss Hitler's anti-Semitism with respect to (a) his personal grudges, and (b) prejudice he learned from others.

9. What divine mission did Hitler come to believe he had?

CHECKING YOURSELF

Exercise 2
Crossword Puzzle

(All answers to this puzzle can be found by studying Chapter Two.)

ACROSS

1. Franz ____, the king of the Austria-Hungary Empire.
5. Before WWI, the German government was a ____.
6. ___ became the president of the new German republic.
9. Kaiser ___ was the German king up to the end of WWI.
12. ___, or Jew-hatred, became the core of Nazism.
13. The German army generals refused to admit ___ in the war.
19. Name for the German army.
21. Hitler wanted Austria to become a part of ___.
22. Hitler lived in the German state of ___.
23. Name for the Russian communists.
25. Social ___, the name of the socialist workers' political party.
27. In 1913 Hitler became a draft ___, fleeing his native Vienna and settling in Germany.
28. Another important German General of WWI.

DOWN

2. Hitler's birthplace was the ___ ___ Empire.
3. A workers' movement that opposed capitalism.
4. ___ Corps were ex-soldiers hired by the German republic to fight the communists.
7. A ___ is someone who believes certain races are superior to others.
8. Hitler lived as a tramp in ___.
10. The socialists patterned their thinking after the ideas of Karl ___.
11. Hitler joined the ___ ___ party.
14. The ___ party tried to overthrow the German republic after the war.
15. Hitler was a soldier in World War ___.
16. An important German army general in WWI.
17. After WWI, Germany became a ___.
18. The surname of Hitler's father until he changed it was ___.
20. Many Europeans believed each nationality was a separate ___.
24. The ___ symbol was used in Austria to represent superiority of the German race.
26. Karl ___, mayor of Vienna, used anti-Semitism to get votes.

Exercise 3
Looking Up Acronyms

Directions: An **acronym** is a word formed from the first letters or syllables of other words. The word **Nazi** is an acronym. Look up its derivation in the dictionary. Notice that it comes from a combination of letters from **Na**tional So**zi**alist, two German words that mean "National Socialist." Look up the derivation of **Gestapo**, another German acronym. Write the original words that it comes from and underline the letters in them that make up the acronym. Do the same thing for these American acronyms listed below.

radar	CARE	scuba	Amoco	Wasp	NASA
Univac	Amerind	Gasp	UNESCO	SEATO	WAC
snafu	NATO	Alcoa	HUD	NOW	

GIVING REPORTS

Topics to Research

1. Hitler's self-image. Good source: *The Mind of Adolf Hitler*, by Walter Langer, Part I, "As He Believes Himself to Be."

2. Pan-Germanism. Good source: *Modern Germany, Its History and Civilization*, by Koppel S. Pinson.

3. Hitler's father and mother, as parents.

4. More on Hitler's early life. Good source: *Adolf Hitler, His Family, Childhood, and Youth*, by Bradley F. Smith.

5. The royal Hapsburg and Hohenzollern families of Europe. Why did Hitler not respect the Hapsburgs?

6. Karl Marx: Include his anti-Jewish feelings and explain why it was paradoxical that he had such feelings.

7. The influence of Dietrich Eckart on Hitler regarding Jews. Good source: *The Life and Death of Adolf Hitler*, by Robert Payne.

8. How were Russian Jews affected by the Bolshevik Revolution of 1917?

9. The *Ostara*, a widely circulated anti-Semitic magazine in Vienna that greatly influenced Hitler's thinking. Good source: *Adolf Hitler*, by John Toland (Volumes I and II).

10. The differences between systems based on capitalism, communism, and socialism.

11. The use of the swastika as a symbol of Aryan superiority by some Austrians during the nineteenth century. Good source: *Hitler*, by Joachim Fest.

12. Personality characteristics and backgrounds of modern dictators.

13. Jews in twentieth-century Germany through World War I.

14. Hitler's attitude toward religion (Christianity and Judaism).

15. A psychological portrait of the young Hitler. Good source: *Hitler's Psychotherapy*, by Norbert Bromberg and Verne Voly Small.

16. The origin of the concept of a master race.

MAKING PROJECTS

Poster and Artwork Ideas

1. On one half of your poster, draw a map picturing Europe before 1918. On the other side, draw a map of Europe after World War I (1918) to point out the new nations that appear.

2. Research the races of people, then make a chart to show the number of different races. Perhaps you can find magazine pictures to illustrate a representative of each race, or draw figures of your own.

A Model Idea

Make a relief map of Europe after 1918 to show the configurations on the ground.

Materials:

1. Either one of these recipes can be used to make your modeling clay:

CLAY-DOUGH

1 cup flour	1 cup water (more or less)
1 cup salt	1 tablespoon alum (optional; from drugstore)

Mix ingredients in bowl. Store in air-tight jar until ready to use. This clay takes several days to harden thoroughly.

MODEL CLAY

1 cup cornstarch   2 cups baking soda $1\frac{1}{4}$ cups cold water

Boil ingredients in pan until mixture looks like mashed potatoes. (Stir constantly over medium heat.) Put in dish, cover with damp cloth until cool enough to handle. Knead a few times before using. This clay dries to a hard cement overnight.

2. Paint or magic marker in shades of brown and green

3. A large flat wooden base

4. Shellac (optional)

Procedure:

1. Make either recipe for modeling clay.

2. Using a topography map of Europe as your guide, shape the clay on the wooden base into different elevations to show mountains, hills, and flat areas. Allow to dry thoroughly.

3. Paint in shades of brown and green to show the various elevations. Provide a color key for your map. Allow to dry.

4. With a black marker, make boundary lines, rivers, names of countries, etc. Allow to dry.

5. For a professional ceramic look, cover with clear shellac.

NOTE: You can use this modeling clay for many projects besides relief maps. For supplementing the study of this Holocaust unit, students have used this clay for shaping synagogues, Stars of David, flags, battlefields, soldiers, ghettos, concentration camps, and other scenes or figures reminiscent of the Holocaust.

AUDIOVISUAL AID SUGGESTIONS FOR CHAPTER TWO

1. Two filmstrips and a cassette entitled *The Roots of Adolf Hitler's Mind.* **SSSS**

2. Rent the 24-minute black-and-white film *Willie Catches On*, which points out how prejudices are taught. **CT**

CHAPTER THREE

Hitler and the Nazis

ORGANIZER OF THE NAZI PARTY

Politics breathed new life into Hitler. He soon took full charge of the German Workers' party. Becoming **Der Fuehrer** ("the leader"), he changed the party name to the National Socialist German Workers' party: abbreviated, the Nazi party. As a cure-all for Germany's many postwar problems, he developed a twenty-five-point party platform, mostly aimed at punishing German Jews. To strip Jews of their German citizenship was one of his first goals. The Nazi party motto became "Germany Awake! Perish Jewry!"

To spread Nazi propaganda far and wide, Hitler began to publish and distribute a Nazi newspaper. In addition, he made the most of the talent he had discovered on the occasion of his first political speech on November 16, 1919—his ability to hold an audience spellbound. As his reputation as a wild and powerful speaker spread, more and more curious people began to flock to Nazi rallies.

Hitler also added glamor to the Nazi party. For the party emblem, he picked a symbol that had fascinated people on every continent for centuries—the **swastika**, or hooked cross. But Hitler changed the age-old swastika. By turning it to a clockwise direction and tipping it on its edge, he created the Nazi symbol, the **hakenkreuz**. This newer symbol, appearing as if it were in motion, was to suggest the Nazi movement, or the party's dual goal of making Germany Jew-free and of conquering the world.

This eye-catching symbol was soon incorporated in the Nazi flag. Placing the black swastika in the center of a pure white circle and centering this on a bloodred background, Hitler created a startling combination that worked like magic on the Germans. They later displayed it on everything imaginable, from armbands to coins. Some of the Nazi flags that hung from buildings during parades were as big as room-sized rugs.

The swastika itself stood for the Aryan or Nordic (German) race. The white color represented the nationalist idea of creating a Greater Germany, a nation of all German-speaking peoples. The red color was for the Nazi movement's idea of all Germans living together.

From the Italian Fascists, led by Benito Mussolini, Hitler borrowed many ideas, including the stiff-armed salute. He also added numerous Nazi songs and slogans.

Discussion Question: Though many Germans called the idea of a superior German race nonsense, there were others to whom this idea had great appeal. Can you explain why the times had something to do with making the idea popular and attractive?

The Stormtroopers

Hitler hired a private army to help him overthrow the German government. He called them the **Sturmabteilung**, meaning the "Stormtroopers," or the SA. Because these fighters wore brown uniforms accented by bold swastika armbands and high jackboots, they sometimes were called the Brownshirts. Some were unemployed ex-soldiers who were angry and frustrated with the German government. Most of the SA, however, were common criminals and cutthroats.

Hitler assigned the SA two jobs: (1) to create so much violence in the streets that the German people would come to believe the present government was too weak to keep control, and (2) to destroy all opposing political parties.

To head the SA, Hitler appointed Ernest Rohm, a tough, scar-faced ex-army officer. Rohm trained the Stormtroopers in street fighting and in starting riots. He also used his connections with the German army and local police to provide the SA with army weapons and to keep them out of jail. Rohm had the backing, too, of many politicians who saw Nazism as the best alternative to both the present democracy, which they had little faith in, and communism, which they feared was becoming a threat.

On Hitler's orders, the dangerous SA men went on a bloody spree. They used their clubs, brass knuckles, and guns on anyone who dared speak out against Hitler. They charged into and broke up others' political meetings by throwing beer mugs and breaking furniture over their heads. Their melees with communists and other political rivals turned the streets of Germany into a wild free-for-all. "Listen to Hitler, or we'll smash your heads in!" became the SA battle cry.

POSTWAR TROUBLES, THE LIFEBLOOD OF THE NAZI PARTY

By 1923, the already shaky German republic suffered two more severe setbacks. Plagued by the shattered war economy, the government lagged behind in paying its war debts to France. Angry Frenchmen reacted by sending troops to take over the heartland of German industry, the Ruhr Valley. Then enraged German workers there walked off their jobs, for they had no intentions of taking orders from the French, their longtime rivals.

As German factories shut down one after the other, the German economy reached a breaking point. A resulting superinflation began to drain every German's wallet. Soon it reached such monstrous proportions that a person's entire life savings could not buy even a quart of milk.

Disgusted with their government, more and more jobless Germans began to listen to Nazi promises of prosperity and restored German honor. Nazi party membership climbed to 56,000. The ranks of the SA swelled to 15,000. And the Stormtroopers felt confident enough to begin beating up Jews in the streets.

THE BEER HALL PUTSCH

The Nazis Take Munich by Force

Late in 1923, Hitler decided the time was right for a Nazi takeover of the German government. According to his plan, the Nazi **putsch** or **coup d'etat** was to take over the state government in the Bavarian capital of Munich first and then to seize the federal seat of government in Berlin.

On November 8, 1923, with 600 armed SA troops and old army General Erich von Ludendorff, now a Nazi sympathizer, at his side, Hitler set off for a beer hall in Munich where 3,000 residents plus all the important Bavarian political leaders had gathered to discuss the worsening German economy. As his Nazis surrounded the beer hall and pointed their machine guns at the entrances, Hitler burst in on the startled crowd, jumped up on a table, fired a shot into the air, and shouted, "The revolution has begun!"

After ordering his SA to lock up the furious political leaders in a back room, Hitler pronounced himself the new dictator of Germany. The beer-happy crowd cheered and applauded.

Meanwhile, the politicians in the back room had sneaked out a back window to call out the police and army to teach the Nazis a lesson.

Hitler, Ludendorff, and the SA began a noisy victory parade through the streets of Munich. The arriving police and army troops opened fire. Sixteen Nazis lay dead. Many were arrested. Although Hitler managed to escape, he too was later arrested and jailed for treason.

The failure of the Beer Hall Putsch showed that Germans were not ready for Hitler yet. In fact, most respectable people considered the wild Nazi leader a joke. They scoffed and laughed at how much he resembled the then-popular comedian Charlie Chaplin.

Hitler Scores a Victory at His Trial

But later, during his trial for treason, Hitler proved that Nazi promises to restore German glory were not falling on totally deaf ears. He acted as his own lawyer. Putting his voice into high gear, he hotly denied being a traitor and voiced his love for the Fatherland. He vowed to become the German leader who would put Germany back on the path to honor and glory.

He swayed both the judge and the jury. The usual death penalty or life imprisonment sentence was laid aside. Hitler received a mere five-year prison sentence. Besides that he had scored a big publicity bonus. Worldwide reporters who had attended the twenty-four day trial now spread the name of Adolf Hitler far beyond the state of Bavaria, where he had been primarily known.

CONVICT IN PRISON

While a prisoner at Landsberg Prison, Hitler decided on a new course for the Nazi party. The Beer Hall Putsch fiasco had taught him that taking the government by force was no longer the answer. From then on, he decided his Nazis would strive for power legally. By having Nazi

representatives gain the majority of seats in the Reichstag, or German house of representatives, in legal elections, they could destroy the German democracy from the inside.

Hitler was released on parole after serving only eight months of his sentence.

MEIN KAMPF

In prison Hitler wrote a biography/Nazi handbook called *Four and a Half Years of Struggle Against Lies, Stupidity, and Cowardice*. Actually, he dictated the ideas while other Nazi prisoners, mostly school dropouts themselves, did the actual writing for him because he was such a poor speller and writer.

After correcting thousands of mistakes in grammar and spelling and persuading Hitler to change the title to *Mein Kampf*, or "My Struggle," a Nazi publisher placed the book on the market in 1925. It sold very poorly. Most readers, in fact, considered it the work of a madman.

But later, after Hitler came to power, millions of Germans bought the book—out of a sense of fear and duty. *Mein Kampf* became the required gift for every occasion, from birthdays to wedding anniversaries. For added safety, every German household placed a copy in full view on a living-room bookshelf. By 1945, Hitler had become a rich man from the book sales. Only one other book in Germany had ever sold as many copies—the Bible.

Still, *Mein Kampf* often remained unread. That is both a sad and scary fact, for in the book Hitler revealed in detail his plans to be the future warlord and dictator of Germany. He later followed these plans as a builder follows a blueprint.

Hitler wrote that he would conquer Europe and that the Slavic lands to the east, especially Russia, would provide Germans with more **Lebensraum**, or living space. Millions later died as he sought to make good on this promise. To create a German master race, Hitler said he would make the Eastern Europeans slaves of Germany and make Europe **Judenrein**, or free of Jews. The result of this pledge and his attempt to carry it out, was the Holocaust.

In *Mein Kampf*, Hitler had given the world public notice, a full warning of his evil intentions. But nobody paid much attention.

THE NAZI CREED

Nazism was Hitlerism, or the beliefs of Adolf Hitler. He poured these ideas into *Mein Kampf*. Here is a short summary:

1. *Men are not created equal. As the most superior race on earth, Germans are true creators of culture. Since only they are capable of solving mankind's future problems, the future of civilization depends on them. Therefore, Aryan blood must be kept pure, or these superior qualities will be lost. Marriages to inferior races are forbidden. Germans must create a pure master race to rule the world.*

2. *Jews, the most inferior race, are the true destroyers of culture. They have deliberately invaded and drained all countries of the world of money and power. Therefore, the future of world power rests on either the rightful German masters or the Jews. Germans must save the world by ridding it of this Jewish poison.*

3. *Slavs, blacks, and Mediterranean peoples rank only slightly above Jews. They are fit to live only as German slaves.*

4. *The German master race will take as much land to the east as it needs for Lebensraum, or extra living space. Political boundaries are nonsense. If others resist, Germany will use its arms and take land by force.*

5. *Democracy and majority rule are stupid. The masses are ignorant sheep that need leading by a brilliant statesman. This divinely appointed leader is Adolf Hitler, who will rule the world with a few chosen elite. The Third Reich, or new German Empire, will last a thousand years. It will be a Nazi totalitarian state with total control of government and the lives of all citizens.*

6. *Propaganda, or a system to spread political ideas, must be used to gain support of the ignorant masses. Since the people are dull and forgetful, propaganda must be limited to only a few points and repeated over and over again in slogans. It is not important that these ideas be true, for people are willing to believe anything. In fact, the bigger the lies, the better.*

7. *Force and fear are the only means to keep the masses under control. Reason and argument have no place in the Third Reich.*

8. *Give the people a single enemy to hate and to blame for all their troubles. Then they will not feel guilty and will aim all their frustrations in one direction. Blame the Jew for everything evil.*

9. *Thou shalt have no other God but Germany! (Hitler even proposes this to be the eleventh commandment.) Christianity is just a scheme created by Jews. Christian love, mercy, and charity must be replaced by pride, willpower, defiance, and hate. Honor not a heavenly Father but the Fatherland!*

Discussion Questions: Why would the Nazi idea of creating a "pure" race be impossible? How does modern advertising use some of the same techniques the Nazi propagandists used?

HITLER CLEVERLY MANIPULATES POWER

The Nazi Party Fades

After Hitler was released from prison, the growth of the Nazi party was slow. The government had temporarily declared the party illegal and banned Hitler from speaking publicly. Even Hitler's leadership was being threatened by others in the party.

Furthermore, between 1925 and 1929, conditions in Germany improved. A new money systetm and foreign loans had eased the bad economic situation. As prosperous times returned to Germany, the German people not only stopped complaining about the government but also stopped listening to the Nazis.

Hitler Builds a Nazi "Shadow State"

Hitler didn't give up. He worked furiously to reorganize the Nazi party. He cleverly laid plans to take over the government when times were right for the Nazis again. He created a Nazi "shadow state." This was a secret, substitute Nazi government—a Nazi state within the state—that would be ready to take over power whenever the democracy was crushed.

To create this Nazi shadow state, Hitler divided Germany into thirty-four districts and appointed Nazi leaders in each. All the districts corresponded to the regular election districts for the Reichstag. These districts were further broken down within the cities, so that a Nazi leader was assigned to cover every city block and even each apartment building. Hitler even planted Nazis in the German-speaking countries of Austria and the Sudetenland area of Czechoslovakia.

Also included in this Nazi shadow state were departments of justice, labor, propaganda, interior, and culture. There was even a cabinet. In addition there were special Nazi clubs for doctors, lawyers, teachers, writers, and children. Together with Hitler, all the party leaders organized and built up the party in each group and in each area. They worked to make the Nazi party strong, and to elect Nazi delegates to the Reichstag.

The Great Depression of 1929 Opens the Door to Nazism Again

In 1929, the Great Depression gave the Nazis their lucky break. Misery and starvation spread all over Germany, allowing Nazism to rear its ugly head once again. By now, Hitler was back in the driver's seat in the party, the party leaders had done their work, and the shadow state was ready to go. By 1933, the stage was set. And through a series of clever political tricks, Hitler and Germany were to become one.

Discussion Questions: Why did Hitler make his Nazi shadow state districts match the regular election districts for voting in Reichstag elections? Why do you think he placed Nazi representatives in Austria and the Sudentenland of Czechoslovakia?

NAZI PARTY LEADERS

Thousands of Nazi leaders helped Hitler to power. Nazism gave the people who gathered closely around Hitler wealth and power. Because of this, they became Adolf Hitler's blind followers who cared nothing about good or evil or the people they destroyed.

Hitler's Top Henchmen

Hermann Goering, who had joined the army in 1921, was the number two Nazi and a drug addict. A well-known pilot and hero of World War I, he used his old war fame to become elected president of the Reichstag. From this position, he helped to destroy the democracy from within.

In the Nazi state, Goering created the Gestapo, or secret police, who hunted down Germans opposed to Hitler. To house and punish these "Nazi enemies," Goering also directed the building of the first concentration camps.

Using his prior experience, Goering became head of the Luftwaffe, or German Air Force, during World War II. By then, however, this air force chief had become so horribly fat he could not even fit into the cockpit of an airplane. Not only did he enjoy food, he also helped himself to a fortune's worth of priceless paintings stolen by his Nazis from Jewish victims of the Holocaust.

When he was asked his feelings toward the Nazi tortures and killings during Hitler's regime, Goering answered, "I have no conscience. My conscience is Adolf Hitler!"

Rudolf Hess, a big man with thick bushy eyebrows and piercing black eyes, was Hitler's third in command until 1941. So mentally unbalanced that his Nazi friends called him "Mad Rudi," Hess suffered from hallucinations and bouts of amnesia. His worship of Adolf Hitler was fanatical.

Once, to please his beloved Fuehrer, Hess took off from Germany for England in an open-cockpit Messerschmitt. He planned to ask Prime Minister Winston Churchill if he wouldn't like to change his mind and join with the Germans against the Russians. His flight took place on May 10, 1941, right in the middle of furious bombing raids between the Germans and the English.

Hess finally was forced to crash-land in an open field in Scotland, where he was captured by a farmer with a pitchfork. Hitler was furious when he heard about his secretary's actions. And the English, who pronounced Hess crazy, kept him in jail until after the war ended.

Josef Goebbels, Hitler's propaganda chief, held the college degree of doctor of philosophy. But he could never keep a job until he became a Nazi. So small that he was almost a dwarf, and handicapped with a disfigured leg, Goebbels was a bitter, nasty man.

As Hitler's "master of the big lies," Goebbels made sure that Germans read only books approved or written by Nazis. All others he simply had burned. In 1933 he ordered that all books written by Jewish, communist, or other "unapproved" authors be removed from bookstore shelves and libraries and thrown into the streets. On May 10 he called for book-burning ceremonies. In Berlin alone, 20,000 books drenched with gasoline went up in smoke.

After Adolf Hitler's death in 1945, Goebbels proved his loyalty to his Fuehrer. Deciding he and his whole family could not stand to live in a world without Adolf Hitler, he had his six young children poisoned. Then he and his wife comitted suicide.

Alfred Rosenberg, the "brains" of Hitler's mob, was a wild fanatic who had been educated as an architect in Moscow before he emigrated to Germany in 1918 and joined the party. Hitler looked up to Rosenberg and accepted all his ideas. It was Rosenberg who gave him the "scientific evidence" proving Germans a superior race and Jews subhumans.

Rosenberg also brought Hitler a fake paper from Russia that "proved" the Jews were conspiring to take over the world. The paper, the *Protocols of the Elders of Zion*, was supposedly the minutes of an international meeting of Jewish leaders who had gathered in a cemetery in Prague to discuss their plans to blow up all the world's cities and take over all world banks and governments. The *Protocols* had long since been proven a total forgery. However, Hitler and his

Nazis had the *Protocols* reprinted in the 1920's, and circulated it widely among the German masses during political campaigns.

Rosenberg also convinced Hitler that the "same Jewish instigators of the Russian Bolshevik Revolution of 1917" were at work in Germany.

Heinrich Himmler, Hitler's SS chief, was the most feared and dreaded Nazi of them all. Bespectacled, with a receding chin and sunken chest, this one-time chicken farmer had been arrested for killing his girlfriend, but was released for lack of evidence. As Hitler's man in charge of the Jewish slaughter during the Holocaust, he well proved his capacity for murder. In command of all extermination or death camps, he personally checked the functioning of the gas chambers and watched executions. He also ordered Nazi doctors to use camp prisoners as human guinea pigs in horrible medical experiments. Once, when asked how he could exterminate helpless, innocent Jewish children, Himmler protested, "But they are animals!"

THE SS—THE "ELITE GUARD"

From the ranks of the SA in 1925, Adolf Hitler handpicked a few top men to serve as bodyguards to him and other Nazi leaders. He called this group **Schutzstaffel,** meaning "Protective Guard," or the SS. Because they wore black uniforms, they were sometimes called "the Blackshirts." Throughout Nazi-occupied Europe, however, they were referred to as "Hitler's Butchers."

In his future German Empire, Hitler planned to use the SS as his elite underlords to help him rule the masses. They and their brides were also to be the parents of the "pure-blooded" master race of superpeople.

By 1933, SS membership was 30,000. Who had joined? Fanatics. Average citizens. Young German boys attracted by the flashy black uniforms with silver trim. Power-hungry people from all walks of life . . . doctors . . . nurses . . . engineers . . . lawyers . . . judges . . . teachers.

Becoming an SS member was no simple matter, however. A prospective SS man had to prove his German blood was "pure" by submitting his family tree dating back to 1750. His family medical records had to be closely examined to prove he had no history of heredity diseases. Besides all that, he had to be tall, blonde, blue-eyed, and athletic. Prospective SS brides had to submit the same records before marriages were permitted.

Once accepted, an SS man took an oath to Hitler in which he swore to kill all enemies of the Fuehrer—even his own brother, if necessary. He received a special SS dagger as a symbol of this "honor." And no law, judge, or court could punish him. In short, the SS became nothing more than a criminal organization, a group of killers with a license.

Special training produced the cold-blooded SS killers Hitler wanted. At grooming schools, trainees exercised, received military training, studied Nazism's theories about their superior race, and ate only special foods suitable for their "pure" blood. By the time they were finished, they had become so puffed up with their own glory that they firmly believed all non-Germans were subhuman.

Divisions of the SS

There were several divisions of the SS. The commandants of all Nazi concentration camps were members of the Death's Head Regiment, who wore skull-and-crossbones insignia on their uniforms. The Gestapo, or secret state police, made Germany a prison. They had spies living in every German neighborhood and even among concentration camp prisoners. They made arrests, searched homes without warrants, dragged people off to prison camps. Eventually their spy system spread around the world.

Another SS agency with agents inside and outside Germany was the SD, or security police, headed by Reinhard Heydrich. They collected intelligence information. Third in command after Hitler and Himmler in charge of the extermination of Jews, Heydrich and his security police handled the organization of the mass murder.

The Einsatzgruppen, or SS political police, were killing squads who moved all about, especially through Poland and Russia. They carried out mass shootings of a million Jews and others. Most of their victims were shot over open trenches, which they were forced to dig first.

Finally, the Waffen SS consisted of SS military units during the Second World War. They became an army within an army. But they were controlled not by the regular army generals but by Hitler and the SS itself. Composed of all volunteers, the Waffen SS were to be the guards of the coming Reich. During World War II, they fought in the battlefields alongside the Wehrmacht (Hitler's new name for the Reichswehr, or German army). However, the Waffen SS also became hunting units for Jews throughout Europe. Wherever they went, they committed horrible crimes against Jews, other civilians, and prisoners of war.

In 1943, when Hitler wanted to increase the size of his forces, he threw the old rule about "pure German blood" for the SS men out the window. He allowed Italians, Dutch, Hungarians, French, Albanians, Russians, Norwegians, Flemings, Croatians, and other "subhuman" races to form their own Waffen SS divisions. Eventually the Waffen SS grew to more than a million fighting men.

The SS had many other departments that operated the dirty business of Hitler's Third Reich. Some of these departments organized slave labor and the handling of vast amounts of Jewish property, which they stole and distributed among themselves.

Discussion Question: Compare the SS, Hitler's killers, to his Nazi chiefs. Were they the same type of people? Compare the SS to the SA.

Chapter Three Review

REVIEWING KEY POINTS

Exercise 1

1. What was the SA's job?

2. As a convict in Landsberg Prison, what new course of action for a Nazi takeover of Germany did Hitler decide upon?

3. Why did Germans stop listening to the Nazis between 1925 and 1929?

4. What was the *Protocols of the Elders of Zion*? How did Hitler use it?

5. The SS was in full charge of the Jewish Holocaust. Name some of the divisions and tell what their duties were.

6. Were the SS killers of Jews all Germans? Were most SS lunatics, or were they what we might consider ordinary people?

7. In what sort of atmosphere did the Nazis thrive?

8. What event gave the Nazis their chance to take over Germany?

CHECKING YOURSELF

Exercise 2
Giving Reasons

Directions: Each incomplete statement in Part A tells about the Nazis in Germany during the 1920's. Part B lists reasons that complete the statements. Number your paper from 1–15. Next to each number, write the letter of the reason that best completes the statement.

PART A—Incomplete Statements

1. Most of the twenty-five-point Nazi platform was aimed at hurting Jews because

2. Hitler chose the swastika as the party emblem because

3. Many unemployed ex-soldiers joined the SA because

4. The SA stirred up trouble in the streets because

5. The SA was not punished severely for causing trouble because

6. Hitler decided to take over the government in 1933 because

7. The French sent in troops to take over the Ruhr because

8. The Beer Hall Putsch failed because

9. Hitler did not get the usual death penalty for treason because

10. Hitler's trial for treason helped rather than hurt him because

11. Most people paid little attention to *Mein Kampf* because

12. Hitler said the future of world power depended on either Jews or Germans because

13. Hitler called Jews the most inferior race because

14. The Nazis came to power in Germany mainly because

15. When Ludendorff became a Nazi sympathizer, it was a forewarning of Nazi success in Germany because

PART 8—Reasons

a. it had fascinated people for centuries.

b. the Germans could not afford to pay their war debts to France.

c. if he, an important, popular figure who had commanded the German troops during World War I, could be sympathetic to the Nazis, so could other "sensible" people.

d. they dismissed it as the work of a madman.

e. they were angry at the government for not being able to find them jobs.

f. they wanted the people to think the government couldn't keep law and order.

g. Germany suffered from many severe postwar problems, which Hitler promised to cure.

h. Hitler wanted to use Jews as the scapegoats for all the problems in Germany.

i. conditions were so bad that most people were fed up with the government.

j. the judge and jury who were disgusted with the government probably faulted it more than Hitler.

k. reporters published the story throughout the world and thus popularized the name of Adolf Hitler.

l. their leader, Rohm, kept them out of jail.

m. Hitler did not yet have enough support to take over the whole country.

n. he said that Jews had already "robbed" the power and that it was up to the rightful Aryan masters to destroy them and take over the world.

o. he believed they were biologically inferior, that is, less advanced in body and mind than any other group of human beings.

Exercise 3
Defining Terms

Directions: List these twenty words on your paper. Next to each word write its definition. Many are German words. All the words have been defined for you in Chapter 3.

1. hakenkreuz	11. Der Fuehrer
2. *Mein Kampf*	12. Sturmabteilung
3. Lebensraum	13. putsch
4. Third Reich	14. Aryan
5. Reichstag	15. Nordic
6. Luftwaffe	16. coup d'etat
7. Reichswehr	17. Nazism
8. Wehrmacht	18. propaganda
9. Schutzstaffel	19. Gestapo
10. Einsatzgruppen	20. SD

Exercise 4
Recognizing Information

Directions: Number your paper from 1–5. One of the points under each statement is **not** true. Write the letter of the **untrue** point next to each number.

1. Nazism was
   a. against using force
   b. against democracy
   c. against Christianity
   d. against Jews

2. The Nazis believed propaganda should be
   a. simple
   b. in the form of slogans
   c. repeated constantly
   d. based on truth

3. The Nazis believed Aryans were
   a. the smartest people on earth
   b. meant by nature to rule over the rest of the earth
   c. entitled to take others' land
   d. willing to discuss these rights with others

4. The Nazis believed in
   a. having a totalitarian state
   b. using fear to rule the people
   c. lying to the people
   d. giving the Germans a voice in their government

5. The Nazis said Jews were
   a. trying to take over the world
   b. human beings
   c. to be blamed for all the evil in the world
   d. the lowest "race" of people on earth

GIVING REPORTS

Topics to Research

1. Hitler's private life and character while he was dictator and warlord. Good sources: *The Horns of the Moon*, by Gene Smith; *Hitler's Hang-ups*, by Mina C. and H. Arthur Klein; *The Mind of Adolf Hitler: A Secret War-time Report*, by Walter Langer.

2. Notorious Nazis. Good source: *The Face of the Third Reich: Portrait of Nazi Leadership*, by Joachim C. Fest.

   Reinhard Heydrich   Gregor Strasser
   Adolf Eichmann   Ernst Kaltenbrunner
   Martin Bormann   Julius Streicher and his anti-Semitic newspaper *Der Sturmer*

3. Rudolf Hess, Hitler's secretary, who later lived in Spandau Prison in Berlin. He died in 1987.

4. The Nazis' twenty-five-point party platform presented on February 15, 1920. Point out how many points were aimed at punishing Jews. Good source: *The Life and Death of Adolf Hitler*, by Robert Payne, pages 143–145.

5. Read aloud the dedication from Hitler's book *Mein Kampf*. Tell who the "heroes" are that he glorifies, what event this dedication commemorates, and from which place the dedication is written.

6. In *Mein Kampf*, read the section entitled "Nation and Race." Though the text is very difficult to understand, try to find ten sentences describing Hitler's contempt for Jews. Read them aloud to your class.

7. The "censored" versions of *Mein Kampf* that were sold in England and France. Tell what was cut out and why.

8. Selected passages from *Final Entries, 1945; The Diaries of Josef Goebbels,* which refer to Jews.

9. Hitler's adult character. Read two chapters entitled "A Man Possessed" and "The Anatomy of a Liar" from the book *Hitler and Nazism,* by Louis B. Snyder.

10. More on Hitler as a politician. Read Chapter 6, "The King of Munich and His Court," from the book *Adolf Hitler,* by Frank Gervasi.

11. Jews as great contributors to the culture of the world (contrary to what Hitler said). Good sources: *An Index to Young Readers' Biographies,* by Judith Silverman; *American Jewish Heroes,* by Rose G. Lurie; *Great Jewish Women,* by Elma C. Levinger.

12. Himmler's *Lebensborn* program.

13. The lyrics of Nazi songs called the "Horst Wessel Song" and "Germany Awake!" (Deutchland Erwache!). Tell who the "hero" Horst Wessel was. Point out how both songs reflect hate and violence.

14. In at least three or four encyclopedias, research the swastika. Tell of its meaning and uses by people throughout the world.

15. Hitler/Nazi propaganda strategies and techniques.

16. The economy of pre-World War II twentieth-century Germany as a contributing factor to Hitler's success.

MAKING PROJECTS

Poster and Artwork Ideas

1. See Number 4 on the previous page. Make a chart of the points that discriminated against German Jews. Use the colors red, white, and black.

2. See Number 14 above. Illustrate how the Nazi swastika differed from the ancient symbol by drawing one next to the other.

3. Find pictures of the uniforms of the SA, the SS, the German soldier, and the U.S. soldier. Draw large pictures of them in color.

Conducting A Classroom Debate

Hitler and his party chiefs may have been deranged fanatics, but his brutal SS killers often were not. Before their Nazi involvement, the majority had been what we think of as ordinary people. This brings up some questions about human nature. Are people by nature good? Or are they basically evil? Or is their morality shaped—for better or worse—by their environment? Think about these questions.

With concrete examples to support your opinion, take one of three sides: People are basically good, people are basically evil, or people's morals are subject to their environment. With your teacher as a moderator, conduct a debate. Arrange the chairs in your classroom like this:

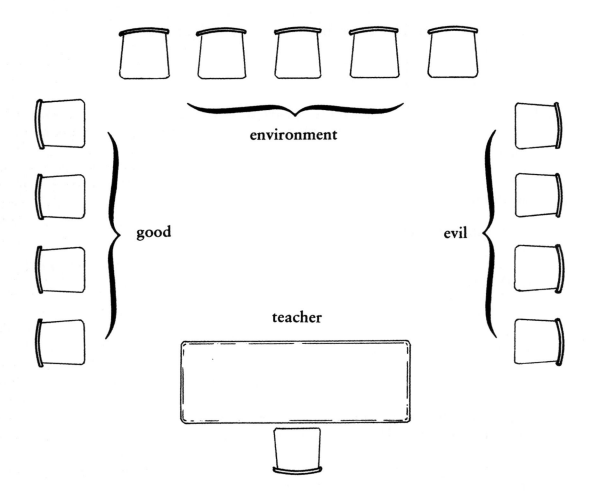

✡ CHAPTER FOUR

Why Germany?

Introduction

Why did the German people accept a dictator like Adolf Hitler? Why didn't they turn away from his anti-Jewish campaign? The answers lie in the German history of three distinct eras: (1) before World War I (up until 1914); (2) during World War I (between 1914–1918); and (3) after World War I (1919–1933).

GERMANY BEFORE WORLD WAR I (up to 1914)

Autocratic Military Leaders: The German Norm

Germans had no tradition of democracy. Authoritarianism, or willing obedience to the orders of an autocrat (a powerful and absolute ruler) had always been the accepted way of German life. In addition, all German leaders had been military men who used soldiers to help them govern.

The First Reich (or German Empire), a part of the Holy Roman Empire for over a thousand years, had been a loosely secured patchwork of farmlands. Peasants worked the land for their noble landlords who in return offered their tenants military protection.

This feudal system lingered on in parts of modern Germany hundreds of years after it had disappeared from the rest of Europe. It existed even after Otto von Bismarck (1815–1898), chancellor of King Wilhelm I (1797–1888), had united all the German lands to form the new nation of Germany in 1871.

In this new German nation, Wilhelm I, once the ruler of the Germanic land of Prussia, now became kaiser, or emperor, of the Second Reich. He, his chancellor Bismarck, and the Junkers, their noble army officers, continued to rule over the new nation with an iron hand. Not only were the Junkers the commanders of the German army, they also held the majority of high government positions. Besides that, they owned nearly all the land of Prussia, now the largest of the twenty-five German states. Prussia held two thirds of the people and land in the new Germany.

Kaiser Wilhelm II (1859–1941), who came to the throne in 1888 and ruled until World War I ended in 1919, was also a hard despot. The racist type of nationalism that was sweeping over the new German nation infected him, too. In fact, Wilhelm II believed Germans were a master race destined to rule the world. Promising Germans a "place in the sun," he began to acquire new colonies and expanded the army and navy to make Germany the strongest military power in all of Europe.

Under Kaiser Wilhelm II, German men had to serve in the military in some capacity until they were forty-five years old. Thus, obeying orders of military authorities had become an acceptable way of life long before Hitler and his Nazis arrived on the scene.

Discussion Question: How did the pattern of authoritarianism and militarism set the stage for a dictator like Hitler?

MODERN GERMAN ANTI-SEMITISM

A By-product of German Nationalism

By the time the new German nation was formed in 1871, German Jews had become thoroughly assimilated into German life. They differed from their neighbors only in their religious worship. A tiny minority comprising about 1.25 percent of the total population, these Jews were mostly middle-class citizens living in German cities. In addition to being involved in their traditional business roles, many had also entered the professions of law, teaching, music, and medicine. However, they were still barred from civil service jobs and officer positions in the army. Despite this, most German Jews were optimistic that anti-Semitism was on the wane. German nationalism was to prove them wrong.

Compared to the other countries of Europe, the German nation was very young. The long-awaited and welcomed unification of German lands had come at the end of three wars that the German army had won easily and quickly. As a result, the proud and victorious German people began to develop a fierce pride in their "German-ness." This intense glorification of themselves and their new nation caused some Germans to go to extremes.

Only true Volk, or German folk, should be citizens of our new state. The true Volk is the German peasant who has been tied to German soil for centuries; we are united by blood, language, traditions, and culture,

claimed the proud Germans. Then they began to question Jewish citizenship:

Jews are not the true German Volk. They are city people whose ancestors lived in the deserts of Palestine. They are an international people without true roots who are tied together not by German traditions and culture but by their own religion and culture. Jews should not be German citizens.

German Nationalism Becomes Racism

Then German nationalism turned to racism. The new discovery of different language groups, including Semitic and Aryan (sometimes referred to as Nordic or Germanic), prompted pseudoscientists to come forth with "racial theories."

Among others, Frenchman Arthur de Gobineau (1816–1882) and Englishman Stewart Chamberlain (1855-1927) said that Aryans and Semites belonged to two different races. They also added the myth that blonde, blue-eyed Aryans were the most superior race, while Semites were the least advanced form of human life. These racists spread tales labeling Jews as carriers of "bad genes and blood" and warning that marriages to them would produce Aryan children with "polluted blood."

Writer Wilhelm Marr, the originator of the word "anti-Semitism," spread the belief that Germans could never live in harmony with Jews, for it was part of "Jewish nature" to take over every country where they lived.

How could such a small, "inferior" Jewish minority have the strength to take over the entire world? Racists seemed to contradict themselves here. They said "Jewish strength" came from the "purity of the Jewish race."

New Problems Intensify Jew-Hatred

Two more situations added fuel to the fires of German anti-Semitism. An economic depression hit in 1873. Racist Jew-haters were quick to point the finger of blame at "selfish Jewish bankers and speculators" who had "manipulated the money market for their own selfish interests." What the accusers ignored were two important facts: (1) the majority of German bankers were non-Jews, and (2) the young German economy had lacked the protective measures to keep it stable.

Then Jewish immigrants fleeing from horrible pogroms in Poland began to pour into Germany. Their Eastern European manners and style of dress not only made them stand out in this modern Western world, but also convinced the racists that Jews were indeed "different."

German Anti-Semitism Becomes a Political Movement

By the late 1800's, German anti-Semitism had become a political movement. A minister, Adolf Stoker (1835–1909), who also served as Kaiser Wilhelm's chaplain, was one of the first Germans to form an anti-Semite political party. Stoker's platform? To make Germany solely a Christian state.

Racist fanatics like Paul de Lagarde (1827–1891) weren't even satisfied with that. They urged their countrymen to drop Christianity altogether because it had Jewish roots. Even the noted German historian Heinrich von Treitschke (1834–1896) called Jews a "German misfortune." He urged an end to Jewish immigration and favored more anti-Jewish discrimination.

In the late 1880's, another group of German citizens climbed on the anti-Jewish bandwagon. They spread a petition urging Bismarck to get rid of Germany's Jews. Nearly a quarter of a million Germans signed the petition.

As ambitious politicians witnessed this popular support, more and more anti-Semitic political parties were formed. Their platforms called for a variety of solutions to the "Jewish problem," ranging from removing Jews from the professions and the universities to expelling them from Germany entirely.

By the turn of the century, some German Jews, disillusioned by racial and political hatred, left Germany. Many migrated to America. But the majority of German Jews stayed because they regarded Germany as their true home. They hoped the storm of new anti-Semitism would pass. It did—temporarily.

But by the time Hitler and the Nazis had entered the German political arena, anti-Semitism again pervaded every level of German society.

Discussion Questions: Why was nationalism in Germany at its peak by the twentieth century? From old religious anti-Semitism, Jews could escape through baptism. Why could they not escape racist anti-Semitism?

Rapid Changes in Germany Create an Uneasy Atmosphere

By the turn of the twentieth century, nationhood and rapid industrialization had brought bold, dramatic changes in Germany.

Industrialization had sharply changed Germany's agricultural face. The new nation had become the leading industrial power in Europe and was second only to the United States in the world. Railroads sliced through once peaceful pastures. Black smoke poured from factory chimneys and polluted the fresh country air.

Major cities had grown overnight. Berlin, for instance, had tripled its population within thirty years.

Germany's traditional two-class system had also gone by the wayside. Once-obedient peasants had left their Junker landlords' estates to pour into the cities where the factories were. A new industrial working class had emerged. So had a new middle class, as more and more people earned money and became property owners for the first time. Now they were shopkeepers, small farmers, and tradesmen.

The first stirrings of democracy were being felt and were threatening the old autocratic government order. Socialist factory workers, demanding more rights and better working conditions, had formed labor unions and their own political party, the Social Democrat party. Many Jews, attracted by the democratic ideals of socialism, had become Social Democrats. Other Jews joined the National Liberal party and the Progress party, which were also moving toward more government reforms.

Although all Germans were extremely proud of their new and powerful nation, not everyone was comfortable with the rapid changes. Fears and tensions had developed. And many of them were frequently heaped on the old scapegoat—the Jew.

Jews Are Blamed for Problems of Industrialization

The aristocratic landlords of the old manorial estates hated and feared giving up their power to city workers who had once been their slaves. They hated the new railroads that broke up their lands, and the crime and social problems brought on by the overcrowding of the cities. Since the cities had always been the centers of Jewish population, some Junkers labeled all the ills of the newly industrialized society "Jewish."

Some wealthy industrialists and big businessmen, eager for more and more profits, resented the competition of Jews in their fields of enterprise. They also blamed "Jewish socialists" for organizing the labor unions that they loathed.

There were people in the new middle class of small businessmen and small farmers who resented Jews, too. Fearful of losing their new

and better standard of living, they complained, "What if these new and larger Jewish-owned department stores cut our trade so much that we won't be able to pay our mortgages? They may force us out of business!" As soon as a money crisis threatened the new booming economy, these middlemen were always quick to say, "It's Jews in finance!" And because they were more comfortable with the old government order, they also feared the factory workers' drive for more political power. Here again they pinned the blame on Jews. They pointed to the few Jewish socialist leaders as the sponsors of the whole workers' movement.

Discussion Question: Why would Jews tend to be liberals and supporters of democratic movements?

GERMANY DURING WORLD WAR I (1914–1919)

Introduction

The internal confusion and tension in Germany mounted with the events of World War I. From the beginning of the war to its very end, Germans were led to believe victory was theirs. It wasn't. They lost the war. But never was the German public told the truth about how and why their nation had been defeated. In the minds of many anti-Semites, Jews again emerged as the scapegoat for this failure.

Wilhelm's Promise of Easy Victory Does Not Come

Kaiser Wilhelm's war cry and military buildup of Germany had triggered an arms race in Europe, divided the nations into two armed camps, and brought them to the brink of war. The assassination of Archduke Francis Ferdinand of Austria-Hungary on June 28, 1914, was just the excuse the nations needed to start the fighting.

As German soldiers went off to battle, their families cheered them on with flag-waving and brass bands. Kaiser Wilhelm had promised they would win the war so fast that the troops would be back home for Christmas. And Germans had no reason to doubt their leader. The glorious Reichswehr, the most powerful army in all of Europe, had not been nicknamed the "army of a thousand victories" for nothing.

By 1916, all the smiles and cheers had faded. The war had dragged on for two long years, hundreds of thousands of German soldiers had died in the miserable rat-filled trenches at the front, and the English blockade of German ports had brought the German people to the point of starvation.

A new wave of anti-Semitism grew. Ignoring the fact that tens of thousands of German-Jewish soldiers were now fighting at the front and that thousands more had already died in battle, Jew-haters began to spread tales that Jewish industrialists were dragging out the war for their own profits.

Not knowing which way to turn, Wilhelm handed the full reins of government over to his general staff. Field Marshal Paul von Hindenburg and General Erich von Ludendorff, the high commanders of the Reichswehr, became both the war directors and military dictators of Germany.

The miserable war dragged on for two more years. In the meantime, however, the Junker generals had done everything they could to keep alive the myth that the German army was indestructible. Carefully screening all war news to the German public, they censored all reports of defeats or setbacks and revealed only news of victories and advances. By the spring of 1918, when their armies had actually defeated the Russians and had pushed the British and French into retreat, they strongly assured the German people that victory was near at last.

But by September 1918, the tide suddenly turned against the German armies once and for all. The United States had entered the war, and the British had a powerful new weapon—the tank. Germany's allies began to give up one by one. Soon the German armies were in full retreat toward home.

Up until this time, no battles of the war had been fought on German soil. And the proud Junker generals had no intentions of allowing the glorious Reichswehr to be disgraced by defeat in their own country.

German Defeat: A "Stab in the Back"

Before their troops were forced to surrender on the soil of the Fatherland, the Junker generals hurriedly worked out a clever scheme to have a cease-fire called but to have others besides themselves call for it.

Off to Kaiser Wilhelm they went, with news that the war was lost and that a truce needed to be declared. To negotiate the truce, the Junkers suggested the kaiser form a new government to include the Social Democrats, representatives of the common people, for the Allies would probably offer better peace terms to such a government.

American President Woodrow Wilson unknowingly played right into the German generals' hands. When the kaiser's son, Prince Max, approached Wilson for an armistice, Wilson insisted on talking not with the warmongering emperor or any of his noble military leaders, but with representatives of the German people.

Smug and satisfied, Ludendorff resigned his commander's post, dressed in false whiskers and dark glasses, and flew off to Sweden. On November 9, 1918, Kaiser Wilhelm fled to Holland, never to return to his homeland. The German monarchy toppled. On the same day, Prince Max handed over the powers of his father's government to Friedrich Ebert, leader of the Social Democrats.

Germany became a federal republic, with Ebert as the new president. Two days later, on November 11, 1918, Ebert sent a group of representatives of the new German republic to Compiègne in France to sign the armistice. World War I was over.

The Junkers' scheme had worked. Afterward the noblemen created a "stab-in-the-back" story. They said their armies had not been beaten on the battlefield but had been "stabbed in the back" by government politicians who had forced the military to quit fighting by insisting on an armistice. They smugly contended that they as the military commanders had on no account asked the enemy for a truce.

Millions of proud Germans chose to believe this lie. Army Corporal Adolf Hitler believed it, too. He would later use this story to destroy the German republic. In his campaign speeches, he would call the signers of the armistice "November criminals" or "Jewish and communist traitors in the government" who had "stabbed Germany in the back."

Discussion Question: Why could the generals get away with saying that they hadn't been beaten in the battlefield?

GERMANY AFTER WORLD WAR I (1918–1933)

Introduction

Except for a brief period, conditions in Germany after the war went from bad to worse. Revolution, disorder, and chaos filled the air. German morale and pride were severely wounded by the war loss. Economic problems reached impossible proportions. Consequently, Germany descended from a democratic republic to a Nazi police state within fourteen short years.

THE NEW DEMOCRACY WAS WEAK

The Weimar Republic Is Blamed for Unpopular War Treaties

The revolutionary government, declared on November 9, 1919, was a democracy. The new German republic came to be called the Weimar Republic, named after Weimar, the town where its constitution was drawn up. The Weimar constitution provided one of the most advanced democracies in the world. But advanced or not, the new republic was doomed from the start.

The signing of the November armistice was the first strike against it. Defeat in the war was just too bitter a pill for most proud Germans to swallow. They preferred to use the government as the scapegoat for the defeat.

Seven months later, on June 23, 1919, the government was faced with signing another unpopular document, the Versailles Treaty, which officially ended World War I. The German people hated this treaty. They called it an unfair, harsh, and dictated peace. The Allies—the United States, England, France, and Italy—had insisted that Germany sign it, but they had refused to allow the Germans any part in drawing up the peace terms.

Not only did the Versailles Treaty blame Germany for causing the war, it also made the Germans responsible for paying 33 million dollars in war damages to surrounding countries. In addition, the treaty deprived Germany of much of her valuable land, such as Alsace-Lorraine and the Saar Basin, areas rich in iron, coal, and industry. All her overseas colonies were taken away, too. The final insult to the traditionally military-minded Germans was the treaty's provision that Germany disarm. The Germans had to strip their army down to 100,000 men, sharply reduce the navy, and eliminate the air force altogether.

Just to be sure the Germans obeyed, the Allies had placed all major German rivers and canals under patrol by international troops. And Allied soldiers were to be stationed off the west bank of the Rhine River for the next fifteen years.

Humiliated by the treaty, many Germans felt anger and resentment toward their government for signing it.

The Republic Has Few Supporters

Apart from bearing the blame for the war loss and the peace terms, the Weimar government was handicapped by lack of support to begin with. Not used to freedom, the majority of Germans, especially the upper and middle classes, felt more comfortable following the orders of a king.

Of the dozens of political parties that sprang up during the fourteen Weimar government years, twenty-five were active. Only a few were dedicated to democracy: the Liberals, the Social Democrats, the Socialist party, and the Catholic Center party. Among these, the Social Democrats, consisting mainly of German workers, were the largest democratic party in the Reichstag. But they did not have a majority. In order to run the government, they always had to form a coalition, or union, with other political parties. As the German republic's pack of postwar problems continued to grow heavier and heavier, it became harder and harder for the Social Democrats to gain supporters.

It Has Many Enemies

Almost from the very minute the republic was declared, it came under attack from both sides. Its strongest enemies were the right-wing Nationalists and the left-wing communists. (Nazis, to the extreme right, did not pose a real threat until after the Great Depression in 1929.)

The Nationalists were the upper classes: the Junker army officers and landowners, the big businessmen. They scoffed at government in the hands of the lower-class workers and looked down their noses at President Ebert, a one-time saddlemaker and now leader of the Social Democratic party. The industrialists hated the workers' unions that demanded a share in their business and profits. What these conservative Nationalists wanted was to restore the old order of government—the monarchy. Even though they outwardly had pledged President Ebert their support, they continually worked and plotted to weaken the new democracy.

The Communist party was comprised mainly of dissatisfied workers who had broken away from the Social Democrats. This split weakened the Social Democrats even further. The communists believed the democratic way of achieving reforms took too long. They wanted to overthrow the present political system in Germany by quick force, as the Russian communists (the Bolsheviks) had done during their proletarian revolution two years before in 1917.

The communists wanted all property and business to become nationalized, or state-controlled, so that all workers would share in the wealth. These German communists took orders and received money, help, and weapons from Moscow in Russia, the headquarters of world communism.

Discussion Question: How were the large numbers of political parties a strike against the Weimar government?

Bloody Revolution Follows the War

Even before the armistice had officially ended the war, news about the shaky German position in the battlefield had leaked out to the German public. Revolution broke out everywhere. Soldiers deserted their ranks. Rioting workers staged antiwar strikes and screamed for Kaiser Wilhelm to abdicate. Sailors at the naval base of Kiel mutinied. Many of them joined communist workers who began to swarm through Germany and to take over many city and town governments.

The minute the communists heard that Prince Max had transferred the government to the Social Democrats, they began to attack the new republic. President Ebert was forced to call on the support of regular army troops and Freikorps (Free Corps), ex-soldiers willing to fight. Deafening machine-gun fire and bloodshed wracked the streets as Germans killed Germans.

The communists didn't give up. In January 1919 they tried to seize the government of Berlin. One thousand communists lost their lives. In May they again attempted to overthrow the government of Munich, and several hundred more died. (At this time, Adolf Hitler, stationed in army barracks near Munich, was serving as a stool pigeon against soldiers who were communist sympathizers.)

Even a group of army officers tried to overthrow the government. In a revolt called the Kapp Putsch in March 1920, a group of Reichswehr officers seized the government of Berlin. When President Ebert called on army troops this time for help, they refused to fire on their own men. Only a strike by socialist workers ended this siege.

Political murders became an everyday occurrence. Between 1918–1922 alone, 300 politicians were shot down. Most were communist and Social Democratic leaders. And because some of these leaders had been Jewish, another wave of anti-Semitism grew. People blamed Jews not only for running the weak, shaky government but also for trying to overthrow it.

By October 1923, the Nazis had gotten into the act. Ebert's troops this time rushed toward Munich to put down Hitler, General Ludendorff, and the Stormtroopers in the Nazis' unsuccessful Beer Hall Putsch.

Like Hitler and his Stormtroopers, other political parties had their own private armies. All waged political wars, scuffled in the streets, and turned Germany into a battleground of civil war.

Adding to all this confusion were labor disputes between communist and Social Democratic workers, who clashed in the streets. Their strikes and demonstrations against factory owners kept tempers on edge. All the while, the Weimar government tried desperately to keep some semblance of order.

Discussion Question: If you were a citizen of Germany at this time, how do you think you would feel about your government?

Hyperinflation Adds to the Misery

The new republic was also plagued with an economy wrecked by staggering war costs and now the huge war debts imposed by the Versailles Treaty. By 1923, Germany lagged behind in her war debts to France, her old rival.

Refusing Germany's plea to lower the payments, angry Frenchmen sent troops to take over the Ruhr, Germany's heartland of iron and steel production, on January 11, 1923. Furious German workers refused to obey French orders, blew up trains, wrecked factories, and went on strike. Massive unemployment resulted.

To help the strikers, the Weimar government placed hundreds of thousands of them on welfare rolls. Then, rather than collecting more taxes to foot the bill for welfare payments and war debts, the German government decided to get even with the French by paying its bills with cheap money instead. It began to print huge quantities of paper money. Without the backing of gold reserves, the value of the German mark began to fall at an unbelievable rate.

In 1914, one German mark had been worth twenty-five cents in American money. By November 1923, the mark wasn't worth the paper it was printed on. One million marks was barely worth one American quarter.

Between January and November 1923, Germans went through a nightmare of money madness. By then, hundreds of paper mills and thousands of printing presses were operating round-the-clock to print the tons of useless paper money the German people needed to live on. Prices skyrocketed by the hour, so that the price of a loaf of bread one day could have bought the entire bakery a week before. People used baskets and suitcases to carry money from place to place. In one city, a man carrying a basketful of money placed it on the sidewalk while he quickly ran into a building. When he got back, he discovered a thief had dumped the money into a heap on the pavement and had stolen the item of greater value—the basket.

The hyperinflation did benefit some Germans. The government was able to pay off its debts with worthless money. The wealthier citizens not only cleared their debts but also used the cheap money to buy property and other goods.

It was the working classes, the people on pensions, and the new middle classes that suffered the horrible effects. Life savings had been wiped out overnight. Starving families stood and begged in the streets for food.

Once again Jew-haters blamed "Jewish politicians in the government and wealthy Jewish financiers" for creating the inflation.

A Five-Year Breathing Spell

Between 1924–1929, good times returned to Germany. Gustav Streseman, the new chancellor elected in 1923, changed the money system and ended the inflation. The French left the Ruhr. Americans poured dollars into the German economy. Germans went back to work and began to enjoy life. To make it easier for Germany to pay her war debts, the Dawes Plan and the Young Plan were worked out with the Allies. Conditions between Germany and England and France improved through treaties signed at the Locarno Conference in 1925. The Weimar government enjoyed a breathing spell from its trials and tribulations.

Without trouble and turmoil, the Nazi party began to die. Bavarian authorities had forbidden Hitler, now in Munich and on parole from Landsberg Prison, to speak in public until 1927. Nevertheless, he still worked feverishly in the background to build up the party again.

The Great Depression of 1929: The Last Straw

In October 1929, the final blow to the republic was struck. In the United States, the Wall Street stock market crashed. The Great Depression soon swept over most of the world. It hammered Germany the hardest. Now the bloodline of American dollars stopped feeding the German economy. When world trade sagged, Germany couldn't afford to buy food imports. Everything in the country slowed to a halt.

A sharp drop in farm prices resulted in thousands of farmers losing their farms and homes because they could not meet their mortgage payments. When the slump spread to the cities, thousands of factories ground to a halt. Bankrupt small businessmen closed their shops. Ruined bankers could pay their depositors only one tenth of the money in their bank accounts. By 1932, nearly 6 million Germans were forced to live in shacks on vacant lots and to accept free soup and bread handouts from government-operated soup kitchens.

As the depression got worse and worse, the suffering Germans looked for drastic change in their government. More and more began to listen to the radical solutions of the communists and the Nazis. Both party memberships grew.

Competing for support, communists and Nazis became bitter rivals. City streets, where they fought savagely, became the center of their power struggle. Once again, murders and violence became an everyday occurrence. In 1931 alone, 300 political murders took place.

The communists and Nazis had another goal: to destroy the republic as quickly as possible. They constantly worked at causing trouble. They organized strikes and demonstrations against the government.

By now, the German people had had it. They were tired of the street fights and political wars. They were tired of being hungry and cold. They wanted no more of a government that could not keep law and order or provide them with food and heat for their homes. They wanted a leader to restore the old order and harmony to Germany.

Their cries of woe were music to Adolf Hitler's ears.

Discussion Question: Why is it true to say that had the 1929 Depression not occurred, the Nazis probably never would have come to power?

Chapter Four Review

REVIEWING KEY POINTS

Exercise 1

1. How long did the First Reich last? The Second Reich? The Weimar Republic? (Give dates and number of years.)

2. Why were the Junker aristocrats so powerful in the new German nation during the Second Reich?

3. How did German nationalism make Jews outsiders in the new nation of Germany?

4. Discuss the "Volk" idea.

5. Why did racists warn Germans against marrying Jews?

6. Why did many politicians see fit to form anti-Semitic political parties?

7. Why did the Prussian aristocratic landowners blame most of the ills of the new industrialized society on Jews?

8. Why were the new middle-class small businessmen resentful of Jews?

9. Discuss how the army high command was able to arrange the stab-in-the-back story to explain Germany's defeat in World War l.

10. How many good years did the Weimar government have? (Give dates.)

11. Which class of Germans were the main supporters of the democracy? Why didn't the Social Democrats, the largest of all democratic parties, have much power?

12. Which two political parties were the strongest opponents of the democracy? What type of government did each of them want instead?

13. What two economic crises weakened the Weimar government even more?

14. When did the Nazis begin to gain power?

15. Which two groups were the Nazis' biggest rivals?

Exercise 2
Recognizing Information

Directions: Number your paper from 1–15. One of the points under each statement is **not** true. Next to each number, write the letter of the **untrue** point.

1. Up until World War I, Germans were used to

   a. autocratic rulers
   b. military rulers

   c.   an agricultural society
   d.   democracy

2. Modern German anti-Semitism was

   a. based on religion
   b. based on nationalism

   c.   based on racism
   d.   based on false racial theories

3. By the time the German nation was formed in 1871, German Jews were

   a. thoroughly assimilated
   b. rural dwellers

   c.   middle class
   d.   mostly business and professional people

4. Anti-Semitic politicians who preceded Hitler also said that

   a. Jews should be expelled
      from Germany
   b. Jews were inferior

   c.   more discriminatory laws against Jews
        were needed
   d.   Jews should be exterminated

5. Rapid industrialization in the late nineteenth century brought about the following changes in Germany:

   a. The power began to slip
      from the baronial landlords
      to the city workers.
   b. The center of life shifted from
      the quiet countryside to the
      noisy, overcrowded city.

   c.   Most people felt more comfortable in
        the new atmosphere.
   d.   The nation became the leading
        industrial country in Europe.

6. Some people used Jews as the scapegoats for all the ills of Germany's new industrialized society, including

   a. pollution
   b. progress

   c.   economic upheavals like inflation and
        depression
   d.   bankruptcy

7. People who preferred the old government order also accused Jews of promoting political movements such as

   a. communism
   b. socialism
   c. democracy
   d. authoritarianism

8. Before World War I, Germans gloried in their state and culture; but after the war ended, their morale hit rock bottom because

   a. they lost the war
   b. they had to pay huge war debts to other countries
   c. they "were stabbed in the back"
   d. they lost all their world prestige

9. To make matters even worse, the German people were led to believe they would win or could have won the war by

   a. the Allies
   b. misleading war reports given by the high army commanders
   c. Kaiser Wilhelm
   d. the fake stab-in-the-back story

10. The Germans hated the Versailles Treaty because it

    a. made them disband their armies
    b. denied them any voice in its peace terms
    c. blamed them for causing the war
    d. ended the shooting in the war before the German army was ready to give up

11. Some German leaders before Hitler were also

    a. evil Nazis
    b. warmongers
    c. obsessed with the master race idea
    d. autocratic

12. The democracy in Germany (the Weimar government) had little chance of success because it

    a. faced the worst economic and political problems in German history
    b. had to pay war debts with money it didn't have
    c. had few democratic supporters
    d. was sabotaged by the Social Democratic workers

13. The stab-in-the-back story was

    a. a lie
    b. believed by the Allies
    c. believed by most Germans
    d. used by Hitler to undermine the government

14. Nazism came to Germany in the 1920's and 1930's because

   a. the Germans had a long
      tradition of Nazism
   b. the Weimar government was
      weak

   c.   a communist revolution filled the air
   d.   severe postwar economic problems
        made most people look for a radical
        change in their government

15. Racist anti-Semites before Hitler said that Jews

   a. had inferior bodies
   b. had inferior minds

   c.   were mixed breeds
   d.   had the strength to take over the world

Exercise 3
Choosing the Correct Answer

Directions: Number your paper from 1–10. Choose the answer below each statement that **best** completes it. Mark the letter of each correct answer on your paper.

1. Willingly following the orders of a powerful ruler is

   a. authoritarianism   b. socialism   c.communism

2. The largest of all German states was

   a. Bavaria   b. Prussia   c.Moravia

3. The ruler who made the German army the strongest in all of Europe during the nineteenth century was

   a. Wilhelm II   b. Wilhelm I   c.Frederick the Great

4. The German word for king is

   a. Junker   b. Volk   c.kaiser

5. The powerful Prussian noblemen were the

   a. Nationalists   b. Junkers   c.aristocrats

6. A unit of money in Germany is the

   a. cent   b. guilder   c.mark

7. The term used to refer to "pure-blooded" German is

   a. Prussian   b. Volk   c. German nationalist

8. The first time democracy came to Germany was

   a. after World War I   b. before World War I   c. during the nineteenth century

9. The German government created an inflation in order to use worthless money to pay her debts to her old enemy

   a. United States   b. France   c. England

10. The main event that opened the German door to Nazism was

    a. the inflation   b. the Great Depression   c. the Roaring Twenties

GIVING REPORTS

Topics to Research

1. Thousands of German Jews fled to America to escape anti-Semitism in Germany during the mid-nineteenth century. What did the following individuals contribute to American society?

   Levi Strauss   Nathan Straus
   Adam Gimbel   Meyer Guggenheim
   Julius Rosenwald

2. The code of behavior of the old Order of Teutonic Knights became the "Prussian spirit" glorified by the Prussian Junker officers and landowners in modern Germany. What was that code?

3. The nature of the German people. Read Chapter 1, "Germany and the Germans," in the book *Modern Germany, Its History and Civilization*, by Koppel S. Pinson.

4. More on anti-Semitism in modern Germany before Hitler. Good source: Read Chapter 2, "Anti-Semitism in Modern Germany," in *The War Against the Jews 1933–1945*, by Lucy Dawidowicz.

5. More on the "Volk" concept. Good source: *The Crisis of German Ideology*, by George Mosse.

6. The German philosopher Johann Fichte (1762–1814), called the Father of German Nationalism. Tell of his philosophy of "German-ness" and his feelings about Jews.

7. The anti-democratic and anti-Semitic writings of Freidrich Nietzsche (1844–1900), another popular German philosopher.

8. "Spartacus Week" in Germany in January 1918, a radical communist movement led by two Germans named Rosa Luxemberg and Karl Liebkecht. Good source: *Sieg Heil!*, by Stefan Lorant.

9. The Stahlhelm, another private army (like the SA) of ex-World War I German soldiers who also opposed the Weimar government.

10. Why did Hitler admire the famous German composer Richard Wagner (1814–1883)? Good source: *Adolf Hitler*, by John Toland, Volumes I and II.

11. Feudalism in Prussia during the late nineteenth century. Good source: *The Rise and Fall of the Third Reich*, by William Shirer.

12. More about the racist thinking of Stewart Chamberlain (1855–1927). Good source: *Hitler*, by Joachim C. Fest.

13. The nature and aims of the Thule Society in Munich, Germany. Good source: *The Life and Death of Adolf Hitler*, by Robert Payne.

14. Details of the Dawes and Young plans regarding Germany's war debts.

15. The Locarno Conference.

16. Jewish industrialists in Germany.

17. The role of Jews in the labor unions in pre-World War II Germany.

18. The economic basis of anti-Semitism in Germany.

19. The relationship between class structure and political parties in pre-World War II Germany.

A Book to Review

The Adventures of Gluckel of Hamelin, by Bea Stadtler, a biography that gives an excellent view of German-Jewish life during the seventeenth and eighteenth centuries.

MAKING PROJECTS

Poster and Artwork Ideas

1. The main provisions of the Versailles Treaty regarding Germany.

2. A graph showing the decline of the German mark from 1918–1923. A table of figures appears in *Hitler and Germany*, by B.J. Elliott.

3. A picture of a Prussian Junker in uniform.

4. A map of unified Germany in 1871.

AUDIOVISUAL SUGGESTIONS FOR CHAPTER FOUR

1. Rent *Part I, The Rise of Hitler*, which reveals how he manipulated his way to power, why his master race idea took hold, and how he and his Nazis overthrew the Weimar government "legally." **ADL**

2. The book *Sieg Heil! An Illustrated History of Germany from Bismarck to Hitler*, by Stefan Lorant, is an excellent pictorial history of this period.

3. Rent *Hitler: Anatomy of a Dictator*, a 22-minute black-and-white film that concentrates on Germany's economic and political problems between World War I and World War II. **LCA**

4. A package of two filmstrips and two cassettes entitled *The Holocaust*—an overview analyzing anti-Semitism and culture in pre-Nazi Germany, Nazi racial theories, and the horrors of the Holocaust. **AVNA**

5. View *Mein Kampf*, a 117-minute black-and-white video, for a look at German fascism and its consequences. This film begins with the rise of Hitler in post-World War I Germany and ends with his defeat in World War II. **EHE**

✡ CHAPTER FIVE

Hitler's Seizure of Power, 1930–1933

Introduction

One year before the Great Depression struck, the Nazis were the smallest political party in Germany. In the 1928 elections, they had polled only 800,000 votes and gained 12 seats in the Reichstag. It was the 1929 crash that provided the turmoil and trouble that not only gave the Nazi party new life but also was the final death blow to the German republic.

ELECTION OF 1930

Hitler had answers to all of Germany's problems. With the help of his fanatical followers, he staged a whirlwind campaign for the 1930 elections. They put on dazzling torchlight parades with thousands of Stormtroopers goose-stepping under swastika banners. Records and films of Hitler's speeches played in beer halls everywhere. The radio carried Hitler's voice to homes in every corner of Germany.

It worked. Some 6.5 million German voters climbed on the Nazi bandwagon. One hundred seven seats in the Reichstag went to Nazi representatives. Next to the Social Democrats' 143 seats, the Nazis now were second. Adolf Hitler was no longer a joke.

Nor were the communists. Coming in third with 4.5 million supporters and 77 Reichstag seats, they too, had proven their strength.

HITLER THE VOTE-GETTER

He Is a Powerful Speaker

What was it about Hitler that moved many good, sensible people to accept him? It was his voice. Judged by many to be the most powerful orator of modern times, Hitler was also said to be a mass hypnotist.

Like a locomotive, Hitler's voice was always soft and even at the beginning of a speech. Then it picked up speed to a rapid fire of ranting, raving, and harsh screaming. All the while Hitler wildly waved his arms and slammed his fists on the podium to make each point. His pale blue eyes bulged and seemed to pin his audience to their seats.

His power over crowds was unbelievable. People listened with openmouthed attention. And they became hysterical right along with him. Women swooned and fainted. Men howled with excitement. To halt their earsplitting screams and thunderous applause instantly, Hitler needed only to raise a hand. After his speeches ended, many in his audiences could not even remember exactly what he had said. They were convinced only that Adolf Hitler was Germany's Messiah, destined to save their nation.

He Is a Demagogue

What did Hitler say to create such hysteria? He was a demagogue, a selfish leader who took advantage of a bad situation. To gain support, he harped on the fears and worries of the masses and played upon their emotions. Then he promised a cure for each and every problem. However, his real motive was not really to help the people but to gain power and money for himself alone. Nevertheless, his technique worked, for there were very few Germans who remained untouched by their country's critical problems. Millions of voters from all walks of life swallowed Hitler's promises.

Unemployed workers went for Hitler's promise of jobs and bread. Small farmers and shopkeepers who were nearly bankrupt accepted his pledge of decent earnings. Thousands of industrialists, hopeful of having their pockets filled with huge profits, also pulled the Nazi lever of the voting machines.

Millions of urban Germans, fed up with the crime and disorder in the cities, welcomed Hitler's promise to restore law and order. And when Hitler vowed to destroy the communists, he calmed the greatest fear of the upper- and middle-class property owners: that the communists would take over Germany and seize all their private holdings and wealth.

Not many voters could resist Hitler's promise to restore honor and glory to Germany. When he said he would tear up the hated Versailles Treaty, refuse to pay the war debts, and make the German army the strongest in all the world, it was exactly what Germans wanted to hear.

Furthermore, Hitler's use of scapegoats for Germany's battered condition freed millions from their own personal guilt. They wanted to believe Hitler when he shouted, "Traitorous politicians in the corrupt republic stabbed the German army in the back and made us lose the war! Down with the November Criminals!" And many, not wanting to be losers, rallied behind Hitler's scream, "We Germans are a master race destined to rule the world!"

What about the "Jewish Question"? This was not a burning issue in the voters' minds. Yes, there were anti-Semitic voters; but the majority of Germans were not against Jews per se. It was Hitler's cure-all campaign that they liked. The Jewish issue was a sideline.

Hitler the orator knew this. So he always proceeded with caution in his attack on Jews. He always waited until he had whipped up the crowds to a frenzy before blasting Jews. "It is they who are the real enemies of our country. They dragged out the war and caused the inflation and depression. The Weimar government is nothing but a Jewish instrument! Free Germany from the Jews!" By then the crowds were willing to applaud anything Hitler said.

Unfortunately, even some of the initially unbiased would come to accept the idea of Jews as "the internal enemy of the Reich." The next several years of Nazi propaganda in the new Nazi state would see to that.

Discussion Question: Assuming you were a jobless, hungry German listening to Hitler's promises, how do you think you would have responded?

CONDITIONS IN GERMANY WORSEN (1930–1933)

Between 1930 and 1933, the depression deepened. To help Germany, American President Herbert Hoover declared a moratorium, or postponement, of Germany's war debts in 1931. Then, at the Lausanne Conference in 1932, the country's debts were cut drastically. Finally, Germany had to stop payments altogether. There was no money.

To make matters worse, the Weimar government stopped functioning. In a state of deadlock, the political parties could not agree on a suitable program to ease the depression. Nazi delegates were pulling one way; communist delegates were pulling another. And the Social Democrats and other parties in the middle could not form a coalition. As a result, the Reichstag was dissolved time after time. New Reichstag elections were held over and over again. A series of new chancellors came and went. It was no use. The republic was all but dead. President Hindenburg (the old war general who had been elected president in 1925) and his cabinet were forced to run the government by passing emergency laws.

HITLER MANEUVERS HIS WAY TO POWER LEGALLY

Hitler's Strategies

Meanwhile, with millions of the masses now behind him, Hitler still needed to do several things before Germany could legally become Nazified: (1) gain support of the Junker Nationalists, (2) crush the communists, (3) destroy the democrats, (4) have his Nazi representatives gain the majority of seats in the Reichstag, and (5) be named chancellor and then president.

Hitler Gains Control of the Nationalists

Moving first to gain the support of the monied classes, Hitler assured businesspeople that they would still be able to own, operate, and profit from their factories in the new Nazi state. He told the aristocratic Junker army officers that they were to rebuild and command the Wehrmacht, the new and great army of the German people.

These groups took the bait. They began to pour millions into Nazi party funds. These Junkers and businesspeople had no real love for Hitler, whom they regarded as a crude nobody. But the logic behind their support went something like this:

Only force can smash the Russian menace of communism in Germany. Perhaps this Hitler barbarian and his band of ruffians are the answer. And they do have the support of the German people. As Germans, at least they are the lesser of the two evils. Later, when Hitler is leader, we'll tame him. He'll be only a figurehead who follows our orders.

Little did they know how violently their plan would backfire.

The 1932 Elections

Ex-army Corporal Hitler decided to run against Hindenburg, former commander-in-chief of the Reichswehr, for the office of president in the 1932 elections. He lost. However, Nazi power was growing steadily. Hindenburg scored 19 million votes to Hitler's 13.5 million. Again the communist candidate came in third.

When national elections were held in July 1932, the Nazis emerged as the largest single political party in Germany, with 230 seats in the Reichstag. Encouraged Stormtroopers began to slaughter hundreds of communist and socialist workers in the streets. Their murderous attacks on unarmed Jews began to increase.

However, in November 1932 when the Reichstag was dissolved and new elections held again, the Nazis lost 2 million votes. Hitler was worried. So were the Junkers and big businessmen, who saw the republic quickly crumbling and communism right around the corner. They decided to move quickly.

Hitler Is Named Chancellor

On January 30, 1933, President Hindenburg named Adolf Hitler the new German chancellor. He had done so very reluctantly, for he despised Hitler; but he had given in to men around him who urged the appointment. The aging president had taken one safety precaution first: He had selected a new eleven-man cabinet including only three Nazis and eight other men who he felt would keep Hitler in hand. He couldn't have been more wrong.

Communists and Democrats Are Hitler's Next Victims

Chancellor Hitler was ready for his next kill: the 100 communist and 121 Social Democratic delegates who stood in the way of a Nazi party majority in the Reichstag. Calling for new elections to be held on March 5, 1933, he set out to destroy his competitors.

On the night of February 24, 1933, Nazi Hermann Goering led a small group of Stormtroopers through an underground passageway leading from his home to the Reichstag building. They carried gasoline with them. Flames soon shot up through the dome and windows of the Reichstag building, gutting it within a few hours.

"The communists did it!" Hitler later screamed. "It's the beginning of another Bolshevik Revolution!" Within twenty-four hours after the Reichstag fire, Hitler had talked the frightened President Hindenburg into signing an emergency law called The Law for the Protection of the People and State. It gave the government the right to arrest or even kill "enemies" of the German nation. With the signing of this law, all civil rights in Germany went down the drain. The Nazi reign of terror began.

Hitler's delighted Stormtroopers became mad dogs. Without warrants, they burst into homes, arrested tens of thousands of people, and dragged them off to prison. When the jails overflowed, the building of concentration camps began.

Communists were not the only ones to be arrested. Hitler used the new law to houseclean Germany of all his political enemies: Social Democrats, Socialists, Catholic Center party members, and trade union leaders. But not many

Jews. Not yet. Special treatment for them was in the planning stages.

The Nazis Gain the Majority of Seats in the Reichstag

Just as Hitler had ordered, elections were again held on March 5, 1933. Frightened by the "new communist revolt," over 17.25 million Germans voted for the Nazis. Still a majority of Germans did not want them. With only 43 percent of the popular vote and 288 seats in the Reichstag, the Nazis needed to gain more ground.

It was the Nationalist party delegates that tipped the scales in the Nazis' favor. Joining ranks with Hitler's men, their support gave the Hitlerites 52 percent of the vote in the Reichstag.

Hitler didn't stop there. Calling them enemies of the state, he ordered the immediate arrest of the 81 communist delegates and dozens of Social Democrat representatives from the Reichstag.

Now the Nazis had the absolute majority they needed.

The Enabling Act Makes Hitler the Absolute Lawmaker

On March 24, 1933, the predominantly Nazi Reichstag passed another new law called the Enabling Act. This law gave Adolf Hitler sole power to make laws "to fight the crisis of the people and the state" without the consent of the parliament or the authorization of the constitution. The Weimar democracy and its constitution were now dead. The Third Reich, with Hitler as the supreme lawmaker, had begun.

Hitler's war on Jews was about to start. On March 26, Hitler gave Josef Goebbels instructions to organize a boycott of Jewish businesses.

Four months later, on July 14, 1933, Hitler made another law that proclaimed the Nazi party the only legal political party in Germany.

All others were outlawed.

Discussion Question: How could the Weimar government be dead if the Reichstag was still in "operation"?

Hitler Destroys the Stormtroopers in Order to Become President

To become absolute dictator of Germany, Chancellor Hitler still needed to be named president. In July 1934, eighty-six-year-old President Hindenburg was ill and near death. Hitler knew he could not gain this office without the support of the Junker army generals. However, there was one problem in the way—his Stormtroopers.

Now that Hitler had made it to the top, the Stormtroopers were getting restless. Rohm and his bullies clamored for a second revolution: "We did all the work to get you where you are. Now give us our due! We want the land, the money, the jobs, and the factories. Down with the Junker aristocrats! Germany's riches belong to us!" Furthermore, Rohm, Hitler's friend and right-hand man for over fifteen years, now wanted Hitler to name him minister of defense and to make the Brownshirts the official People's Army of Germany.

The proud generals, with the aristocratic "von" before their names, would not hear of this. To make the Brownshirts—that band of drunkards and misfits—the official Wehrmacht was, to them, out of the question. Before they would allow that, they threatened to knock the Nazis out of politics and to bring a Hohenzollern prince back to the throne.

Hitler knew that these well-trained Prussian soldiers and their powerful military weapons could overthrow him. He also realized that only they, and not his crude band of SA streetfighters, could conquer Europe and lead Germany to new glory. He decided his Stormtroopers had to go.

Hitler made a bargain with the army high command. He asked them to support him for president after Hindenburg's death. In return, he promised to destroy his SA and to give the old generals the same privilege they had enjoyed under the kaiser—a share in government power. In addition, Hitler assured them that they alone would bear arms and command.

The old monocled, high-booted officers shook hands with Hitler on the bargain. However, they really had other ideas. They reasoned that since they had used Hitler once before as their puppet to crush the communists and the republic, they could now use him to destroy the SA gangsters who were ravaging the country. Once that was done, they were sure they could tame this ex-corporal. So they thought.

In the end, the officers were to learn a bitter lesson: Hitler was no man's puppet, and his SS would become far more deadly and powerful than the SA had ever been.

Meanwhile, on June 30, 1934, Hitler and his SS began their massacre of the Stormtroopers. In a two-day shooting spree, later referred to as the Rohm Blood Purge, the SS gunned down more than a thousand of their Nazi SA brothers. Rohm, too, was shot to death. After this, the SA faded away.

HITLER BECOMES DICTATOR OF GERMANY

On August 2, 1934, President Hindenburg died. The day before, Hitler had made another new law, combining the offices of chancellor and president into one. Creating a new title for himself, Hitler became Reichsfuehrer, or leader of the Reich.

He also became commander-in-chief of the army. Within hours after Hindenburg's death, Hitler made all army personnel swear an oath of allegiance—not to their country but to him.

The army was his. The government was his.

On August 19, 1934, Hitler announced a plebiscite, or a direct vote of approval, of the people on his becoming Reichsfuehrer. Of the more than 43 million who cast votes, 38 million approved Hitler as their leader.

It seemed the people were his, too.

And just as he had once planned while a convict in Landsberg Prison, Adolf Hitler and the Nazis had come to power legally.

German Jews had voted in the election, too. Al Lewin, a Holocaust survivor who was an eight-year-old living in Berlin at the time, says:

I couldn't vote, of course, but my father did. I remember he told us all about it. There was a voting booth. An SS man stood watching. Hitler said he made it legally. Yes, that's true. But as for the counting of the votes, we didn't know the actual number for sure. It wasn't really a free and open situation like we have in this country. Someone was there watching over the vote-counting.

Chapter Five Review

REVIEWING KEY POINTS

Exercise 1

1. Why do demagogues like Hitler succeed only in troubled times?

2. What other political party besides the Nazis gained a foothold in Germany after the depression?

3. What was the biggest fear of the propertied classes during this time? What did Hitler promise he would do for them?

4. What did he promise to do for the German workers? the middle class, small businessmen, and farmers?

5. How did Hitler remove the shame of defeat in World War I from the German people?

6. How did he restore the intense German nationalism that had prevailed during the Second Reich?

7. Why was the Weimar democracy unable to function from 1930–1933?

8. What was the logic behind the monied class's support of Hitler?

9. Which two political parties were the strongest opponents of the Nazis?

10. What prompted Hindenburg to name Hitler chancellor?

11. How did Hitler arrange to have the Communist party destroyed in Germany?

12. What party formed a coalition with the Nazi representatives in the Reichstag to give them the majority of votes to run the government?

13. Why did Hitler destroy the SA?

CHECKING YOURSELF

Exercise 2
Filling In the Dates

Directions: Number your paper from 1–8. For the blank space in each statement, provide the correct date to make the sentence true.

1. In _____ the Nazis were the smallest political party in Germany.

2. The Great Depression struck in _____.

3. In _____ the Nazi party became the second largest political party in Germany.

4. By _____ Hitler's Nazis were number one in size.

5. Hitler was named chancellor on _____.

6. In _____ the Nazi representatives gained the majority of votes in the Reichstag.

7. On _____ Hitler and his SS killers executed the Stormtrooper leaders.

8. Hitler became president and absolute dictator of Germany on _____.

Exercise 3
Matching Terms with Definitions

Directions: Number your paper from 1–10. Match each word or phrase in Column I with a phrase from Column II. Use each item only once. Write the correct letter after each number on your paper.

COLUMN I	COLUMN II
1. demagogue	A. What Hitler called the signers of the armistice of World War I.
2. "November Criminals"	B. What many Germans called the communists.
3. "Russian menace"	C. The massacre of the Stormtroopers.
4. Reichstag fire	D. The law that destroyed all civil rights and freedom in Germany.
5. The Enabling Act	E. The law that made Hitler the supreme German lawmaker.

Exercise 3 (continued)

COLUMN I	COLUMN II
6. Rohm Blood Purge	F. A vote of approval.
7. plebiscite	G. Hitler ran against him for president.
8. The Law for the Protection of the People and State	H. The title of Adolf Hitler, the dictator of Germany.
9. Hindenburg	I. A Nazi scheme to incriminate the communists.
10. Reichsfuehrer	J. A leader who feeds off the fears and prejudices of the people.

GIVING REPORTS

Topics to Research

1. Article 48 of the Weimar Constitution and how it made dictatorial powers possible in Germany.

2. The role of Franz von Papen in Hitler's rise to power.

3. Alfred Hugenberg's role in helping Hitler to power.

4. More on Hitler's strategies in seizing power in Germany. Good source: *Hitler*, by Joachim Fest (read the chapter "Legal Revolution").

5. More on the Rohm Blood Purge. Good source: *Hitler, Mad Dictator of World War II* (Chapter 10), by John Devaney.

6. Hitler's "explanation" of the Rohm Purge to the Reichstag in July 1934.

7. The role of General Kurt von Schleicher in Hitler's rise to power. Find out why he was shot during the Rohm Purge.

8. Marinus van der Lubbe, the retarded communist who was accused, tried, and executed for causing the Reichstag fire.

9. Short biographies of these great German thinkers and writers who saw through Hitler's fake promises and tried in vain to warn their fellow citizens: Henrich Mann (1871–1950), Thomas Mann (1875–1955), Bertolt Brecht (1898–1956).

10. The role of communism as a spur for Hitler's plans.

Books to Review

1. *Reichstag Fire: Ashes of Democracy*, by John Pritchard (one of the series of *Ballentine's Illustrated History of the Violent Century*).

2. The following are good short biographies of Hitler: *Horns of the Moon*, by Gene Smith; *Hitler and Nazism*, by Louis Synder.

3. *The Nazi Voter*, by Thomas Childers, an examination of the social foundations of fascism in Germany from 1919–1933.

4. *The Nazi Seizure of Power: The Experience of a Single German Town, 1930–1935*, by William Sheridan Allen.

MAKING PROJECTS

Poster and Artwork Ideas

1. List Hitler's campaign promises for the 1930 elections.

2. Create a front page of a newspaper featuring the Nazi explanation of the Reichstag fire.

3. Create a front page of a newspaper featuring Hitler's explanation of the blood purge of Rohm and the SA.

4. Make a picture of Hitler at the speaker's podium giving a wild speech.

5. Make a graph of the Nazi rise to power, indicating their election results from 1928–1933.

6. Picture the Reichstag fire.

AUDIOVISUAL AID SUGGESTIONS FOR CHAPTER FIVE

1. Rent *Puppets*, an 11-minute black-and-white film on totalitarianism in which a marionnette introduces Hitler and other despots and explains how they have used scapegoats to gain power and to ultimately strip their underlings of all freedom. **ADL**

2. Rent *Rise to Power*, a 25-minute black-and-white film on how Hitler and his Nazis maneuvered their way to power. **MSU**

3. Show the first 20-minute segment ("Rise of the Nazis") of *Witness to the Holocaust*, a documentary. **ADL**

4. Show *Hitler: The Whole Story*, based on Joachim C. Fest's book *Hitler.* **NDR**

The Third Reich: A Terror State, 1933–1945

FEAR AND PROPAGANDA WORK

Hitler's Germany became a totalitarian state in which Nazis were the absolute masters of 66 million people. Without warrant or trial, they searched homes, tapped telephones, opened mail, imprisoned and executed thousands of innocent persons. They gave citizens no rights, no freedom of choice, no privacy. Only the good of the state mattered. Individuals didn't count.

Rule by fear was the Nazi way. Citizens soon learned that prison and hard labor awaited anyone who dared speak out against Nazis or their policies. Not even a harmless remark about a Nazi figure was tolerated. For instance, one young German secretary was jailed for two years because she had told her office friends a joke about Fuehrer Hitler.

The plainclothes Gestapo were the watchdogs of the Reich, constantly snooping and searching for Nazi "enemies," they lived and worked among citizens in every neighborhood, school, office, and factory in Germany. They had unlimited powers to arrest, to jail, or to kill anyone they pleased. Their victims had nowhere to turn for help. Local police were under the jurisdiction of the SS. So-called people's courts, composed of only loyal Nazi judges and lawyers, could not and would not interfere with Gestapo actions. As a result, most Germans who opposed the Nazis learned to keep their mouths shut and to mind their own business.

Propaganda was another Nazi control device. Propaganda slogans were drummed at the public over and over again like broken records: "Jews are Germany's enemies! The will of the Fuehrer is the will of the people! Aryans are the master race!" This effective propaganda technique worked. Soon many Germans came to accept Nazi ideas.

There was a reason, too, why Hitler frequently staged huge rallies in the big cities. It was to overwhelm the public with Nazi power and might. At such times, giant-sized Nazi flags were draped down the sides of tall buildings. Hundreds of thousands of uniformed soldiers goose-stepped down the cobblestone streets, a sea of swastikas dancing on their armbands. For hours on end, the deafening clack of their jackboots seemed to drum "Power! Power! Power!" into the spectators' heads.

Such big demonstrations of Nazi muscle swept average Germans off their feet. Most often they reasoned "Who am I to question the wisdom of the Fuehrer?"

No phase of German life in the Third Reich escaped tight control. Citizens soon learned that as long as they didn't question and did exactly what they were told, life was not really that unpleasant.

In the war on Germans Jews, Hitler moved slowly until fear and propaganda had done their work to suppress public outcry. In 1935 he passed special laws that made the mistreatment of Jews the civic duty of all Reich citizens. By then, most Germans who opposed the anti-Jewish laws kept silent for fear of their own lives.

As Al Lewin recalls:

. . . we had many non-Jewish friends who often visited us in the evenings. After a while, they began to look around twice before walking into our apartment. And some stayed away because they were afraid. From what my relatives told me, things were much worse in small towns where everyone knew everyone else.

Discussion Question: Assuming you were friends of the Lewins, what would you have done?

NAZI CONTROL OF LABOR

Under Hitler the depression vanished as Germany became a war machine. Unemployment lines disappeared as German men were called up to serve in the armed forces, to work in the war factories, or to build the **autobahns**, the superhighways built to aid the speedy transport of troops and military equipment. The profits of this economic boom went, however, not to workers but to the big company owners and Nazi leaders.

Workers were treated like robots. The Nazi Labor Front, which replaced all labor unions, forbade laborers to strike or to have any say about wages or working conditions. Hours were long; wages were low. By 1936, the average worker's weekly take-home pay was less than seven dollars.

A worker had no choice of jobs. Like a soldier, he was drafted and assigned to a special job whether he liked it or not. To keep tabs on performance, employers kept a written work report card for each employee. If absent from work without a good excuse, the worker was fined or sent to prison.

With the depression still fresh in their minds, most German workers accepted this regimentation—to them, a regular job and bread on the table were worth it.

Discussion Question: Why did the Nazi party truly not represent the workers of Germany as its party name—National Socialist German Workers' party—suggests?

CONTROL OF THE CHURCHES

Hitler Wants to Stamp Out Christianity

The Jewish religion was not the only one to come under Nazi attack. Christianity was under fire, too. Holocaust survivor Al Lewin comments on this:

I was in Dachau prison with a priest. He was more scared than I was. He had been jailed because he had refused to say during one of his sermons what the Nazis had told him to say. A belief in Jesus Christ was competition for Hitler, too. You really can't believe in two gods. Hitler wanted people to accept what he said as holy. He'd rather you listened to one of his speeches on a Sunday morning.

Although brought up a Catholic, the adult Hitler considered Christianity a nonsensical "Jewish invention" and the Bible "a pack of lies." He developed a long-range plan to stamp out Christianity in Germany. To erase Christianity from the next generation, he planned to shape young minds with Nazi propaganda in a compulsory organization for children called Hitler Youth. To steer adults away from Christian doctrine, he planned to use the pulpits of Germany as Nazi propaganda instruments.

He Tries to Nazify Protestant Churches First

Because Catholics looked to the Pope in Rome for leadership, Hitler figured it might be easier to Nazify the Protestant churches of Germany first. He passed a law making the state the controller of all church affairs. Then he tried to unify the twenty-nine different Protestant congregations in Germany into a single National Reich Church under the leadership of an obscure Nazi minister. In addition, all German ministers were ordered to both swear an oath of allegiance to Adolf Hitler and promote his doctrines in their Sunday sermons.

Hitler's plan didn't work. While some ministers did go along with the government, others could not stomach Nazi ideas. They rebelled, demanded an end to government control of churches, and openly criticized Nazi treatment of Jews.

SS punishment was soon in coming. They threw more than 800 ministers into concentration camps, closed their churches, and confiscated their property. Thereafter, fear of brutal SS tortures and death in Nazi prisons forced the majority of ministers to keep silent on Nazi policies.

Roman Catholics Are Next

Hitler also warred against Roman Catholics. In 1933, he signed a concordat, or treaty, with Pope Pius XII that guaranteed Catholics the right to manage their own affairs so long as they kept out of politics. But almost as soon as the ink dried on the paper, Hitler violated the concordat. Catholic teachers were dismissed from schools. Crucifixes that adorned classrooms were replaced with swastikas. The Catholic press was censored and their youth organizations outlawed. And thousands of priests and nuns were arrested and thrown into concentration camps.

In 1937 the Pope issued an encyclical called "With Burning Sorrow." It criticized Hitler for breaking their agreement and for spreading hatred toward Christ. Smuggled into Germany, the Pope's letter was read by brave priests from pulpits all over the country.

Hitler Postpones Attack on Churches Until War's End

Once the war started, Hitler eased up on his attacks against Christianity; he knew that churches helped to lift the people's morale. Thus, throughout the Nazi regime, the churches remained open and better attended than ever before.

But Hitler fully intended to resume his war on God once the war had ended. His fanatical Nazi friends, bent on the idea of a strictly German faith in the coming Reich, begged him to enforce the worship of Thor, Odin, and other pagan gods once upheld by their Germanic tribal ancestors. But Hitler had his own thirty-point plan that he planned to enforce for the future National Nazi Church. A few of his points:

1. *The swastika is to replace all crucifixes in churches.*

2. *The Bible is to be banned in Germany.*

3. *The replacement of the Bible—Mein Kampf, the most outstanding book of human morals ever written—is to be the basis of all religious sermons.*

4. *The following concept of Christ shall be conveyed: Christ was not a Jew. He was a leader who tried to rid the world of all Jews but instead was destroyed by them. Adolf Hitler is the replacement of Christ, the new Messiah who will carry on Christ's work. Through Hitler, the Third Reich will be Jew-free.*

Discussion Question: Do you think Hitler's plan for Nazifying Christianity would have worked?

CONTROL OF COMMUNICATIONS AND CULTURE

With absolute power over all newspapers, books, radio, theater, films, and even artwork, Josef Goebbels, Hitler's propaganda chief, placed the German people on a strict diet of Nazi propaganda. Before a book was published or a film or play presented, Goebbels' censoring committees, in charge of every field of communication and culture, first had to approve the work on two accounts: (1) The composer had to be a "racially pure Aryan," and (2) the work had to promote Nazi ideology.

As added insurance, the Nazis also eliminated all "non-Aryan influences" from these fields. All Jews and other "inferiors" were forced out of their professions. Their businesses were shut down. Tens of thousands of books written by non-Germans were burned to ashes.

On one occasion in 1937, Hitler himself kicked giant holes into priceless paintings that he didn't like. At the time, he was in a Munich art museum choosing "proper German art" for public display. And since he hated and labeled abstract modern art as "Jewish garbage," no German artist of the Third Reich was allowed to create it. Nor were German musicians permitted to play the music of Jewish composers.

Bored with the incessant Nazi propaganda bombarding them from every direction, many Germans stopped buying books and attending theaters. Some even risked tuning in to the English BBC radio station, even though they knew the Nazi penalty for that was death.

Because of the Nazis, Germany lost much talent. Many of the outstanding Germans in culture and communication were Jewish. They either fled from Germany during the early years of Nazi tyranny or were later destroyed in the Holocaust.

CONTROL OF YOUTH AND EDUCATION

Hitler Becomes the "Big Father" of German Youth

That many Germans opposed Nazism was no surprise to Hitler. That's why he used terror tactics to keep people in line. But Hitler knew that the minds of children, on the other hand, could be shaped like clay. As he once stated in a 1933 speech, "If an adult says, 'I will not come over to your side,' I will calmly answer, 'Your child belongs to us already.' What are you? You will pass on!"

As the "Big Father," Hitler assumed command of German children. He took over their upbringing, their education, even their leisure time. His Nazis forewarned parents that interference or failure to cooperate would result in imprisonment or in having their children sent to other Nazi homes to be reared.

He Wrecks the German School System

In the education of youth, Hitler cared nothing about reading, writing, and arithmetic. He once said:

I do not want an intellectual education. I want young people who will grow up to frighten the world . . . arrogant, violent, unafraid, cruel youth who must be able to suffer pain. Nothing tender and weak must be left in them!

Hitler wrecked the once highly acclaimed German school system by turning it into a Nazi training center. From the university level down to the elementary school, every course was Nazified. Brilliant Jewish teachers and professors (Albert Einstein was one) were fired. By the time Hitler was finished, some German youth had become so brainwashed, they actually turned their anti-Nazi parents in to be jailed.

A Typical School Scene in Nazi Germany

Imagine yourself in a typical elementary or secondary school in the Third Reich. Staring you in the face at the front of the classroom is a huge picture of Adolf Hitler. Law requires you to stand and salute it at least ten times a day. At lunchtime you recite a prayer to the Fuehrer thanking him for your food

All loyal Nazis, your teachers—who belong to the Nazi Teachers' League—have sworn an oath to Hitler promising to make you a Nazi and to use *Mein Kampf* as the foundation of all their teaching. This means, above all, that you must learn to hate Jews passionately and to believe you are a member of a master race that will rule the world by force. Since you will provide that force, you must be taught to lose your fear of death.

To drill Nazi ideas into your mind, all your textbooks have been rewritten. You also study a new course called "racial science." Math problems deal with bombs, soldiers, planes, machine guns. Stories in your reading book call the Jews "devils," "scum," even "poison mushrooms." You are warned that one Jew, like one poison mushroom, can destroy a whole town. Even the games you play with your classmates teach you to hate Jews. One of your favorite games is called "Jews, Get Out!"

He Takes Charge of After-School Hours, Too

To fill young minds with Nazism after school hours, Hitler organized two youth groups: Hitler Youth for boys from six to eighteen, and the League of German Maidens for girls from ten to eighteen.

A juvenile version of the German army, Hitler Youth became compulsory after 1936. Boys were drafted into it. As members, they attended military camp, trained to be soldiers, and studied Nazism. They also swore an oath to the Fuehrer, promising to give up their lives for him if necessary. A dagger, engraved with the words "Blood and Honor," was the graduation diploma from Hitler Youth.

For boys with strong Nazi feelings and qualities of leadership, six more years of training in one of Hitler's special schools for Nazi leaders lay ahead. Others went on to serve in the Nazi Labor Service, where they worked cultivating fields or building roads. After that, they laid down their shovels and took up arms for two more years in a branch of the military.

In their organization, girls too became fully indoctrinated into Nazism and prepared to deal with war. They wore uniforms, went backpacking on long marches, and learned survival techniques. However, not soldiering but mothering was to be their main role. The more Germans there were, the better the Fuehrer liked it, for more future soldiers and more Aryans were needed to fill up the living space Germany was to gain in her conquered lands. Consequently, one idea was repeated over and over again to German girls: "It is your duty to bear children for the Fatherland. The Fuehrer wills it! Marriage is unimportant!" As a result, many young teenagers—children themselves—became mothers, and there was little their heartsick parents could say.

After high school, eighteen-year old girls went on to serve a year working on farms or in homes caring for children of large families. This free baby-sitting service was another way to encourage German women to have more babies.

By the time German boys and girls had graduated from twelve years of Nazified education in schools, plus Hitler Youth or League of German Maidens, is it any wonder that many of their minds had been thoroughly poisoned by Nazism?

Discussion Questions: How do you think such schooling would affect you? Why were textbooks rewritten?

CONTROL OF THE ARMY

By 1938, Hitler had Nazified all public institutions except one: the army high command. Up to now he had given them elbow room, for he had needed their support. To appease them, he had followed through with all his promises: the massacre of his SA friends, the smashing of the communists, the rearmament of Germany. Moreover, the Junker generals had been busily at work during the past six years, training a half-million new servicemen and testing their new weapons.

Now, however, had come the time for a showdown. There was one part of their bargain that neither the Junkers nor Hitler intended to keep—that together they would share government power. Monarchists at heart, the old aristocratic generals could never be Nazis. They fully intended to replace Hitler once he had served their purposes. And because they felt Germany was not yet militarily strong enough, they did not like what now seemed to be Hitler's intention: to launch another war. Some of them secretly plotted to assassinate the Fuehrer.

Hitler struck first. In a quick and bloodless fashion, the Gestapo arranged several embarrassing scandals to force the generals to resign. Loyal Nazis filled their posts. And no one raised a finger to help the fallen generals.

By now, it was too late. Every serviceman had already sworn an oath of loyalty to Hitler, the commander-in-chief of all armed forces. Such oaths were never taken lightly. Furthermore, Nazism had already infiltrated all levels of the armed services.

Hitler's clamp on Germany was now complete. His all-out war on Europe and on Jews was next.

Discussion Question: In your opinion, why didn't Hitler have the Junkers executed?

THE NEW ORDER

With Germany firmly in his grip, a Nazified Europe was Hitler's next goal. He called his future plans for a Nazi-controlled Europe the **New Order.**

First, Hitler intended to make his old dream of uniting all German-speaking peoples come true. To form the New Greater Germany, he planned to annex, or join, to Germany his homeland of Austria, the Sudetenland of Czechoslovakia, Alsace-Lorraine, Danzig, Memel, and other scattered areas housing German-speaking peoples.

Then, because Germans needed more farmland and living space, his armies would simply take over the Slavic lands to the east—Poland, Russia, and Czechoslovakia. All Slavic leaders and intellectuals were to be murdered, and the remaining people were to be slave laborers for the Reich. German settlers would take over all Slavic land and property.

The remaining European countries would also come under Nazi rule. Nazi "protectors," or governors, would be the overseers. All industrial goods, raw materials, resources, wealth, and foodstuffs were to be shipped to Germany.

And all of Europe was to be made Jew-free.

THE NAZI CONCENTRATION CAMP OR KZ

Not an Ordinary Jail

The KZ, or Nazi concentration camp, was

very different from an ordinary jail or prison. Normally, criminals are removed from society and forced to live in prison to pay for their crimes. In a Nazi prison, on the other hand, criminal guards held sway over decent people who had broken no laws. These guards committed countless crimes against their prisoners every day. In fact, Nazi law gave camp chiefs a license to murder, starve, and torture prisoners. SS doctors even used camp prisoners as guinea pigs for horrible medical experiments.

The camp masters, a special division of the SS called the **Death's Head Unit**, had complete charge of all Nazi prison camps after 1934. They generally chose prisoners who were sadists, hardened criminals, or murderers to help them manage other prisoners within the camp. These prisoner guards, called **Kapos**, were granted special privileges by the SS and were usually as vicious as the SS themselves.

Camp Victims

Who were the camp victims? Germans who were Hitler's political enemies, such as communists and socialists, were the first to be carted off. Then followed every other German Hitler wanted out of the way: Protestant church leaders and ministers, Catholic priests and nuns, trade union leaders, Freemasons, Jehovah's Witnesses, common criminals, homosexuals. Within six months after he had become chancellor in January 1933, Hitler had shoved 25,000 of his own countrymen behind bars.

Numbering more than fifty within a single year's time, the camps could hardly be built fast enough. Dachau (the first Nazi concentration camp), Mauthausen, Flossenbürg, Theresienstadt, Buchenwald, Gross-Rosen, Sachsenhausen, Ravensbrück (the "women's camp"), and Bergen-Belsen (a transit camp for prominent Jews that could be used as hostages) were among the most notorious built on German soil. Once the war began and Hitler increased his

stranglehold, Nazi prisons spread all over Europe. The number of camp inmates increased to millions.

Except for Jewish political enemies, Hitler did not declare open season on the Jewish community until 1938. But from then until the war ended, millions of Jewish children, women, and men suffered inside the Nazi barbed-wire pens.

Other camp victims included hundreds of thousands of prisoners of war, other Nazi-declared "inferior races" such as Poles, Russians, Slovaks, Gypsies, and countless war victims from all over Europe.

Labor Camps

The Nazis did not allow the enormous reservoir of manpower within their prisons to go to waste. Many concentration camps became labor camps that provided the Reich with a cheap way to run its industries. Camp guards forced prisoners to perform hard labor for twelve to fifteen hours a day, six days a week. A slave laborer's diet? Watery soup, phony coffee, and a few slices of stale bread made of sawdust. And no pay.

When labor-camp workers collapsed from starvation and overwork, the Nazi slave drivers did not care, for the Gestapo were always busy arresting healthy replacements.

Although a few lucky inmates were released from these concentration camps during the early years of the Reich, Nazi law forbade them, under penalty of death, to reveal any of their camp experiences.

Death Camps and Transit Camps

By 1941, Hitler had decided upon a "final solution" to the Jewish Question—a plan to make all of Nazi-occupied Europe Jew-free. How? By the mass murder of the entire Jewish population. Two new types of Nazi camps built expressly for this killing operation appeared in 1941 and 1942, while the war was in full progress. These were death camps and transit camps.

Not concentration camps in the true sense, most of the death camps were equipped not for housing and holding prisoners but only for killing them. All death camps were located in Nazi-occupied Poland. (See Chapter Nine.)

Transit camps, which grew up mainly in the countries of Western Europe, served as tempo-rary collecting centers for Jews on their way to the death camps in Poland. While held at the transit camps, Jews were put to forced labor.

Discussion Question: How did the Nazi prisons show a true picture of the criminal nature of the Hitler regime?

Chapter Six Review

REVIEWING KEY POINTS

Exercise 1

1. Discuss the many ways that Nazis used fear to control the masses.

2. How did Hitler cure mass unemployment in Germany?

3. Why did the Nazis allow the churches to remain open during the war?

4. Discuss how the Nazis used the following as propaganda devices: schools, communication, culture, churches, youth groups, rallies.

5. Discuss how children were taught to hate Jews and to be warlike.

6. Why did Hitler wait until last to Nazify the army?

7. Discuss Hitler's plans for the "New Order."

8. Compare a Nazi prison and an ordinary prison.

9. Which "enemies" did Hitler do away with first?

10. What year did the German-Jewish community come under full Nazi attack? Who did the Nazis wait until then?

CHECKING YOURSELF

Exercise 2
Recognizing True and False Statements

Directions: Number your paper from 1–15. If the statement is true, write +. If it is false, write 0.

1. A Nazi victim could call the police for help.

2. A Nazi victim could prove his or her innocence by going to court.

3. Nazi propaganda was effective in making people think the way the Nazis wanted them to think.

4. Silence and lack of protest in the Third Reich meant agreement with Nazi policies.

5. Hitler claimed to be the replacement for Christ.

6. A worker in the Third Reich could quit his job if he didn't like it.

7. Jews were excluded from all institutions dealing with education, communications, and culture.

8. Hitler did not expect Germans to rebel against Nazism.

9. The only institutions in Germany that did not become Nazified were the churches.

10. Before attacking Jews on a full scale, the Nazis concentrated first on getting all citizens in line through terror tactics and propaganda.

11. Hitler waited two years before declaring an all-out war on Germany's Jewish community.

12. A typical Nazi prison was similar to an American prison for hardened criminals.

13. Hitler saw children as the future bearers of Nazism.

14. Tens of thousands of non-Jewish Germans suffered Nazi torture, too.

15. Most death camps were equipped to hold and house prisoners.

Exercise 3
Completing the Statements

Directions: Number your paper from 1–16. Provide the correct answer for the blank space in each sentence below by using a word or phrase from the list.

terror state	New Greater Germany	Kapos	concentration camp
Third Reich	New Order	KZ	death camps
Gestapo	Nazi Labor Front	Dachau	transit camps
autobahns	Hitler Youth	labor camps	Goebbels

1. Hitler ordered the building of _____ so that military equipment could be quickly transported across the state.

2. _____ was the first German concentration camp.

3. A _____ camp is a place where large numbers of people are held prisoner.

4. The _____ replaced all labor unions in the Third Reich.

5. _____ was Hitler's propaganda chief.

6. _____ was a compulsory Nazi youth group for German boys aged six to eighteen.

7. _____ were temporary holding stations for Jews on their way to the death camps.

8. Another name for a Nazi concentration camp was _____ .

9. The _____ was to be Hitler's new nation housing all German-speaking peoples in Europe.

10. _____ were places that were built expressly for killing Jews.

11. Europe under Nazi control was Hitler's so-called _____ .

12. Germany under Nazi rule was called the _____ .

13. The _____ were camp prisoners who became guards for the SS in exchange for special privileges.

14. Under the Nazis, Germany became a _____ state based on rule by fear.

15. The _____ were the watchdogs of the Reich.

16. _____ were camps where prisoners were forced to do heavy work.

GIVING REPORTS

Topics to Research

1. More about the Nazi Labor Front under Robert Ley.

2. Nazi art. What ideas did it project? Locate pictures to show to the class.

3. Dr. Leo Baeck (1873–1956), the leader and spokesman for the German-Jewish community during the Hitler years.

4. Baldur von Schirach, chief of Hitler Youth.

5. The effect of the Nazification of schools at the university level.

6. Albert Einstein, German Jew whose coming to the United States backfired against the Germans in their war effort. Tell how.

7. The Volkswagen, a product of Hitler's personal design and campaign promise that all German workers of the Third Reich would be able to own this low-priced car. Find out if Hitler fulfilled this promise.

8. Nazi camp prisoners were identified by "badges" that varied in color and shape depending upon the prisoner's "status." Jewish prisoners wore a yellow star. Find out the types of badges worn by other prisoners such as communists, clergy, Jehovah's Witnesses, and so on.

9. The response of the Catholic Church and other churches inside and outside Germany to the arrest and treatment of clergy and lay people in concentration camps.

10. The story and accomplishments of Albert Einstein and/or other German-Jewish professors who were fired from their positions, left Germany, and were able to continue their work elsewhere.

11. Famous art destroyed by Hitler and the Nazis.

12. Medical experiments carried out by SS doctors.

13. More about the Hitler Youth.

Books to Review

1. *Nazi Culture: Intellectual, Cultural, and Social Life in the Third Reich*, by George Mosse.

2. *Friedrich*, by Hans Peter Richter, reveals life in Nazi Germany through a story of friendship between two German boys—one Jewish, one non-Jewish. Excellent.

3. *Holocaust*, by Gerald Green, a novel focusing on a German-Jewish and non-Jewish family under the Nazis.

4. *How Democracy Failed*, by Ellen Switzer, based on interviews with Germans who recall life under Hitler.

5. *Inside the Third Reich*, by Albert Speer, Hitler's economic coordinator of the German war effort, gives a candid look at Nazi Germany.

6. *Education in the Third Reich*, by Gilmer W. Blackburn, explores the effort by the Nazis to control the minds of the youth.

7. *The Other Victims: First-Person Stories of Non-Jews Persecuted by the Nazis*, by Ina Friedman, who interviewed Gypsies, Jehovah's Witnesses, and other religious figures, as well as members of other groups who were persecuted.

8. *Children's Literature in Hitler's Germany: The Cultural Policy of National Socialism*, by Christa Kamenetsky, a look at the Nazi creation of new literature, the manipulation of traditional literature, and the control of the written word in general in order to support Nazi beliefs.

9. *The HJ* (Hitler Youth), Volume 1, by J.R. Angolia.

Making Projects

Poster and Artwork Ideas

1. Picture a huge Nazi rally or a parade. Good source: *The Nuremberg Rallies*, by Alan Wykes.

2. Picture a typical schoolroom of the Third Reich.

3. Picture Hitler's enemies standing behind a barbed-wire fence.

4. Make a map showing the German-speaking areas Hitler wanted to join to Germany.

5. Make a collage of your impressions of life in the Third Reich.

Model Idea

Make a model of a concentration camp. Include prisoner barracks, SS barracks, watchtowers, camp "hospital," a train-loading platform (use tracks from a miniature railroad set), a barbed-wire fence (string chicken wire along a miniature fence). Use modeling clay or small boxes for the structures, and glue firmly to a base of masonite or wood.

Audiovisual Aid Suggestions for Chapter Six

1. Rent *Part II, Nazi Germany: Years of Triumph—1933–1939*, a 28-minute black-and-white film of how millions of Germans became puppets of the Third Reich. **ADL**

2. *Hitler and the Germans*, two filmstrips and a cassette on the Nazification of Germany. **SSSS**

3. Rent *Swastika*, a 90-minute black-and-white Nazi propaganda film made up of Nazi newsreels and home movies portraying a "glorious" Hitler and Nazi Germany. **RBC**

4. View *Heil Hitler: Confessions of a Hitler Youth*, a 30-minute color and black-and-white videotape of an in-depth interview with Alfons Heck, who became a prominent member of Hitler Youth. **AVP**

The First Solution to the Jewish Question, 1933–1938

Introduction

From his first political speech, Hitler promised to free Germany from Jews, the "internal enemies of the Fatherland." Not until 1939, however, did he ever publicly say he would **kill** them. In fact, during the early years of the Third Reich, it seemed Hitler had no clear-cut policy for getting rid of the German-Jewish community.

In the years before the war started, 1933–1938, his first moves were to "free" Jews from German life by (1) stripping them of their German citizenship, (2) using harsh discrimination laws to pressure them to leave the country, and (3) finally expelling them from Germany.

Exactly when did Hitler make the decision to exterminate European Jews? We don't know for sure. Historians are divided in their opinions. Some say Hitler planned genocide right from the very beginning of his political career but waited until invading Russia in 1941 so that the mass killings would be covered up by the war's confusion. Others insist Hitler may have thought about mass murder but that he did not decide to carry it out until events of the war and world reaction to the Jewish Question gave him no other choice.

The real answer lies buried with Adolf Hitler. Perhaps by the time you finish your study of the Holocaust, you will have your own opinion.

JEWS IN MODERN GERMANY

Introduction

Hitler accused Jews of controlling Germany, of dragging out World War I, of losing World War I, of creating the inflation and depression—all for their own personal gain. Could any of this have been true?

The Background of German Jews

Here are some World War I figures: Of the 100,000 Jewish soldiers in the German armed forces, 80,000 had served on the front lines, thousands had been decorated for bravery, and 12,000 had died fighting for the Fatherland. Would a group promoting a war for personal gain allow so many of their husbands, fathers, and sons to fight and die in it?

A tiny minority, Jews constituted barely one percent of the total German population. Of 66 million German people, only 525,000 were Jews. From 1900 on, the German Jewish population had been steadily shrinking for a number of reasons, including an ever-increasing number of intermarriages, conversions to Christianity, and a low birthrate.

Most Jews lived in German cities. For instance, Berlin, with 160,000 Jews, held almost one third of Germany's entire Jewish population. Shouldn't Hitler have wondered why "Germany's enemies" didn't try to increase their size or to spread themselves out more?

Did the Jews control the German economy? Ninety-eight percent of German bankers and brokers were non-Jewish. Could a two-percent Jewish membership have pulled enough weight to drag the economy into depression or create inflation?

And consider this. While there were many wealthy German Jews, the vast majority were average, middle-class people. Some, too, were poor and struggling. Moreover, thousands of Jews who had lost their jobs and life savings during the depression had joined the long unemployment lines with everyone else.

Was the Weimar government "Jewish" as Hitler said? Of the two hundred sixty cabinet members who served between 1919 and 1933, seven were Jewish; and of these, four were only part Jewish. The most influential, Foreign Minister Walter Rathenau, was assassinated in 1922. Could that small a number of Jewish politicians have dictated German government policies during the Weimar years?

As for Hitler's accusations that communism in Germany was a "Jewish menace," not one communist delegate in the Reichstag in 1933 was Jewish.

Did Jews really control big business? Involved in commerce, approximately sixty percent of German Jews remained in their traditional roles as merchants, traders, and salesmen. Businesses such as the garment industry, shoes, furs, leather goods, grains, large department stores, and advertising were controlled by Jews. However, non-Jewish Germans overwhelmingly dominated such important businesses as iron and steel, petroleum, and chemicals.

The two areas where Jews were represented in the highest proportion in relation to their small numbers were in the professions—medicine (ten percent), journalism (five percent), and law (fifteen percent)—and in the number of university students (ten percent). Many Jews had also entered such fields as science, engineering,

art, and music. Were these furriers, artists, doctors, lawyers, scientists, and store owners the "dangerous enemies" Hitler was talking about?

It is also difficult to understand how Hitler could have accused Jews of "poisoning" Germany when so many had received worldwide recognition for their contributions not only to German culture but to the welfare of the world. For example, by 1933 eleven of the thirty-eight Germans who had won the Nobel Prize for outstanding accomplishments were Jewish.

German Jews, the Most Assimilated in the World

Moreover, German Jews were the most assimilated Jews in the world. Accepting German culture as their own and considering themselves more German than Jewish, large numbers of them had loosened or even cut their ties with their Jewish traditions. Many had gone even so far as to take more German-sounding names to make their "German-ness" complete.

And although Hitler preached about racial differences between "true Aryans" and "inferior" Jews, not even his propaganda chief Goebbels could tell the difference. Holocaust survivor Frieda S., who lived in the German town of Saarbrueken in 1935, recalls:

The Nazis were staging a huge parade which was to pass right in front of our house. We Jews were told we were not allowed to watch it. Our shades had to be drawn, our doors shut. However, my twelve-year-old son Richard was caught up in the excitement and begged me to let him out of the house. In spite of my warnings, he stole out of the house to watch the parade. Goebbels, who marched in the parade and stopped to shake hands with the crowds who lined the sidewalks, spotted my son. He looked at Richard's fair skin, blue eyes, and blonde hair and proudly proclaimed to the crowd, "What a fine-looking Aryan boy!"

Discussion Question: Imagine yourself as a German Jew at this time. How would you feel about being labeled "an enemy"?

ATTACKS ON JEWS AND JEWISH PROPERTY, 1933–1938

The Boycott of Jewish Businesses, 1933

Soon after Hitler was named chancellor in January 1933, his SA and party chiefs were itching to begin clearing Jews out of Germany. They had already done much to harass them: robbing, beating, and even killing them in the street; vandalizing Jewish cemeteries, synagogues, and other properties. So brutal were these attacks that American Jewish leaders and others from abroad had raised loud protests and threatened to boycott German goods if the assaults didn't stop.

But Hitler was not yet ready for an all-out war on Jews. Many things had to be done first. The wrecked German economy had to be put in order. The takeover of Jewish businesses and other properties would require time and organization. In addition, the German public had to be primed through Nazi propaganda and terror tactics into accepting the eviction of Jews.

To satisfy temporarily his Nazi hounds' thirst for blood, and to use Jews as a political tool, Hitler announced a one-day boycott of Jewish businesses to be held on April 1, 1933. But first he commanded German-Jewish leaders to halt the foreign protests by sending letters abroad denying reports of Nazi attacks. Threatened with renewed violence, German Jews had no other choice but to comply.

Then a Nazi propaganda announcement spread the warning that the coming boycott of Jewish businesses was in punishment for the "lies about the Fatherland" which German Jews had spread to other countries.

The boycott lasted not one but three days. To mark Jewish businesses, the Stormtroopers smeared buildings with bright paint in the form of Jewish stars, the word **JUDEN** (meaning "Jew"), and ugly degrading pictures supposedly depicting Jews. They plastered anti-Jewish posters everywhere. SS and SA guarded doors to Jewish establishments and warned shoppers not to enter. When violence and looting took place, forewarned German police did not interfere.

Anti-Jewish Laws of 1933

Using the boycott as an opportunity to further "punish" German Jews, Hitler passed several anti-Jewish laws in 1933.

On April 7, a civil service law fired all non-Aryans except Jewish war veterans from their government positions. A non-Aryan was defined as any German with even one Jewish grandparent. As a result, 28,000 Jewish public employees lost their jobs. They included teachers, judges, lawyers, railroad personnel, doctors and nurses in public hospitals, radio and stage entertainers.

An April 21 law that forbade the kosher method of butchering meat was a direct blow against orthodox, or strict Jews, whose religious customs required the eating of only kosher foods—those foods especially prepared according to religious law.

Another April 25 law discriminated against Jewish children. It strictly limited the number of Jewish students to be admitted thereafter to public schools and universities. Now many Jews had to provide their own schools for their children.

Books by Jewish authors were ordered destroyed. On May 10 in Berlin, Goebbels turned the burning of thousands of volumes into a public celebration. He announced that the spirit of the new Nazi state was born in the ashes of the books that lay smoldering in the streets.

By the end of the year, many Jews felt they had suffered enough. Thirty-seven thousand left Germany to make their homes elsewhere.

1934–1935: A Cooling-off Period

For the next two years, there was no further action on the Jewish Question. Hitler was busy with other things. Laying plans for war, he had yanked Germany out of the League of Nations in October of 1933. Then he began to secretly rearm Germany—a direct violation of the Versailles Treaty. He also was busily maneuvering his way to total power: building concentration camps, slamming political opponents behind bars, and staging the massacre of his SA friends in July 1934 to seal his bargain with the army commanders. With their approval, on August 3, the day after President Hindenberg's death, Adolf Hitler became absolute dictator of Germany.

During this two-year period, 50,000 more Jews poured out of Germany. However, at least 10,000 of the refugees soon decided to come back to their homes and families. In the absence of new anti-Jewish laws, and with the violent SA hooligans out of the way, they and other German Jews believed that the worst of the Nazi anti-Semitic storm was over.

The Nuremberg Laws, 1935

In March 1935, Hitler boldly and openly violated the Versailles Treaty by sending German troops into the demilitarized Rhineland and by passing a new draft law in Germany. None of the war-weary European nations moved to stop him.

The new German draft law raised the Jewish Question again. Were German Jews going to be drafted, too? The answer was not long in coming.

At a mass rally in Nuremberg on September 15, 1935, Hitler announced the Nuremberg Laws. The Reich Citizenship Law and The Law of Protection of German Blood and Honor defined German citizenship as being based on race and blood. Only German **Volk** (folk) could be citizens. No person was permitted to become a **naturalized** citizen. In other words, being born in Germany did not make Jews citizens even if their ancestors had migrated to Germany a thousand years before.

Overnight, German Jews became stateless. They lost all political rights. They could not vote, serve in the army, or hold public office.

Furthermore, the Nuremberg Laws forbade marriages between Aryans and Jews. Even extramarital relationships (relationships outside marriage) between Aryans and Jews became a crime against the Nazi state. Furthermore, Jews were not allowed to fly the Nazi flag or to hire Aryan female servants less than forty-five years old.

Legal Definition of Jew and Aryan

What about the hundreds of thousands of Germans with "Jewish blood"? The Ministry of the Interior, fortunately not yet a totally Nazified body, settled this heated argument.

These people were considered Jews:

1. *A person with three Jewish grandparents.*

2. *A person who had two Jewish grandparents and who was a follower of Judaism.*

3. *A person who was married to a Jew and who had two Jewish grandparents.*

4. *Any child born to a Jewish parent after September 15, 1935.*

For all other Germans with "mixed blood," the Nazis created a new category of people called **mischlinge**. Considered neither Jew nor Aryan—for the time being—mischlinge were further divided into two more categories, depending upon whether the number of Jewish grandparents was one or two.

Mischlinge were considered Reich citizens, but only second-class citizens. The Nuremberg Laws did not apply to them, but strict laws governed whom they could marry. And though allowed to serve in the army, they were never permitted to become officers.

All Germans had to produce baptismal records to prove their backgrounds. Once established as Aryan, Jew, or mischlinge, everyone had to carry identification cards at all times to prove his or her status.

The mischlinge status for the moment concerned only the Jews of Germany. Later, as Hitler took over Europe and nearly all of European Jewry, even a trace of "Jewish blood" condemned a person. Many a horrified Christian found himself or herself locked up in a Nazi prison simply on the basis of having one Jewish ancestor. Eventually, that trace of Jewish ancestry was to make the difference between life and death.

Discussion Question: Imagine yourself in this situation: You are a devout Christian just like both of your parents and two of your grandparents. Yet you are labeled and punished for being Jewish. How would you feel?

1935–1938: Pressures Force Thousands of Jews from Germany

Until 1938, no new anti-Jewish laws were passed, nor were there any more organized boycotts. Instead, Nazis began to apply subtle pressures from the inside to force Jews to leave Germany. Owners of small businesses and shops were "persuaded" to sell their businesses to Aryans at half the real value after buyers and suppliers had blackballed their stores.

Nazi supporters refused to sell Jews real estate or to reserve places for Jews at hotels. Unashamed, they hung signs from their establishments warning Jews to stay away.

Thousands of outstanding Jewish athletes competed for places on the 1936 German Olympic teams; all were rejected. The Nazis later explained the absence of Jewish athletes by saying they had not been good enough to qualify. While Olympic spectators from all over the world toured Berlin, Hitler played down these injustices by ordering all **JUDEN VERBOTEN** (Jews Forbidden) signs temporarily removed from public places.

By the late 1930's, Hitler's anti-Jewish campaign had prompted one fourth (150,000) of Germany's Jews to leave their homeland.

Nazis and Emigration

The Nazis were more than willing to let Jews go. When the Jewish Zionist Organization began to train future émigrés to Palestine in agricultural skills so that they could make a living in their new home, the Nazis nodded in approval. When German or international Jewish organizations worked to help their people relocate in other countries of the world, Nazi emigration officials often bent over backward to provide departing Jews with visas and other necessary papers.

So why didn't more Jews leave? Attachment to their homes was the biggest reason. Hope that Hitler would fall was another. Because large Jewish businesses and many Jewish professionals continued to operate without Nazi interference, many were convinced that the Nazi storm would pass. Moreover, the relaxed Nazi emigration policy led Jews to believe that if things got too bad, they could always pick up and leave Germany without too much difficulty.

According to Holocaust survivor Sam Gottisman:

To many of us who remained in Germany, persecution almost came to be a fact of Jewish life. For instance, one afternoon a uniformed man climbed aboard the bus I was riding, checked every passenger's identification papers, then told me to step outside in the road. The bus left. There I was in the middle of nowhere. Was I angry? By now, I had come to the point of saying, "This is the price I have to pay for being Jewish!"

Al Lewin, who was thirteen at this time, says:

My father, who owned a good business in Berlin, kept reassuring that nothing bad would happen to us. After all, he and many other Jews had served in the first war. That had to count for something. And we did have five years of doing almost what we wanted to. Of course, freedom was over for everyone—Jews as well as non-Jews. With us Jews, it didn't happen overnight. It was a slow process. We had almost learned to live without freedom. Then by 1938, it became so bad that we really wanted to leave. But it was too late, for we could no longer get out of Germany.

1938: JEWS ARE FORCED OUT OF GERMAN LIFE ALTOGETHER

Introduction

By 1938, all German Jews had come to the same conclusion as the Lewins. At last Hitler was ready to move aggressively in both his wars—the war on Jews and the war on Europe. Militarily, Germany was now a powerhouse, and Hitler anticipated weak resistance from the other countries of Europe. And in his coming all-out war on German Jews, he knew he risked little protest from the German public; fear of

Nazi punishment and acceptance of Nazi anti-Jewish propaganda had seen to that.

As 1937 came to an end, Hitler gave Hermann Goering, his minister of economics, the order to begin channeling all of Germany's economy toward a supreme war effort. This was also the signal to cut Jews out of German life altogether. Already stripped of political rights, they were now to be eliminated socially and economically as well.

Economic Segregation

The first step to Aryanization, or German takeover of Jewish property, came in April 1938 when Nazi law required Jews to register all their belongings—real estate, stocks, bonds, art treasures, everything.

The actual takeover began in October 1938. Goering set the selling price for all Jewish property at 5 to 10 percent of its actual value. Jewish owners had no choice but to sell. It was the law. In the case of businesses jointly owned by Jews and Aryans, the Aryans were instructed to "phase out" their Jewish partners.

Not only were Jews stripped of their businesses. All their personal properties, such as stocks, bonds, and savings accounts, were automatically transferred to the Nazi Finance Ministry. Jews were also compelled to hand in their jewelry and other valuables.

Jews in all walks of life lost their livelihood. Lawyers were disbarred. Doctors lost their licenses to practice medicine. Hereafter, they were considered "medical attendants," privileged to care only for "their own kind." No Jew could be a broker. And Aryan employers were "persuaded" to dismiss their Jewish help.

Social Segregation

Jews quickly became public outcasts. They were banned from all places of entertainment such as beaches, resorts, theaters, and parks.

Even public restrooms were off-limits to them. Nor were the necessities of life easily had. Public schools and hospitals were reserved for Aryans only. Bold signs warned Jews not to enter barbershops, bakeries, drugstores, public transportation facilities, and many grocery stores. Shopping for Jews was restricted to only a few stores and during certain hours of the day.

Laws that came after 1938 made Jews easier to identify. They were forced to wear the yellow star. As a middle name, Jewish men had to adopt Israel; Jewish women, Sarah. In addition, Jews who had legally changed their names to Aryan-sounding ones were forced to take back their original names.

Many Nazi discriminations were utterly ridiculous. For example, Jewish musicians were forbidden to play the music of German composers such as Bach or Mozart. Aryan veterinarians were forbidden to care for dogs belonging to Jewish owners. And, to top that, in order to avoid the crossbreeding of "Jewish" and "Aryan" dogs, their owners were compelled to walk their animals at different times of the day.

As if things were not bad enough, cruel Nazis looking for sport often went out of their way to humiliate Jews. At various times, they forced them to perform such mortifying tasks as scrubbing the streets on their hands and knees; parading through laughing, mocking crowds; or bathing the feet of bystanders and then drinking the water. Jews were even forced to lick the streets. It seemed no act was mean enough.

Discussion Question: In Chapter One, reread medieval Roman laws against Jews. Compare them with Nazi laws.

Hitler's War on Europe Brings More Jews into the Nazi Fold

While Jews in Germany were suffering a nightmare of persecution, Hitler had moved aggressively in his war on Europe. The first two countries fell without a fight. In March 1938, when Hitler's armies invaded his homeland of Austria, many Austrians greeted them not with bullets but with waves and cheers.

Although much against her will, Czechoslovakia gave up part of her land to Germany the following September. In an agreement known as the Munich Pact, Hitler had convinced France, England, and Italy that the Sudetenland of Czechoslovakia rightfully belonged to Germany because it housed 3.5 million German-speaking people. He also promised to make no more demands for land.

With the annexation (absorption) of these two lands, Hitler realized his boyhood dream of uniting all German-speaking peoples into a New Greater Germany. Unfortunately, along with this union 180,000 Austrian Jews and 130,000 Czech Jews fell under the Nazi anti-Jewish rules and regulations.

A NAZI POGROM: KRISTALLNACHT, OR "NIGHT OF BROKEN GLASS"

The Entire Jewish Community Comes Under Attack

On November 9 and 10, 1938, the Nazis launched their first organized, full-scale attack on Jewish communities all over Germany and Nazi-controlled Austria. During this twenty-four-hour bloody spree, Nazis disguised as ordinary citizens in civilian clothing brutally murdered over a thousand Jews in the streets, burned down hundreds of their synagogues, smashed tons of window glass in Jewish homes and businesses, and dragged 20,000 Jews off to concentration camps. Because glass lay shattered everywhere, the incident is referred to as Kristallnacht, or Night of Broken Glass.

Holocaust survivor Frieda S. remembers the incident well:

*My husband and several other men were
forced to put on their prayer shawls and
skull caps and then to stand before our
synagogue and sing a continuous song
until it burned to the ground. The SS
draped hundreds of prayer shawls all
along the fence surrounding the synagogue and set them afire, too.*

Insult was added to injury when the pogrom
ended. Jews were ordered to clean up the mess.
They were denied all insurance payments for
damages to their property. Even worse, the
entire Jewish community was fined 1 million
Reichsmarks for causing all the trouble.

Kristallnacht Is Nazi Punishment

All this Nazi fury was aimed at Jews because
a few days earlier, in Paris, a seventeen-year-old
Jewish boy named Herschel Grynszpan had shot
Ernst von Rath, a Nazi official. Von Rath died of
his wounds on November 9.

Why had Grynszpan killed the Nazi?
In March 1938, the Polish government had
declared that all Polish nationals who had lived
abroad for the past five years were no longer citizens of Poland. The Nazis reacted furiously to
this ruling, which affected thousands of Polish
Jews now living in the Reich, for they detested
Poles almost as much as they hated Jews. "Obey
Polish laws? Offer Germany as a refuge to Polish
Jews? Ridiculous!" answered Nazi officials.
Immediately the Gestapo began to round up the
Polish Jews. On October 18, 1938, they packed
12,000 of them into cattle cars and trucks and
dumped them at the Polish border. There the
stateless Jews remained.

Ultimately, the Polish government decided to
accept them. However, that decision was not
made until midwinter. In the meantime, the
homeless people were forced to take shelter in
crude tents, abandoned shacks, and stables.
Many died from exposure, illness, and hunger.

Among the group of forlorn Jews had
been Herschel Grynszpan's aged parents. When
Grynszpan received a letter from them describing their misery, he went berserk, stormed into
the German embassy in Paris, and shot Nazi
official von Rath.

Kristallnacht, the One and Only Nazi Pogrom

Kristallnacht was the first and last Nazi
pogrom. After this, Hitler ordered Goering to
speed up the Aryanization of Jewish properties
so that all would be confiscated by December
30, 1938. He also called a halt to any further
outbreaks against Jews and placed the handling
of the Jewish problem solely under the authority
of the SS and Gestapo. From here on, the SS
were to follow a highly organized and more efficient plan of attack.

**Discussion
Questions:**   Why did the Nazi marauders
disguise themselves as civilians?
Why was Kristallnacht obviously
well organized? If you were a
non-Jewish German observing
this violence, would you have
tried to stop it?

1938–1939: Jewish Emigration Becomes a Mad Scramble

The horrible events of 1938 had turned emigration into a mad scramble, for now every Jew
in Nazi territory wanted out. But emigration
required more than a Jew's willingness to leave.
Money was needed for travel and resettlement.
A foreign country had to be willing to accept
him or her as a permanent resident. And with
the Fuehrer's new order—that Jewish emigrants
leave Germany with no more than the equiva-
lent of four dollars in their pockets—how could
people prove to a host country that they could

support themselves and their families?

International Jewish organizations came to their beleaguered brothers' support. Families in faraway lands promised to shelter incoming relatives.

German Jews tried desperately to get out before the Nazis liquidated all their assets. A visa became the most sought-after possession. Wealthier Jews were able to leave first. Oftentimes, poor Jewish families pooled their resources just to get one family member out, usually a child. This became a pattern for most families: younger ones first, then elders.

Unscrupulous people began to take advantage of the Jews' desperate situation. Emigration became a racket. Gestapo members often bled emigrants of huge sums for visas that later proved to be worthless. For some lucky Jews, underground escape methods such as secret ships to Palestine became a safe way out. But in other instances, the secret convoys never made it.

Other factors compounded the emigration problem. That hundreds of thousands of German Jews wanted out was bad enough. But also trying to escape Nazi tyranny were thousands of non-Jewish Germans who hated the Nazis. So were hundreds of thousands of Austrian and Czech Jews, whom Hitler had ordered to leave their countries. Adding to the confusion were Jews seeking refuge from persecution in Poland. And finally, Nazi movements in Rumania and Hungary were pressuring Jews there to seek new homes elsewhere.

Then the Nazis themselves made the emigration situation impossible. They began to expel Jews.

Nazis Deport Jews

A blonde, ruthless Nazi giant, SD chief Reinhard Heydrich was put in charge of the Central Emigration Office for Jews. He and his assistant, Adolf Eichmann, another cold-hearted Nazi who headed the emigration centers in Vienna and Prague, decided to expel Jews from Nazi lands.

In March 1938, Eichmann used a new pressure tactic to evict Austrian Jews. He threatened them with life imprisonment unless they left. Then he forced wealthier Jews to pay the transport costs of those in need. Setting up a special bank account for this purpose, he ordered his SS squads to collect from the deportees, deposit their money, and then later withdraw it to pay the required fares to railroad officials. It worked. In less than a year, he managed to ship out 100,000, or one half of Austria's Jewish population. Using the same tactics, he began to deport Czechoslovakian Jews.

Meanwhile, Hershel Grynszpan's parents, along with 12,000 other Jews who had been driven out and forced to stand and freeze on the Polish border, were the first to be expelled from Germany by Heydrich's order of October 1938.

A Refugee Crisis

By the end of 1938, a severe refugee crisis had developed. With hundreds of thousands of Jewish refugees pouring out of Germany and other lands, the immigration quotas of countries willing to receive them were now filled up. To date, only an additional 150,000 German Jews had managed to find new homes. Many more hundreds of thousands there and elsewhere wanted out, but there was no place for them to go.

Now stripped of all their rights and possessions, hundreds of thousands of stranded Jews stood hopelessly in long lines at Jewish soup kitchens set up to feed the hungry. Frantic, the caged-up Jews cried for help. Adolf Hitler also screamed out to the world, "You criticized us Germans and shed tears of pity at the way we treated our Jews. Now they are yours! Take them!" To spur the world to react, he ordered the arrest of thousands of Jews on the condition they be released from prison only if they emigrated.

It is sad to say there were few takers.

WORLD REACTION BECOMES INACTION

The Evian Conference

Early in 1938, American President Franklin Delano Roosevelt's voice had called out to the world to help the Jewish refugees. Four months passed before thirty-two nations of the world accepted Roosevelt's invitation to discuss the refugee crisis.

In the meantime, daily newspapers of the free world continued to print front-page stories of new Nazi atrocities. Hitler had also seized more European soil and brought added thousands of Jews under Nazi tyranny.

But when the thirty-two nations convened in Evian-les-Bains, France, in July 1938, they did nothing to help ease the Jewish plight. About all they did was talk at this Evian Conference. When the issue of raising their immigration quotas came up, the representatives just shook their heads. One spokesman said, "We have our share of Jews. We don't want to invite any racial problems." Except for the tiny Dominican Republic, not one nation opened its doors to Jews.

The United States Bars Entry, Too

So many restrictions governed an immigrant's passage into America that United States quotas for incoming Austrian-German refugees had not even come close to being met between 1933 and 1937. The combined quotas for immigrants from those two nations was approximately 27,000 a year. Yet only 30,000 Jews had been allowed to resettle in America during the entire five-year period of Hitler's rampage. In spite of this, the only concession America was willing to make at the Evian Conference was that from then on it would allow in the full yearly quota.

Why didn't Americans open up their doors and hearts to the Jewish victims? One reason was the aftereffects of the 1929 Depression. Many millions of Americans were now unemployed, and they did not welcome more job competition from incoming refugees. Nor was anti-Semitism dead in America. Nazi agents had done their best to spread hate-filled propaganda against Jews. They warned that Jewish immigrants might be German spies or communists bent on taking over the United States. And there were anti-Semitic Americans who tried to influence their congressmen against an open-door policy for Jewish victims.

Not even German children were made an exception. In 1939 the United States Congress refused to pass the Wagner-Rogers bill, a proposal for admitting 20,000 Jewish and non-Jewish German children above the regular quota limit. The Congressmen had barred these children even though they offered no job competition, were to be cared for by thousands of volunteers, and would be reunited with their families once conditions in Germany permitted safe return.

Discussion Questions: Do you think that people generally welcome or shun foreign immigrants? If the normal United States quotas for German-Austrian immigrants could have been met between 1933–1937, figure out how many Jewish lives could have been saved.

Palestine Shuts Her Door

Palestine, the ancient home of the Jewish people, had bolted its doors shut, too. The British, who now controlled Palestine, were concerned because Arabs there were complaining about too many incoming Jewish refugees. To appease the Arabs, the British issued the British White Paper of 1939, which was to severely limit Jewish immigration for the next five years. It allowed in 25,000 Jewish immigrants for the first year, then only 10,000 for each of the following four years. After that, Jewish immigration into Palestine was to end altogether.

Desperate Jewish Refugees Take to the Seas

Willing to do anything to get away from Nazi terror, thousands of Jews took to the seas. In dilapidated, leaky boats that they had somehow managed to buy or rent secretly, the desperate Jews wandered from port to port begging authorities to let them in. Most often they were turned away and forced to return to German lands.

In 1941, when the dangerously overcrowded *Sturma* carrying 769 Rumanian Jewish men, women, and children was turned away, it roamed the seas for two months. Then it sank. All but one person aboard drowned.

The story of the *St. Louis* voyage is another tragedy. In May 1939, all 937 German refugees who set sail for Cuba aboard this ship had American passports. Cuba was their immediate destination, however, because their passports did not permit immediate entry into the United States, and Cuba had granted them permission for a temporary stay.

As the *St. Louis* sailed across the Atlantic, the Cuban president had a change of heart. Swayed by anti-Semitic citizens who had raised their voices to protest the entry of the Jewish immigrants, he claimed the *St. Louis* passengers had illegal permits. When the *St. Louis* docked, only thirty passengers with special papers were permitted to come ashore. The Cubans barred the rest.

So did the United States. The United States Coast Guard was ordered to keep the ocean liner away. For more than a month, the *St. Louis* wandered aimlessly at sea. Finally, France, England, Holland, and Belgium agreed to share the passengers. Of these four countries, however, only England would successfully resist a Nazi takeover in the oncoming war. Therefore, it was only England's share of the *St. Louis* cargo who were destined for a new lease on life. The rest were to be swallowed up again in the Holocaust.

Discussion Questions: Imagine yourself as a passenger aboard the *Sturma* or the *St. Louis*. How would you feel about yourself? about the world? Put yourself in the place of a border guard. Would you allow the Jewish refugees in?

WORLD WAR II BRINGS MILLIONS OF JEWS UNDER NAZI RULE

Hitler broke the Munich Pact on March 15, 1939, when he sent his troops in to seize the entire country of Czechoslovakia. There the Nazi protectorates of Moravia and Bohemia were set up.

This meant not only tight Nazi control over all Czech affairs but also Nazi racist laws against Jews living there. Now the total number of Jews under Nazi rule swelled to approximately 750,000.

On August 23, 1939, Germany signed a pact with her old communist enemy, Russia. In this Nazi-Soviet Pact both countries agreed to two things: (1) not to attack one another, and (2) to conquer Poland jointly and divide Polish territory between them.

Keeping their bargain, the Germans charged into western Poland on September 1, 1939. Two weeks later Russian forces smashed into eastern Poland. Then Great Britain and France, who had pledged to support Poland in the event of war, jumped into the battle. World War II had begun.

Caught in the middle, Polish forces fought back desperately, but it was a losing battle. In less than a month, Poland fell to the Germans and the Russians. After the victors divided up her territory, the country of Poland ceased to be.

Poland had the largest Jewish population in Europe: 3.3 million.

Russia had swallowed up eastern Poland and her 1.5 million Jews. Hitler divided his share of Polish territory into two sections. He wanted western Poland with its half-million Jews to be used as added living space for German homesteaders and farmers, so he incorporated this area into the Reich. Then he renamed central Poland the Government General and placed it under tight control with Hans Frank as the Nazi governor. There were 1.3 million Jews living in this area.

With millions of Jews now living in Nazi-controlled lands, forced emigration was certainly no longer Hitler's answer to his Jewish Question. He decided there was a need for a **new** solution.

The German-Soviet Division of Poland
SEPTEMBER 1939–JUNE 1941

Chapter Seven Review

REVIEWING KEY POINTS

Exercise 1

1. On what aspect are Holocaust scholars divided in their opinions?

2. Discuss the Nazi anti-Jewish laws of (a) 1933 and (b) 1935.

3. Who were the mischlinge? Discuss the different categories.

4. Discuss how German Jews were segregated socially and economically.

5. What goal of the "New Order" did Hitler achieve in 1938? 1939? How did this add to Jewish problems?

6. Before a Jew could emigrate, what requirements did he or she have to meet?

7. Discuss why many German Jews decided to remain in Nazi Germany.

8. Who else besides German Jews were trying to escape Nazi tyranny or other persecutions? How did this create a refugee crisis?

9. Discuss several reasons why the United States refused to allow more Jewish refugees in. What about Palestine?

10. How many Jews were living in Poland at the time of the Nazi-Russian invasion? Compare this figure to the German-Jewish population.

CHECKING YOURSELF

Exercise 2
Matching Dates with Events

Directions: Match each date in Column I with an event from Column II. Write the letter of each event next to the appropriate number on your paper.

COLUMN I	COLUMN II
1. 1933–1938	A. Nazis expelled or deported Jews from Germany
2. 1933	B. a "cooling-off" period during which no new anti-Jewish laws were passed

Exercise 2 (continued)

COLUMN I	COLUMN II
3. 1934–1935	C. laws cut Jews out of civil service jobs
4. 1935	D. the period of the "First Solution"
5. 1938	E. laws stripped Jews of citizenship and political rights

Exercise 3
Filling in the Spaces

Directions: Number your paper from 1–10. The paragraph below has numbered blanks that require correct answers. Provide an answer for each blank. Write each answer on your paper beside the number corresponding to each blank space.

Hitler's charge that Jews were the "internal enemy" of Germany was ridiculous because ____(1)____ German-Jewish soldiers had fought for their country in World War ____(2)____. Nearly ____(3)____ had died in battle, and ____(4)____ had been decorated for bravery. Besides that, Jews were such a tiny minority that they made up only ____(5)____ of the total German population. In addition, German Jews, like all other German citizens, had lost their jobs and life savings in the ____(6)____ . And in no way did statistics show they "controlled" either the ____(7)____, the ____(8)____, or the ____(9)____ as Hitler claimed they did. Finally, so many had broken ties to their Jewish traditions and had embraced German culture as their own that German Jews were known as the most ____(10)____ Jews in the world.

Exercise 4
Working a Crossword Puzzle

All the answers for this crossword puzzle are terms that have been explained in the preceding chapter.

ACROSS

1. The Nazi takeover of Jewish property was called the _____ process.
5. _____ had the largest Jewish population in Europe.
9. The initials of the American president during this time.
12. Hitler joined his homeland of _____ to Germany in 1938.
13. Nazis created the _____, a new category of Germans with "Jewish blood."
16. When the Nazis and Russians signed the Nazi-_____ Pact, they agreed to attack Poland.

DOWN

2. A _____ _____ developed in 1939 when immigration quotas filled up.
3. Jews had to wear a _____ on their clothing.
4. A country's immigration _____ limited the number of immigrants.
6. Hitler seized this part of Czechoslovakia in September of 1938.
7. Thirty-two nations of the world met at the _____ _____ to discuss the Jewish refugee crisis.
8. The ancient home of the Jews.
10. The first and last Nazi pogrom.

ACROSS

18. Jews who sailed to Cuba on the _____ _____ were turned away from there and the U.S.
19. In 1938, Heydrich and Eichmann _____ Jews from their lands
21. Nazi law in 1933 prohibited the preparation of _____ meat.
22. The _____ Laws of 1935 stripped Jews of their German citizenship.
24. Adolf _____ was head of Jewish emigration in Austria and Czechoslovakia.
25. _____ enforced dozens of laws against Jews.
26. Hitler called _____ the "inside enemy" of Germany.
27. Hitler broke the _____ Pact when he invaded Poland in 1939.
28. In 1938, Jews came under the jurisdiction of the SS and _____.
30. The First Solution to the Jewish Question ended when World War _____ broke out in 1939.

DOWN

11. A German word meaning "Jew."
14. Hitler's _____ _____ to the Jewish Question was to "free" Germany of Jews.
15. Nazi law in 1933 cut Jews out of _____ _____ jobs.
17. In _____ _____ ceremonies, Nazis set afire all works by Jewish authors.
18. The _____ sank with 769 Jews aboard.
20. The British _____ _____ of 1939 barred Jews from Palestine.
23. The first official Nazi action against Jews was a _____ of their shops.
24. By 1938, every Jew in Germany wanted to _____.
29. About _____ million more Jews fell under the Nazis when Hitler conquered Poland in 1939.

GIVING REPORTS

Topics to Research

1. German-Jewish Walter Rathenau, his role in the government and his assassination. Good source: *Sieg Heil: An Illustrated History of Germany from Bismarck to Hitler*, by Stefan Lorant.

2. Did American Jewish leaders believe the letters sent from German Jews in 1933 denying Nazi attacks on their communities?

3. Why did Hitler exempt German-Jewish veterans from the anti-Jewish civil-service laws of 1933?

4. Special laws governing mischlinge. Good source: *A Holocaust Reader*, by Lucy Dawidowicz.

5. How did Nazis "handle" mischlinge after 1939?

6. More on the 1936 Olympics. Good source: *While Six Million Died*, by Arthur Morse.

7. The Herman Goering Works, Goering's huge industrial complex. Include how much it was worth and how Goering came to own it.

8. More about Kristallnacht. Good sources: *Never to Forget*, by Milton Meltzer; or *Crystal Night*, by R. Thalmann and E. Feinermann.

9. The names and accomplishments of the eleven German-Jewish Nobel Prize winners.

10. The Haavara Agreements of August 1933 concerning Aryanization of Jewish property.

11. More about the response of the United States and other countries to the refugees from Germany.

Books to Review

1. *Voyage of the Damned*, by T. Gordon and M. Witts, relates the ill-fated journey of the *St. Louis*.

2. *Mischlinge, Second Degree: My Childhood in Nazi Germany*, by Ilse Roehn.

3. *The Devil in Vienna*, by Doris Orgel, a novel of a Jewish girl and her best friend, the daughter of a Nazi.

4. *Journey to America*, by Sonia Levitin, recounts how a German-Jewish family flees from Hitler.

5. *Hitler and the Nazis*, by Arnold Rubin, dealing with the refusal on the part of the people throughout the world to believe what was going on.

6. *The Jews Were Expendable*, by Monty Noam Penhower, a documented study that shows the Allied agenda did not place much importance on saving the Jews.

7. *The Abandonment of the Jews*, by David S. Wyman, concerning the failure of the United States to help Jews during the Holocaust.

MAKING PROJECTS

Poster and Artwork Ideas

1. List the Nuremberg Laws of 1935.

2. List the anti-Jewish Laws of 1933.

3. Picture a shop with the sign JUDEN VERBOTEN.

4. Picture Kristallnacht.

5. Picture a German-Jewish family wearing yellow stars on their clothing.

6. Divide a poster in half. Label one side "Medieval Anti-Jewish Laws" and the other "Nazi Anti-Jewish Laws." Now list those that are the same under both headings.

7. Create a front page of a newspaper explaining the Nazi version of Kristallnacht.

8. Create a front page of a newspaper explaining the Nazis' reasons for the German boycott in 1933 of Jewish businesses.

Conducting an Experiment

Pretend you are a Jewish student living in Germany between 1933 and 1938. Wear a yellow star on your clothing. Make a list of special restrictions for Jews. These restrictions should limit your activities and set you apart from everyone else. For example, as a Jew you may use only certain stairways or sit only in a special section of the cafeteria. Give this list to your teacher and classmates. Arrange to have them behave like anti-Semites, or Jew-haters. Spend part of your school day being "persecuted." Then give an oral or written report describing your feelings during this experiment.

AUDIOVISUAL AID SUGGESTIONS FOR CHAPTER SEVEN

1. *The Camera of My Family: Four Generations in Germany*, a filmstrip and cassette portraying the complete destruction of a German-Jewish family in the Holocaust. **ADL**

2. The book, *The Yellow Star: The Persecution of Jews in Europe 1933–1945*, by Gerhard Schoenberner, an excellent pictorial record of the Holocaust with nearly 200 photographs, plus official Nazi records.

3. The book, *The Holocaust: Maps and Photographs*, by Martin Gilbert, an excellent collection depicting the history of the Holocaust.

4. View *More Than Broken Glass: Memories of Kristallnacht*, a 57-minute documentary in color and black-and-white of Jewish life in Germany before and during the Holocaust. **EM**

✡ CHAPTER EIGHT

The Second Solution to the Jewish Question, 1939–1941

EASTERN EUROPE HOLDS HALF THE WORLD'S JEWS

When Hitler's armies invaded Poland in September 1939, they cut right into the heart of European Jewish life. Seven million Jews—half the world's Jewish population—lived in Eastern Europe at this time. Three and one-third million lived in Poland alone. More than 2 million lived in the European part of Russia. Rumania was third, with a Jewish population of 800,000. The remaining Jews were scattered throughout the other countries of Eastern Europe: Estonia, Latvia, Lithuania, Hungary, Yugoslavia, Bulgaria, Greece, and Albania.

How do these population figures compare to Jewish population figures in the rest of Europe? Of the central European countries—Germany, Austria, and Czechoslovakia—pre-Nazi Germany had held 525,000 Jews, or nearly half the total population of the area. In all the Western European countries that would ultimately come under Nazi rule in World War II (France, Italy, Belgium, Norway, Luxembourg, Holland, Denmark, Finland) there were barely a half-million Jews.

Of the 9 million Jews in occupied Europe, 6 million—or two of every three—would eventually be killed by the Nazis. By far the greatest number of Jewish victims—4 million—were from Eastern Europe. Three fourths of these Eastern European Jews were from Poland.

Why were so many more Jews living in the East than in the West, and why were such large numbers in Poland and Russia? To answer that, let's take a brief look backward at Poland before the Nazi invasion.

THE JEWS OF EARLY POLAND

Poland, a Refuge from the Crusaders and Pogroms of the West

As you recall from Chapter One, harsh persecutions between the eleventh and fifteenth centuries (the Crusades, the expulsions, libel, the Black Death) had forced most Jews of Western Europe to flee their homes. Most had migrated eastward.

Invited by Polish kings to bring trade and boost the economy of this backward land, the bulk of German Jews resettled in Poland. They did not disappoint the Polish rulers. By stimulating trade and building up towns, they helped spur progress. In return, the appreciative kings granted Jews the freedom to develop and run their own communities. Many monarchs also made Jews their tax collectors and the managers of their estates. Up until the seventeenth century, Jewish life flourished in Poland. It was a welcome relief from the dark years of persecution in German lands.

Anti-Semitism Sparks Persecution in Poland

The good life for Polish Jews didn't last. The old pattern of resentment began to creep in. Clergymen, motivated by religious bias, began urging kings to restrict Jews. The rising middle class, wanting a better life for itself, began to resent the Jewish monopoly of trade and business. And the peasants, who hated paying taxes to their noble landlords, started to take it out on the Jewish tax collectors and overseers.

Peasant resentment toward Polish rulers reached a peak in the seventeenth century. By now, Polish nobles had come to rule over many subject peoples including Ukrainians, Lithuanians, and White Russians. It was the Ukrainian peasants, led by Bogan Chmielnicki, who rebelled first. Between 1648 and 1657 Chmielnicki led his Cossacks, or Ukrainian fighters, to riot against Polish noblemen and the Jews who ran their estates. Polish peasants and other subjects joined in. By the time the massacres had ended, hundreds of thousands of Jewish men, women, and children had been slain. Polish Jewry was all but destroyed.

Jew-Hating Russian Czars Rule Polish Jews Until World War I

Between 1772 and 1795, the country of Poland disappeared from the map. Its land area was partitioned and taken over by Austria, Prussia, and Russia. Most Polish Jews came under the harsh rule of the Russian czars, who had been notorious Jew-haters throughout the ages.

The czars, who had always banned Jews from settling in their lands, had no intention of allowing them to enter the interior of Russia now. They confined Jews right where they were, in the territory that had once belonged to Poland. Known as the Pale of Settlement, this area was like a vast ghetto that stretched all along the western Russian border. Non-Jews lived in the Pale, too, but Jews had to crowd into their own towns, called **shtetls**, and could not leave the Pale without permission.

The czars were not only hard on Jews. Ruling with an iron hand, they kept all the masses in a state of poverty while they and their nobles lived in luxury. But whenever the suppressed people grew restless and dissatisfied, the czars used Jews as the scapegoats. They spread the old ritual murder charges against Jews and provoked peasants to rise up against Jewish communities.

Many Russians who wanted to break out of the czars' grip formed revolutionary groups to overthrow them. A few young Jews also joined this effort. Finally, Czar Alexander II was assassinated in 1881. When his successor, Alexander III (1881–1894), discovered that one Jewish girl had been among the group of assassins, he sent his men out to incite mobs to attack the Jewish shtetls. One violent pogrom after another wiped out countless Jewish men, women, and children.

The next czar, Nicholas II (1894–1917), who ascended the throne in 1894 and was to be the last Russian emperor, continued to oppress the masses and to organize bloody pogroms against the Jewish communities. In the meantime, over a million and a half Jews had fled from Russia to escape czarist terror.

In March 1917, after Russia had suffered heavy losses in World War I, a revolution broke out and czarist rule in Russia toppled. The government was taken over by a moderate group who set up a more democratic system. Jews were delighted with their newfound equal rights and freedom. Some even held positions in the new government. But it didn't last long.

The Bolsheviks (Russian communists) revolted against the democratic regime eight months later. A terrible civil war began. In the middle of all the confusion, bloody pogroms against the Jewish communities claimed more than 50,000 Jewish lives.

One of the leaders of the Bolshevik Revolution was a Jew named Leon Trotsky. But the overwhelming majority were non-Jewish Russians. Nevertheless, Nazi leader Adolf Hitler saw fit to label the entire Bolshevik party "Jewish." That, of course, was ridiculous. Under communist rule, Jewish life in Russia became more oppressive than ever.

Discussion Question: If you saw the movie *Fiddler on the Roof,* discuss how it depicts Jewish life in a particular time and place.

The *Protocols of the Elders of Zion*

In 1905, during the reign of Czar Nicholas II, a new myth about Jews spread throughout Russia and added to their long list of troubles. It was the *Protocols of the Elders of Zion,* a fake document that purported to be the minutes of a meeting of international Jewish leaders who had congregated among the tombstones in a Prague cemetery to discuss plans to take over the world. The devil himself was supposedly in charge of this meeting. Some Russian Jew-haters living in France had fabricated this fantasy and sent it to the czar's secret police. However, even as much as Czar Nicholas disliked Jews, he dismissed the *Protocols* as nonsense. But the common people didn't.

The *Protocols* continued to spread, and in the process it picked up added details. It was not taken too seriously in Russia until the Bolshevik Revolution in 1917. By then, it had spread like wildfire through many other countries of Europe. Even the United States had its own version and a surprising number of believers in the forgery. This was despite proof beyond doubt that the document was totally false.

In the 1920's and 1930's, Adolf Hitler used the *Protocols* as "proof" that Jews had not only "taken over Russia" but also were plotting to control Germany and the rest of the world.

MODERN EASTERN JEWS DIFFER FROM GERMAN JEWS

Eastern Jews differed from their German counterparts in several ways. In terms of lifestyles, very few Easterners were professionals or owners of large businesses. The majority were lower middle-class small shop owners, tradesmen, or industrial workers.

Unlike Jews of Germany, Eastern European Jews did not assimilate into the culture around them. Long unwelcomed and isolated from the outside world, they had not been given that chance. As a result, Jews of the East had remained a very distinct group from their neighbors in every respect. Whereas most Eastern Jews lived in cities and towns and worked in commerce, industry, and trades, most non-Jewish Eastern Europeans were rural dwellers involved in farming. Many of those in the countryside were poor, unskilled, and uneducated. So the strong emphasis that urban Jews had always placed on education resulted in another difference. The very low rate of intermarriage between the two groups also served as a reminder of their separateness.

Jewish cultural differences also sharply set them apart from the surrounding community in the East. Separated from the outside world, Jews had strengthened and developed a rich culture of their own within their communities. They had their own style of dress. They even spoke a different language.

While Eastern Jews communicated with the gentile world in its native tongues, among themselves they spoke their own language of Yiddish, the medieval German brought along by their migrating ancestors from the West and combined with local Polish and Russian words. This language was not only spoken every day but also used in Jewish books, newspapers, theaters, and schools. Even the printed Yiddish stood out, for it was written not in the familiar Roman alphabet but with Hebrew lettering. Thus, Eastern

European Jews had created a Yiddish culture all their own.

Furthermore, Jews of the East had made little attempt to modernize or modify their religious practices. Traditional or Orthodox Judaism was still strong among them. This, too, set them apart in a predominantly Christian world.

Nor did Eastern Jews respond to Zionism the way German Jews had. As a reaction to their persecution, more had joined the Zionist movement, the combined effort of Jews and non-Jews throughout the world to establish an all-Jewish state in Palestine in the hope that such a homeland would free Jews from persecution once and for all.

On the other hand, most German Jews were more attached to their "German-ness" than to the idea of an all-Jewish state. They felt that assimilation or blending into the Christian world was the true solution to anti-Semitism. With a strong attachment to their fatherland, many had no desire to move to a faraway land.

EASTERN JEWS MORE AT A DISADVANTAGE UNDER NAZI RULE

Under Nazi rulers, Eastern Jews were at a greater disadvantage than German Jews. Their differences in language, dress, and culture made them easier to distinguish from the rest of the population. The Nazis scorned and ridiculed their traditional habits, often setting men's beards on fire or cutting them off with their bayonets. They even branded the foreheads of many poor Jews with the Star of David.

That many millions of Eastern Jews were already concentrated in the cities also made it easier for their tormentors to surround and eventually to destroy them.

Finally, the Nazis were able to turn the long-standing Jew-hatred among the Eastern local populations to their advantage. In many cases, they were able to persuade Lithuanians, Poles, Ukrainians, and Russians to aid them in their anti-Jewish activities.

Only in one way did Eastern Jews fare better than German Jews. Their long experience with pogroms and local hostility had made them more conditioned to handle Nazi pressure. Throughout the Holocaust, many German Jews who had so earnestly believed themselves to be true Germans became bitterly disappointed and disillusioned. In the Nazi ghettos and camps, they fell prey to despair and suicide more often than their fellow Jews from the East.

Discussion Question: If you were a German Jew, would you also have been bitterly disappointed?

ANTI-SEMITISM IN MODERN POLAND

After World War I ended, Poland became an independent nation. The 3.3 million Jews within the new Polish borders constituted 10 percent of the total Polish population. But Jews were not the only minority in Poland. One third of the population was made up of Germans, Lithuanians, White Russians, and Ukrainians.

The Poles, who were proud of their new nation, frowned upon all the minorities. Jews especially were resented. During the 1920's and 1930's, a wave of Polish nationalism combined with long-standing religious anti-Semitism and frustration from an economic depression. Nazi ideas about government and race had also seeped into Poland. The result was violent pogroms, murders, boycotts against Jewish businesses, and anti-Jewish laws. There were even movements to force Jews out of the country during the 1930's.

Polish Jews reacted to the hostility in one of

two ways. Despite violent anti-Semitism, the majority of Jews considered Poland their rightful home and wanted to remain there, while maintaining their rights as a minority group. In fact the Bund, a socialist political party made up of Jewish workers, defended their right to live in Poland with their fists. They formed their own militia and met the violence of the pogroms head on.

To others, however, emigration became the answer. But when they joined the flood of German refugees trying to flee Nazi tyranny, filled immigration quotas locked them in. Fewer than 120,000 were able to leave during the troubled 1930's. So when Hitler's troops came crashing into Poland in September 1939, most of the Jewish community was still intact and at the Nazis' mercy.

Nearly 3 million Polish Jews would be dead within the next five years.

Discussion Question: Why did local hostility work against Jews under Nazi rule?

THE SECOND SOLUTION TO THE JEWISH QUESTION, SEPTEMBER 1, 1939– JUNE 22, 1941

A Temporary Move

With the Nazi-Russian conquest, the country of Poland again disappeared from the map. Western Poland became Reichland; central Poland, the "Government General" under Nazi rule; and eastern Poland, Russian territory.

World War II was in full swing. Emigration had come to a standstill. This meant millions of Jews were now shut off from the outside world. Hitler's problem of how to make Nazi lands Jew-free needed a new solution.

Hitler came up with a second—but only temporary—answer. Down the chain of command went his order to Reinhard Heydrich, SD chief and now head of the Reich Security Office (RSHA), the Fuehrer's new department assigned to handle the Jewish Question.

The order? All Jews were to be moved eastward to the Government General. There they would be held in ghettos to be set up in larger cities with access to major railroad lines. This accessibility to railways was of utmost importance, for Jews were to be eventually evacuated from these collection centers. In addition, a Judenrat, or council of Jewish elders, was to be assigned to each town and city and finally in each ghetto to carry out Nazi orders.

In the meantime, until the Fuehrer decided upon where and how all ghettoized Jews could be removed from Nazi lands, they were to be put to forced labor. A deliberate starvation policy and absolutely no medical help were also in order for the Jewish slave laborers. Why? Because the Fuehrer's new policy was "The more Jews that die off, the better. For the fewer there are, the lesser our Jewish problem!"

During the period that this Second Solution was in effect, however, an organized Nazi system of mass murder was not yet apparent.

Roundup and Relocation of Jews

Soon after the Nazi occupation of Poland came Heydrich's eviction notice to Polish Jews. Western Poland was now living space for Germans only. Except for Jews in the city of Lodz, who were to be confined in a ghetto there, all Jews and all Poles were to relocate in the Government General, where Jews would be confined in certain sections of large cities. Jews already living in the Government General were to move into the big-city ghettos. Direct orders to move were usually given on the spot.

Survivor John F., who was living in the Polish town of Tuszyn, describes this typical scene:

I was eleven years old. At 4:00 in the morning on December 26, 1939, my family was awakened by the Gestapo pounding on our door. They gave us a half-hour to pack. We could take only what we could carry on our backs. We were not allowed to take along animals. My dog kept barking at the men. Then he started to run after me. They shot him. I was more upset about my dog than anything else. We walked twenty-five miles to the Piotrkow ghetto. There were 40,000 people jammed in here. From our nice home, we came to one room for our whole family.

Discussion Question: Assuming you were an "evicted" Jew, what would you take along in that backpack?

Aryanization of Property Is Instant

All property left behind became the property of the Reich. While the Aryanization process had taken several months in Germany, in Poland it was done on a moment's notice. Mark Stern was a sixteen-year-old Polish Jew managing his father's factory at this time. He recalls:

My father had temporarily gone off to eastern Poland to hide because we had heard the invading Nazis planned to murder all male Jews. (They did, in fact, murder many thousands of Poles—Polish clergy, professionals, and government leaders—as well as Jews.) But he was never to come back. Russian troops there shipped him off to a labor camp in Siberia where he later died.

In the meantime, I had taken over the family business. One day, the Gestapo walked into our building and asked me to hand over the keys. They said, "By order

of the German occupation, we have to take over your business." I told them I would like to be employed in the business in order to support my mother and younger sister. They replied, "This is a German business now. We don't hire Jews."

Discussion Question: How would you have reacted to the Gestapo order?

Families Walk to the Ghettos

All families were expected to find their own transportation to the Government General ghettos. What a sad, strange sight they made. In the dead of winter, hundreds of thousands of uprooted families trudged over endless miles of country roads, bundles on their backs, babies crying, the aged weary and limping, parents tearful of leaving their homes behind.

Tens of thousands took a chance and headed toward Russian territory instead. But this proved only a temporary reprieve; later, most would either be sent by the Russians to forced labor camps in Siberia or become caught up in the Nazi war on Russia.

When the weary travelers arrived at their destination, they couldn't believe their eyes. The ghettos were always in the slum sections of cities. But now many of the dilapidated buildings had been bombed out by the recent German invasion. Everywhere, mobs of exhausted, bewildered families stood waiting to move into these miserable quarters. The Jewish leaders assigned by the Nazis to organize this mass of humanity into the cramped ghettos threw their hands up in despair. How could tens of thousands of people fit into a handful of broken-down buildings?

Discussion Question: Imagine yourself and your family in this situation. What would your thoughts and feelings be at this point?

Ghettos Are Sealed Off

The Piotrkow ghetto, where John F. and his family settled, was the first Polish ghetto to be established in November 1939. In about a year, the other major ghettos were sealed off. Lodz, the second largest ghetto, was sealed shut in April 1940. The Warsaw ghetto—which became the largest of all, with over a half-million people—was walled off in November 1940.

Cattle Trains Bring Jews from Other Nazi Lands

In spite of all the confusion and the severely overcrowded Jewish quarters, Heydrich gave the signal to begin dumping Jews from other Nazi-occupied lands into the ghettos, too. Chief Engineer Adolf Eichmann's system of cattle trains provided the transportation. In October 1939, cattle trains carried Jews from Austria and Czechoslovakia to the Polish ghettos.

When German Jews heard rumors of their possible deportation to Poland, they grew frantic. They looked for every means to escape. They still desperately tried to emigrate, usually in vain. Some, who were lucky enough to have good and brave friends to protect them, went into hiding. Suicides were an everyday occurrence. In February 1940, their fears became reality. The Gestapo began the first roundup of German Jews.

More often than not, the cattle cars became vehicles of death. Men, women, and children were packed in so tightly, there was neither room to sit nor to breathe. Babies, expectant mothers, the weak, and the aged—all were jammed into these unheated, windowless traps. Often the journeys took several days, especially later in the war when mass deportations began from far-off places of Europe. To the agony and embarrassment of the poor souls within, a barrel or bucket was the only bathroom facility. For those who could wait, there was a daily fifteen-minute stop in the nearby fields. En route, indescribable suffering, crying and whining children, moans of discomfort were all in vain. Occupied with their own misery, few aboard could offer comfort to the others. By the time the trains came to a final stop, frostbite, sickness, and hunger had taken their first toll.

A Jewish Reservation: A Final Solution?

In 1939 the SS chiefs came up with a possible final way to clear all Jews out of Europe. It was to concentrate millions of Jews on a reservation, or separate Jewish state. There, under Nazi control, Jews would labor for the Reich. Two possible locations were cited.

The first was a large area near the Polish city of Lublin. The final plans included shifting much of the native population to other areas. The Nazis began to experiment with this idea. Eichmann's first transports of 1939 began to dump tens of thousands of Jews into the already crowded Lublin ghetto. But the Nazis neither expanded the area nor provided additional housing for the new arrivals. In mid-January, nearly 80,000 relocated Jews were scattered everywhere and dying like flies. Once every inch of shelter had been taken up, homeless Jews lay frozen on sidewalks and in open fields surrounded by electrical barbed wire. Without proper sewage facilities to accommodate the masses of people, the water system soon became contaminated and undrinkable. Typhus and starvation wracked those within. By the spring of 1940, the idea of the Lublin reservation was put aside.

At this same time, the Nazis were dreaming up another fantastic scheme. They reasoned that perhaps Madagascar, an island off the southeast coast of Africa, might be a good site for the Jewish state. However, at the time of their plan, Madagascar still belonged to the French. To implement the plan, Hitler needed to first conquer France, take over the island, ship the

25,000 people already living there to some other place, and then cart 4 million Jews over the ocean. Until the war was over, the Jews would remain in the Polish ghettos.

The Madagascar plan fizzled out. Hitler did indeed conquer France, but his war didn't end there. He made plans for a new war on Russia. With this, a new solution to the Jewish Question had to be found.

Historians are divided in their beliefs concerning Hitler's true intentions regarding a Jewish reservation. Some say Hitler used the idea for propaganda purposes only. Why? To fool both Jews and the world in order to cover up his real plan to eventually exterminate the Jewish people. Other historians believe Hitler seriously considered using this alternative, but that events of the war made the setup impossible. These same scholars believe Hitler gave the command for genocide only as a last resort.

Discussion Question: What do you think?

THE NAZI GHETTOS

They Are Worse Than Medieval Ghettos

In some respects, Nazi ghettos were like medieval ghettos. Both had high walls to isolate the Jewish community from the world outside. Guards stood watch at the gates. But there the similarities end.

Unlike the ghettos of old, which locked Jews in only at night and allowed the daily passage of both Christians and Jews in and out of the ghetto gates to engage in commerce, Nazi ghettos were sealed traps. No Jew could leave. And signs posted on the outer walls warned outsiders **EPIDEMIC! DO NOT ENTER!** It is true that in some Eastern European cities, Nazi ghettos were not actually walled. However, there, too, guards prohibited trespassing in areas to which Jews

were confined. In all, Nazi rules forbade Jews to walk even in their own streets between 7:00 P.M. and 5:00 A.M.

All Are in the East

With only one exception—the ghetto-camp of Theresienstadt in Czechoslovakia—all ghettos were located in the cities of Eastern Europe. The first were located in Nazi-occupied Poland. After the Germans attacked Russia in 1941, ghettos spread to other cities in Eastern Europe.

Warsaw, with over a half-million Jews, was the largest. Other ghettos holding tens of thousands of occupants were Lodz, Cracow, Lublin, Radom, Lwow, Vilna, Bialystok, Kovno, and Riga. There were also dozens of smaller ones.

Why were ghettos set up in cities of the East and not the West? First, a majority of Europe's Jews were already concentrated in Eastern cities; it was a simple matter to push them into a corner and surround them with walls. In contrast, Western European Jews were not only much fewer in number but also widely dispersed among the general population. To ghettoize them, too many non-Jews would have had to be shifted.

They Do Not Last Long

In all, more than 3 million Jews were locked up in ghettos. Some ghettos also contained thousands of Gypsies, thrown in by the Nazis as another inferior race.

None of the ghettos lasted for more than a few years. They were never meant to be more than temporary holding stations. The ghetto occupants disappeared for several reasons. They were slowly and deliberately starved to death. Or they froze to death. Sometimes dreadful illnesses killed them. Forced labor also took a heavy toll. And after 1941, Nazis cleared out all remaining ghetto prisoners and sent them off to nearby gas chambers.

In summary, the two main reasons why Nazis set up ghettos were (1) to concentrate Jews into small areas, and (2) to provide feeding stations for forced labor in the beginning and for the gas chambers in the end.

LIFE IN THE WARSAW GHETTO

A Living Hell

Nazi ghettos were living hellholes. Overcrowding, starvation, cold, disease, forced labor, and death plagued every ghetto resident. Let's examine life while it lasted in the largest ghetto of all: Warsaw.

Just imagine this: Shove more than a half-million people into slightly more than one square mile of space; contaminate the water supply; throw in tuberculosis, typhoid, and body lice; take all winter clothing away from the inhabitants; give them no medicine at all; allow them only a quarter of the food ration relegated to Germans; and work them to the bone. Now you have a picture of the Warsaw ghetto.

The Warsaw ghetto had wall-to-wall people. Four families were squeezed into space normally allotted to one. Others lived in hallways, basements, attics. And the daytime streets were always teeming with humanity. With no place to go, most just paced the streets, feeling a kind of security in the crowds.

Death was an everyday companion. Corpses strewn over the sidewalks became so commonplace, most passersby hardly took notice. A few, however, occasionally bent over to cover the dead with newspapers. In due time, the ghetto "undertakers" would make their daily rounds, load the corpses on their carts, and bring them to a final resting place in the ghetto cemetery.

Ghetto residents constantly battled the winter cold. This deadly enemy froze not only fingers and toes but water pipes in unheated buildings. One by one, bathrooms went quickly out of order and added to the misery. When the residents ran out of coal, they began to tear down buildings for firewood. During the two winters of Warsaw's existence, more than 70,000 people died terrible deaths. Many thousands were orphaned children who had sat huddled in snow-covered streets, barefooted, dressed in rags, and begging for food.

Discussion Question: With your calculator, figure out how much space was available per person in Warsaw.

Warsaw Jews Make the Best of It

However, total misery does not convey a true and complete picture of the Warsaw ghetto. Jews did not just sit around and wait to die. They made the best of what they had. In spite of the inhuman conditions, the Nazis broke neither the Jews' spirit nor their zest for life.

In every little patch of dirt they could find, the Jews planted vegetable gardens. When these filled up, they carried dirt to the rooftops and planted there. Their leaders taxed everyone for a few pennies or a few tablespoons of food. From the proceeds, they opened public soup kitchens to feed the starving. Sometimes the soup they dished out had been boiled from straw; nevertheless, it was hot and would stay hunger pains for the moment.

Smuggling food into the ghetto became a regular practice. Children were the quickest, most expert smugglers of all. They dug holes under walls, climbed through slimy sewers, and—their pockets loaded with potatoes or carrots—darted past SS guards. Many a child was spotted and shot down. But this didn't stop the little band of smugglers.

Nor could anything stop the Jewish love of learning. When the SS banned schooling, the Jews didn't listen. Hidden away in back rooms, classes were conducted routinely. Adults too had their own courses of study, lectures, and

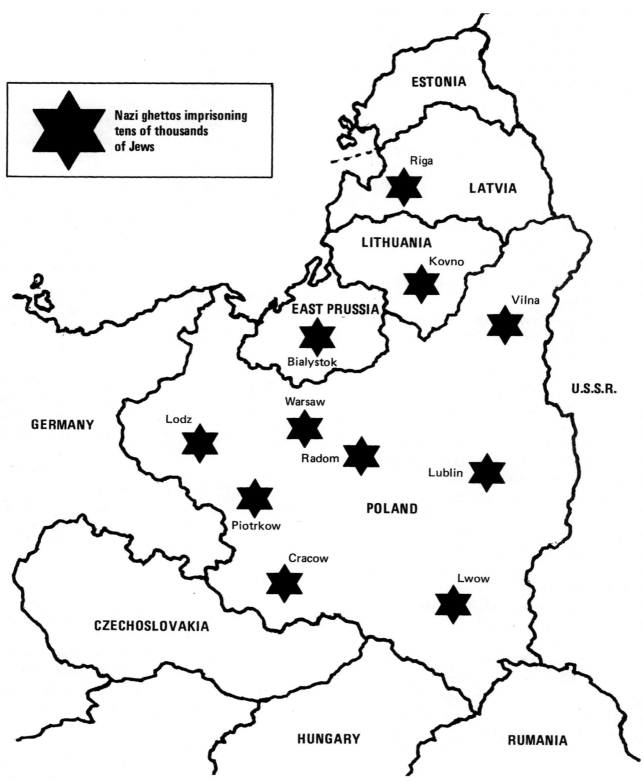

THE LARGEST NAZI GHETTOS

discussions. Later, when the Nazis tolerated the idea of education, thousands of Warsaw children and adults attended classes on all levels.

One group of Warsaw doctors even did an important study of the most common malady among them—the effects of starvation on the human body. The results of their research are still being used in the medical world today.

Although it was strictly forbidden, and countless people involved were arrested and executed, several underground newspapers were published every single day.

Several Warsaw writers who wanted the world to someday know their story kept records of life as it was then. One was a learned historian named Emmanuel Ringelblum. Working with a staff, he set up an archives, or collection, of all Nazi announcements and public records having to do with Jews under the occupation. He also kept a very accurate diary. Then this wise man had all these records buried underground. After the Nazis burned the Warsaw ghetto to the ground, Dr. Ringelblum's records remained unharmed and lived on to tell their story.

Warsaw Jews also maintained their love of culture. Hunger did not rob actors, musicians, and singers of their talent. With what little strength they had, they performed to help others forget their discomfort. Stage plays and concerts continually brightened this otherwise bleak atmosphere.

And all the suffering did not dampen Jewish religious spirit, either. Throughout the two years of life in the ghetto, religious services and study remained an important part of Jewish life.

Discussion Questions: Would you have the courage to make the best of life in Warsaw? If you were a German soldier guard at Warsaw, what would you do if you saw a child smuggling in food? If you were a Warsaw Jew, why would you want to go to school under such conditions?

FORCED LABOR

Ghettos and Labor Camps Provide Slaves

When a Nazi decree in 1939 made all Jewish men and women between fourteen and sixty-five slave laborers for the Reich, the ghettos became bottomless free-labor reservoirs. In addition to ghettos, a huge network of labor concentration camps sprang up all over Nazi-occupied Europe. Seizing the opportunity for this cheap labor and huge profits, owners of large German industries such as IG Farben and Krupp worked out deals with the SS. Then they either built their factories near the ghettos or camps or else erected labor camps beside their mines and stone quarries. Sometimes industry moved right inside the ghettos. In the Government General alone, more than a hundred labor camps kept prisoners slaving.

Pushed to work a dozen nonstop hours each day by merciless Nazi slave drivers, and wasted to skin and bones by the deliberate starvation policy, the life expectancy of workers narrowed down to an average of a few months.

Not only Jews were used as slave laborers. So were millions of other Europeans and concentration camp prisoners. Jews, however, comprised the largest part of the Nazi labor force. And they, especially, became targets for Nazi abuse.

A Holocaust Survivor Tells His Story of Slavery

John Y. survived nine forced-labor camps—three in Poland and six in Germany. First sent from the Piotrkow ghetto to the Polish labor camp Hortensia, where he worked in a glass factory, John recalls:

Poles slaved in the factory, too. However, they worked one shift. We Jews worked two, one inside the factory and the other, outside.

In all nine labor camps, SS guards patrolled us on the outside of camp during labor duty. But after work hours, Kapos, who were prisoners themselves and usually sadists and hardened criminals, managed us inside the camp. Most were as cruel as the SS.

For me, Buchenwald was the most "bearable" of all because it had running water, crude beds, and bathrooms, at least. Mittelbow and Northhausen were the worst. In Northhausen, as in all camps, roll call—held outside in all types of weather and lasting always for several hours—began and ended each day. All prisoners had to be accounted for . . . the ill . . . even those who had died during the night. Prisoners had to drag the sick and dead to roll call to be officially counted. If by chance a prisoner was missing, those in line had to remain standing until he was tracked down. I remember once having to stand at attention all night long in freezing weather because one prisoner was unaccounted for. People were dropping from exhaustion, only to be forced to stand again or else. Some died from weakness and exposure. By morning, the "escaped" prisoner was discovered dead in the camp.

The name of the game in all camps was survival. Food and hunger were all we ever thought of. People did anything for food. Stealing. Fighting. Those who smoked died first. Why? For just a puff from a cigarette, they gave their rations away . . . their shoes . . . their sweaters. Where did prisoners get cigarettes? SS guards on labor duty smoked and threw their butts away. Prisoners collected them,

then fashioned their own cigarettes to either smoke or to use for bartering.

Bathing? Once a month guards sprayed us with ice-cold water from fire hoses while we stood shivering in unheated barracks. Meanwhile our clothing was collected for delousing in huge washing and drying machines. That is, all the clothing of 6,000 prisoners at once. After sleeping naked all night, we had to get up much earlier the next morning to go through the agonizing confusion of trying to find clothing that fit. Never was one's own clothing found. Either we ended up squeezing into pajamas three sizes too tight or else swam in ones too big. All the while, camp guards stood back and laughed at our fury and confusion. Oftentimes in cold weather, we had to go to work in clothing that was still wet.

Medicine for the sick? Nothing at all. Not even aspirin.

The work day? At Mittelbow, our day began at 4:00 A.M. Bathroom time meant a walk with guards to a certain section of a nearby field. Breakfast? A slice of dry bread and coffee. If you wanted to wash your face, you used your coffee. There was no water for bathing. Next, an eight-mile march to the train station. After the train stopped, another eight-mile hike to the stone quarry. Work began at 8:00 A.M. and lasted until 6:00 P.M. There was no lunch. No water to drink all day, even in the blistering sun. SS guards with dogs continuously watched over us.

After the march back to the station, the train ride, the march to camp, and roll call, it was nearly midnight. Supper was stale bread and watery soup and coffee.

From the kitchen, we had to walk through a long dark corridor. If we were off guard or sick or weary, other starving prisoners often grabbed our food.

After a few months of this routine, my twenty-five-year-old cousin who was working beside me in the stone quarry said one day, 'I've had it.' He lay down on the ground. That was suicide. The SS guard killed him right in front of me.

Discussion Question: How would you have reacted if you were the Jewish slave laborer? the guard on duty?

Jews Do Much Work

Without the slave labor of Jews, Hitler never would have gotten very far in his war effort. With the war in full swing and most German men at the front, Jewish manpower assembled parts and ran machines in the armaments plants. Jews dug trenches for German soldiers along the front. They built bridges, railroads, and airstrips. They even erected the very factories and labor camps where they slaved and lived.

Jews had mixed emotions about their labors in the war effort. On one hand, they hated helping their bitterest enemy to win a war they hoped with all their might the Nazis would lose. On the other hand, they had no choice. Many figured that work meant survival, and that as long as their services were needed perhaps the Nazis would let them live.

They Are Not Rewarded

But few Jewish slaves had such luck. Hitler used and then abused them. By 1941, the Jewish labor force was directed to another task, building gas chambers and crematoria. Once this death machinery began to work, Hitler would not allow it to slow down, not even when it

jeopardized his war effort.

As the ghettos were quickly emptied, Hitler ordered the destruction of the Jewish labor force next. By 1943, German war factories were experiencing a critical shortage of laborers. Furthermore, trains carrying Jewish victims to the death camps in Poland were interfering with the flow of military transports and troops to emergency battle areas. German industrialists and army commanders began to complain about the shortages and delays.

Hitler didn't care. Even as his armies began to lose the war, he ordered the genocide speeded up. The killing of Jews took priority over everything else.

THE JUDENRAT, OR JEWISH COUNCILS

Nazis Make Jews Their Spokesmen

Hitler was an evil genius. He carried out hideous crimes against the Jewish people. Even worse, he forced them to participate in their own destruction. By compelling Jews to issue Nazi orders in their own communities, he was able to destroy them with the least amount of resistance. Thus, whenever Nazi forces took over new territories, the first thing they did was to strong-arm Jewish leaders in every town and city into being Nazi spokesmen.

In the ghettos, the Jewish executors of Nazi policies were called the **Judenrat**, or Jewish councils. The number of councilmen ran anywhere from a dozen to twenty-four members, depending upon the size of the Jewish community it governed. The SS also assigned a Jewish police force, not only to keep order in each ghetto but also to follow the Judenrat's instructions. The number of policemen varied with the size of the community, too. Warsaw, for example, had 2,000 Jewish policemen.

Who chose the Judenrat? The vast majority of Jews shied away from this involvement, but in the beginning, a few who had always been leaders in their communities volunteered to be councilmen with the idea, "Perhaps, if we cooperate, we can negotiate with them and save our communities." In most cases, however, the SS handpicked the Judenrat by pointing randomly at individuals whom they judged to be the weakest.

Rule by fear was the Nazi way. Nazi instructions to the Judenrat were simple: Follow orders or die. When too many Judenrat members chose death, the Nazis bent others to their will by threatening to wipe out the entire ghetto. If orders were not followed explicitly, Nazi soldiers often carried out mass shootings of ghetto men, women, and children to show they meant business.

Discussion   Would you have agreed to
Question: become a Judenrat member?

The Judenrat Is Always in a Predicament

Left with no choice, and praying for an early Allied victory to free them, the Judenrat's main goal became to keep as many people alive as possible for as long as possible. With full responsibility of running the broken-down ghettos, distributing supplies, and seeing that Nazi orders were carried out, the Judenrat was in a constant predicament.

How could they distribute food fairly when there was never enough to go around? How could they repair leaking rooftops or broken plumbing when they had no tools or supplies? And when Nazis moved their factories inside the ghettos and ordered the Judenrat to run them and to organize the ghetto labor force, how could they refuse?

Conflicts soon arose whenever hungry and sick ghetto workers begged their leaders for more food. But having no alternatives, the Jewish leaders had to turn down their starving brethren. Moreover, not many of these wasted creatures were eager to report for grinding labor. Under serious pressure to comply with Nazi wishes, the Judenrat had to order the Jewish police to round up the unwilling workers. Now the Judenrat and the Jewish police faced the hostility of their own people.

It is true that a few Judenrat members cooperated too willingly with the SS. And some Jewish police performed their duties with zeal almost equal to that of the Gestapo. But these Jews, a rare exception, were usually very frightened human beings only trying to save their own skins.

As conditions in the ghettos worsened, so did the relationship between the Jewish communities and the Judenrat. Angry Jewish workers began to sabotage Nazi efforts whenever they could. In the factories they damaged machines, set fires, and made defective articles. As always, the SS vented their fury on the Judenrat: "Turn in the resisters or your families. A hundred other Jews shall die each day until the offenders are caught!" No matter what they decided, the Jewish councilmen couldn't win.

Judenrat Is Forced to Make Selections for the Death Camps

The final insult came in 1941 when the Judenrat was ordered to select thousands of ghetto residents to report each day for "deportation and resettlement in the East." When they later learned that the deportation trains were heading to the death camps, many councilmen committed suicide. But other Jewish decision-makers were forced to take their places. The selections had to be made. Hoping to still hold the line, the Judenrat pointed to the beggars, the aged, the ill, and the dying in the ghetto streets and hospitals.

With thousands boarding the cattle trains to the death camps every day, the ghettos were quickly emptied of Jewish inhabitants. And after they had fulfilled their jobs, the Jewish police and the Judenrat were shoved onto the trains, too.

Discussion Question: How would you have reacted if you were in the Judenrat's position?

MORE AND MORE JEWISH VICTIMS

This chapter has dealt mainly with the two-year (1939–1941) plight of 3 million Polish Jews in the Nazi ghettos and camps, and the thousands of deported Jews from Germany, Czechoslovakia, and Austria who also shared in the misery of ghetto and labor-camp life.

However, by June 1941, there were still over 130,000 Jews living in Germany. Thousands more remained in Nazi-controlled Austria and Czechoslovakia. Most lived in poverty and hunger. New anti-Jewish laws had stripped them of such things as food and clothing rations, telephones, fur coats. Many thousands had been taken into "protective custody" in Nazi concentration camps and put to forced labor.

In the meantime, Hitler's armies had not stopped at Poland. Between September 1939 and June 1941, in a lightning war such as the world had never seen, the Germans had overrun Denmark, Norway, Belgium, Luxembourg, Holland, France, Greece, and Yugoslavia. Three other nations—Hungary, Bulgaria, and Rumania—had decided to help the Germans hold the line. Nearly all of Europe had fallen into Nazi clutches.

All Jewish citizens in the last three nations had quickly become victims of the Nazi anti-Jewish laws including the wearing of the Jewish star, the seizing of all Jewish property, and forced labor.

In the conquered countries of Western Europe, however, the SS did not charge in and begin torturing Jews as they had done in Poland. They had to conduct their anti-Jewish campaign at a slower pace, for anti-Semitism was not a popular feeling in the West. Some local populations, in fact, bravely resisted Nazi laws against their Jewish citizens. The SS did not allow this show of support to stop them. But they did have to take the time to "condition" the native peoples and to teach Jewish defenders a lesson. They punished them so severely that resistance soon narrowed down to only a few who were willing to risk their own lives.

Chapter Eight Review

REVIEWING KEY POINTS

Exercise 1

1. Two thirds of the Jewish Holocaust victims were Eastern Europeans. Why?

2. Did the fact that Poland had formed a new nation in 1918 have anything to do with local resentment toward Jews? Explain.

3. Why was the Second Solution to the Jewish Question only temporary?

4. Under Nazi invaders, why did all Poles—Jews and non-Jews alike—have to move out of western Poland? Where did they go?

5. Discuss life in the Warsaw ghetto.

6. How did Hitler use and abuse Jewish slave laborers?

7. Why had the ghettos disappeared by 1942?

8. Why did Nazis force Jews to be their spokesmen? How did they do it?

9. Name the countries that fell under Nazi rule between September 1939 and June 1941. How were Jews within the occupied countries affected?

10. In the countries of Western Europe, why did the SS move more cautiously in their anti-Jewish activities?

CHECKING YOURSELF

Exercise 2
Citing Differences

Directions: German Jews and Jews in Eastern Europe responded differently to the non-Jewish culture around them. Make a chart like the one below. To the left are phrases that describe the way German Jews responded to certain phases of non-Jewish culture in which they lived. To the right, under the heading "Jews in the East," tell how the Eastern Jews behaved differently from their German counterparts. Avoid using the word **not**. The first difference has been provided for you.

JEWS IN GERMANY	JEWS IN THE EAST
1. assimilated into the culture around them	1. kept and practiced their own traditional culture
2. spoke the same language as their neighbors	2. _____ _____
3. most sent their children to public schools	3. _____ _____
4. dressed like every other German	4. _____ _____
5. modernized their Jewish religion so as not to be so different	5. _____ _____
6. in some cases, converted to Christianity	6. _____ _____
7. changed their names to make themselves more "German"	7. _____ _____
8. frequently intermarried with non-Jews	8. _____ _____

Exercise 2 (continued)

JEWS IN GERMANY	JEWS IN THE EAST
9. lived intermingled in the non-Jewish communities	9. _____ _____
10. believed assimilation was the answer to erasing prejudice against Jews	10. _____ _____

Exercise 3
Making the Correct Choice

Directions: Number your paper from 1–26. Beneath each incomplete statement are three answer choices. Choose the one that best answers each statement and place the letter of that answer beside the corresponding number on your paper.

1. During the Holocaust, most of the Jewish victims were living in

   a. Western Europe   b.   Central Europe   c. Eastern Europe

2. At least half of the Jewish Holocaust victims had lived in

   a. Germany   b.   Poland   c. England

3. The ancestors of most Polish Jews had migrated from

   a. Germany   b.   Russia   c. England

4. Polish and Russian Jews had experienced terrible pogroms

   a. between the seventeenth and nineteenth centuries
   b. between the nineteenth and twentieth centuries
   c. both a and b

5. When Nazis arrived in Eastern Europe and began to persecute Jews, many of the local populations viewed such treatment with

   a. shock   b.   disbelief   c. indifference

Exercise 3 (continued)

6. The percentage of Jews in the total Polish population was

   a. 10 percent   b. 1 percent   c. 5 percent

7. When the Nazis evicted all Jews and other Poles from their homes in western Poland, it was during the

   a. winter   b. spring   c. summer

8. Ghettos of Nazi-occupied Europe were set up in the cities of

   a. Eastern Europe   b. Central Europe   c. Western Europe

9. The so-called Second Solution to the Jewish Question was

   a. death to all Jews
   b. imprisonment, slavery, and starvation
   c. eviction and takeover of Jewish property

10. The largest ghetto of all was

    a. Warsaw   b. Lodz   c. Piotrikow

11. Most Polish Jews got to the ghettos by

    a. cattle trains   b. cars   c. walking

12. Except for Lodz, all the ghettos in Nazi-occupied Poland up to 1941 were located in

    a. the Government General   b. western Poland   c. eastern Poland

13. The section of Poland taken over by the Russians in 1939 was

    a. the Government General   b. western Poland   c. eastern Poland

14. The chief engineer in charge of the system of cattle trains that transported Jews from all points of Europe into Nazi hands was

    a. Heydrich   b. Eichmann   c. Himmler

15. Nazis talked about establishing a Jewish reservation on the island of

    a. Madagascar   b. Corsica   c. Australia

Exercise 3 (continued)

16. Nazi ghettos and medieval ghettos were

    a. completely different   b. similar in some respects   c. the same

17. Nazi ghettos lasted

    a. about two years   b. throughout the war   c. about five years

18. The SS set up ghettos mainly to

    a. isolate and concentrate Jews in small areas
    b. remove them from the general population
    c. both a and b

19. Nazi labor chiefs and German industrialists exploited Jews and other prisoners by

    a. forcing them to be slaves
    b. earning huge profits at their expense
    c. both a and b

20. Jewish slave laborers were

    a. both adult men and women
    b. adult men only
    c. males and females from fourteen to sixty-five years old

21. Jewish slave laborers performed their work because

    a. they knew they would be compensated later
    b. they had no choice
    c. they wanted to please the Nazis

22. Most of the Judenrat of the ghettos performed their duties with the idea of

    a. saving at least some Jewish lives
    b. trying to save themselves
    c. serving the Nazis

23. The position of the Judenrat in the ghettos was one of

    a. advantage   b. disadvantage   c. envy

24. Some people in the ghettos were

a. non-Jews
b. Jews from Germany and Austria
c. both a and b

Exercise 3 (continued)

25. In the countries of occupied Western Europe, the SS carried out their war against Jews

    a. just as they had in Eastern Europe
    b. not at all
    c. more slowly but just as surely

26. By June 1941, Nazis had some degree of control over all Jews in continental Europe except those in

    a. Russian territories   b. Greece   c. Norway

GIVING REPORTS

Topics to Research

1. More on the *Protocols of the Elders of Zion*. Good sources: Two books by Norman Cohn: *The Truth About the Protocols of Zion* and *Warrant for Genocide.*

2. What American auto tycoon Henry Ford said about the *Protocols* in articles published in *The Dearborn* [Michigan] *Independent.*

3. How did the Bund and the Zionists respond to the Nazis? Good sources: *The War Against the Jews*, by Lucy Dawidowicz.

4. Mordecai Rumkowski, the leader of the Judenrat in the Lodz ghetto.

5. Moses Merin, leader of the Judenrat in the ghetto of Sosnowiec.

6. Hans Frank, the Nazi governor of Poland.

7. The Nazi treatment of non-Jewish Poles.

8. More about the Judenrat. Good sources: *Judenrat*, by Isaiah Trunk.

9. The ghetto/camp of Theresienstadt (Czech—*Terezin*), the so-called "model camp" used for Nazi propaganda purposes. Find out how Hitler used it, what "type" of prisoners were sent here, and what the real truth was about Theresienstadt.

10. From *Never to Forget*, by Milton Meltzer, read aloud to your class songs once sung by ghetto Jews (page 87), slave laborers (page 94), condemned Jews (page 116), and partisans (page 159). Tell how all the songs reflect hope and courage. Good source for more songs: *Thirty Songs of the Ghetto*, by H. Kon.

11. Social life and conditions in other ghettos besides Warsaw.

12. More on Eastern European Jews. Good source: *World of Our Fathers*, by Milton Meltzer.

13. The **kahal**, the governing council of Jewish communities dating back to sixteenth-century Poland. In what respects was it similar to the Judenrat? How could this tradition of the kahal have made Polish Jews more receptive to the idea of a Judenrat, at least at first?

14. Surviving the Holocaust through art. Give an illustrated talk using *Artists of Terezin*, by Gerald Green; or *The Book of Alfred Kantor*, by A. Kantor.

15. More on the pogroms in Russia at various times in history.

Books to Review

1. *In the Hell of Auschwitz*, by Judith Newman.

2. *The Warsaw Diary of Adam Czerniakov*, by Adam Czerniakov.

3. *The Warsaw Diary of Chaim A. Kaplan*, by Chaim A. Kaplan.

4. *Fragments of Isabella: A Memoir of Auschwitz*, by Isabella Leitner.

5. *Liliana's Journal: Warsaw 1939–1945*, by Liliana Zuker.

6. *Night*, by Elie Wiesel, a powerful autobiographical novel of life in Nazi prisons based on the author's own experience.

7. *I Never Saw Another Butterfly*, edited by Hana Volavkove, a collection of drawings, songs, and poems of children who lived in the ghetto/camp of Theresienstadt.

8. *Never to Forget: The Jews of the Holocaust*, by Milton Meltzer, views the history of the Holocaust through survivor's testimonies.

9. *Survival in Auschwitz: The Nazi Assault on Humanity*, by Primo Levi, is based on the author's own experience.

10. *The Survivor*, by Des Pres.

11. Choose selections from the following anthologies of Holocaust literature: *Out of the Whirlwind: A Reader of Holocaust Literature*, edited by Albert Frielander; *Anthology of Holocaust Literature*, edited by Jacob Gladstein.

12. *Human Behavior in the Concentration Camp*, by Elie Cohen.

13. *Schindler's List*, by Thomas Keneally, is about Oskar Schindler, a German Catholic industrialist who builds a factory-camp to protect Jews in Poland, thereby saving many Jewish lives.

14. *With a Camera in the Ghetto*, Zvi Szner and Alexander Sened, editors, showing pictures by Mendel Grossman, a Jewish photographer of the Lodz ghetto in 1941 and 1942.

15. *And the Violins Stopped Playing: A Story of the Gypsy Holocaust*, by Alexander Ramati, a novel based on notes given to the author by a Polish Gypsy, concerning his experiences with the Nazis from 1942–1945 in Poland, Hungary, and Auschwitz.

16. *Dry Tears: The Story of a Lost Childhood*, by Nechama Tec, a Polish Jew who describes her childhood experiences during the Holocaust.

17. *The Lost Childhood*, by Yehuda Nir, who as a young Polish-Jewish boy, with his mother and sister, posed as Catholic and survived.

18. *The Warsaw Ghetto: A Christian's Testimony*, by Wladyslaw T. Bartoszewski, who returned from Auschwitz in 1941 and served as a liaison between Jewish ghetto leaders and the Polish underground.

19. *Lodz Ghetto: Inside a Community Under Siege*, edited by Alan Adelson and Robert Lapidua; it contains German and ghetto documents.

20. *Auschwitz: A History in Photographs*, Indiana University Press, consisting of photos taken by Nazis, by prisoners, and by liberating Soviets.

MAKING PROJECTS

Poster Ideas

1. Make a map of the Pale of Settlement (consult Martin Gilbert's *Jewish History Atlas*).

2. Make a map showing the distance of Madagascar (now called the Malagasy Republic) from Europe.

3. Picture the Warsaw ghetto streets in the daytime.

4. Show Nazis evicting Jews and other Poles from their homes in western Poland.

5. Picture the arrival of Jewish families to the ghettos.

6. Make a collage or mural of your impression of ghetto or camp life.

7. Choose a poem from *I Never Saw Another Butterfly* (mentioned on p. 132) and print it on your poster paper. Surround it with pictures depicting camp life.

8. Picture Jews boarding cattle trains.

9. Picture Jewish slaves at work in a stone quarry or foundry.

A Model Idea

With modeling clay, make a figure of a Jewish prisoner. Place a yellow star on his or her striped prisoner clothing.

LEARNING ABOUT A HOLOCAUST EXPERIENCE FIRSTHAND

1. Invite a Holocaust survivor to speak to your class.

2. Interview a Holocaust survivor and report what you learned to your class. (Have pertinent questions in mind before going to the interview.)

PUTTING ON A PLAY

Present one or several scenes of one of the following:

1. *I Never Saw Another Butterfly,* by Celeste Respanti, a play centering on the lives of Jewish children in Theresienstadt (Terezin).

2. *Wonders of Heaven* (or *Cat in the Ghetto*), by Simon Wincelberg, a play revealing life in a Nazi ghetto through the experiences of a Jewish boy.

AUDIOVISUAL AID SUGGESTIONS FOR CHAPTER EIGHT

1. Rent *Warsaw Ghetto*, a 51-minute black-and-white on-the-spot motion picture of ghetto life taken from SS files. **ADL**

2. Rent *The Last Chapter*, a 90-minute film portraying 1,000 years of Jewish life in Poland and its ultimate destruction by the Nazis during the Holocaust. **BLP**

3. View the powerful movie *Schindler's List*, based on the book by Thomas Keneally, concerning Oskar Schindler's efforts to save Jews in Poland.

4. View *Image Before My Eyes*, a 90-minute documentary in color and black-and-white, dealing with Jewish life in Poland from the late nineteenth century until the time it was destroyed during the Holocaust. **SWC**

✡ CHAPTER NINE

The Final Solution
to the Jewish Question, 1941–1945

HITLER'S WAR ON RUSSIA BECOMES HIS ALL-OUT WAR ON JEWS

He Calls Russia the "Center of the Jewish World Conspiracy"

Back in 1923, Hitler wrote in *Mein Kampf* that "Russia is the center of Jewish Bolshevism" and that "the Jewish Bolsheviks who seized Russia in 1917 are conspiring to rule the world."

Sixteen years later, in a January 1939 speech, he screamed the same warning, "International Jewish financiers are trying to plunge the world into another world war so they can grab world power. These Bolsheviks shall not win in the end, for I will annihilate the Jewish race in Europe first!" That it was Hitler himself who sparked World War II by invading Poland eight months later is a matter of history. Furthermore, this threat was Hitler's first public statement about **killing** all Jews.

To Attack Russia Is Part of Hitler's Plan All Along

Hitler did not sign the 1939 Nazi-Soviet Pact in good faith. He did it for one reason only: to gain Polish territory without Russian interference. When Poland and the rest of Europe were firmly in his grip by 1941, Hitler turned his guns to Russia, a goal that he also predicts in *Mein*

Kampf: "We Aryans shall conquer all lands stretching from Germany to the Ural Mountains in Russia to provide us with more living space!"

He Prepares Two Armies for Two Enemies

Hitler remained true to both his threats. His war on Russia became his all-out war to wipe out the "international Jewish conspiracy." On June 22, 1939, two German armies invaded Russia. The regular armed forces charged ahead to destroy the Red Army, the obvious armed enemy. And right behind them was the Einsatzgruppen, a separate army of killers assigned to zero in on Jews, whom Hitler had accused of "conspiring to rule the world."

THE FINAL SOLUTION TO THE JEWISH QUESTION IS GENOCIDE

Genocide had become the Final Solution to the Jewish Question. No European Jew was to remain alive. Throughout the Russian campaign, the Einstazgruppen were to shoot Jews on the spot. In Poland, death camps equipped with gas chambers were to wipe out the millions now held in the nearby ghettos. Jews in other parts of Nazi-occupied Europe were to be carried by Eichmann's cattle trains to the death camps in Poland.

Hitler's order for extermination of the Jewish people would remain in effect until the end of the war. On what day did he give the order? No one knows the exact date because the written order has never been found. Many authorities believe the Nazis deliberately destroyed it. Others insist the command would have been given only by mouth. In any case, Holocaust historians debate the issue. Some say Hitler planned the mass killings all along and used World War II as a means to accomplish them. Others argue that he did not make that decision until the Russian invasion and that it was events of the war that led to genocide. Whatever the case may be, the missing order is truly not a missing link. Literally tens of thousands of other available records on the Holocaust make it one of the most documented crimes in history.

JEWS IN THE SOVIET UNION

Did Jews control communist Russia as Hitler said?

When Russia fell under communist rule in 1917, authorities did grant Jews equal rights. They even outlawed any further attacks on Jewish communities. For a while, they also granted Jews the privilege of having their own Yiddish schools, newspapers, and other institutions.

However, the Jews' seemingly good fortune didn't last long. Although outlawed, anti-Semitism didn't disappear in the minds and actions of the local populations. And after a few years, the Soviet government began an anti-Semitic campaign on its own.

Judaism came under attack first. Jews were allowed to speak Yiddish, but Hebrew was forbidden. So were religious schools for Jewish children. Doors on training schools for rabbis were bolted shut, too. And a ban went up on the manufacture and sale of religious articles such as Jewish prayer books and prayer shawls.

To remove all Jewish influences, many religious and community leaders were arrested and shipped to Siberia to labor in concentration camps. Jewish organizations such as the Bund and the Zionists were out. Furthermore, Jews were forbidden to communicate with relatives or friends living outside Russian borders. By the 1930's, even the Yiddish institutions were being phased out. In other words, in communist Russia there was only one way of doing things—the communist way.

Moreover, since communism forbids the private ownership of business, the Soviet system of government had hurt Jews the most. Before the Bolsheviks had taken over Russia, three fourths of the Jewish community had been involved in small trades and commerce. The communists, however, stripped them of all their property. Thereafter, they were forced to become farmers or state employees. In short, communists tolerated only Jews who were willing to give up their Jewish identity, religion, and culture. It is true that some, especially the young, gave in and joined the new regime. A few even became part of its leadership. Not the vast majority of the Jewish community, however. Once again, they found themselves outsiders.

It must be remembered, too, that Jews in Russia were only a very tiny minority. They numbered 3 million, just a little more than 1.5 percent of the total Soviet population. Even in the southwest provinces of the Ukraine and White Russia where most Jews were concentrated, they still represented only five people out of every hundred.

In all, the Russians held nearly 5 million Jews under their authority as of September 1939. Besides the 3 million in their own country, they had "inherited" 1.5 million from western Poland and over 300,000 from the Baltic countries of Estonia, Latvia, and Lithuania after the Red Army had invaded and taken over those countries.

Discussion Question: Do you think this picture justifies in any way Hitler's vision of Russia as "the center of Jewish Bolshevism"?

THE EINSATZGRUPPEN— SS SPECIAL ACTION FORCES

Unlike the SA barroom brawlers or the deranged Nazi chiefs who surrounded the Fuehrer, Heinrich Himmler's four-squad, 3,000-man Einsatzgruppen team was a group of quite ordinary men. Among them were many college graduates, engineers, teachers, lawyers, and other professionals. Yet they became brutal, cold-blooded killers of hundreds of thousands of unarmed, defenseless civilians.

How could these men have put their consciences aside? Didn't they know such actions violated German army regulations as well as all international laws of war? It was Himmler and Heydrich who put these killers' minds at ease. Assuring the men that SS personnel were subject neither to the German army code nor to anyone else's rules, the Nazi chiefs promised to assume full responsibility for all the Einsatzgruppen's actions. They asked only that the men do a thorough job. That they did.

When the German armies attacked Russia, the Einsatzgruppen, spread out to cover Russian territory from the Baltic Sea in the north to the Black Sea in the south, went in behind them. From the rear, they worked from west to east, gunning down local communist officials and other political leaders; Gypsies; and all Jews, including women and children.

The overwhelming majority of Einsatzgruppen victims were Jews. Sometimes the killers just stormed into Jewish communities and shot up the whole place. On other occasions, they marched the Jews to the outskirts of towns, lined them up beside ravines, antitank ditches, or self-dug graves—then shot them down. Bulldozers finished the job with a soil cover. Or else gasoline fires disposed of the remains.

The SS killing squads didn't always work alone. In some instances, the regular army pitched in with rounding up Jews or even with the shooting. In all Russian territories, local Jew-haters also lent a willing hand. For example, in Odessa, a Ukrainian town near the Rumanian border, occupying Rumanian troops shot down 60,000 Jews without any help at all from the Einsatzgruppen.

The site of the largest Jewish massacres occurred in the ravine of Babi Yar outside the city of Kiev in the Ukraine. There, on September 29 and 30, 1941, the Einsatzgruppen gunned down 34,000 Jews in thirty-six hours. A short time later, 50,000 more Jews along with tens of thousands of other Russians were murdered here.

Occasionally, Russian Jews were herded into ghettos for short periods to perform some sort of labor required at the time. Then the above scene was repeated over and over again. Within a year the Einsatzgruppen had executed approximately a million Jewish men, women, and children—about 333 murders per killer.

Discussion Questions: Do you think you could commit a crime if you had first been assured you would not be punished for it? Would you follow an order of a superior if it violated your personal moral convictions?

GAS VANS

After witnessing an Einsatzgruppen execution for the first time in October 1942 and becoming ill at the sight, SS Chief Himmler resolved to "improve" the system of mass murder. Soon after, he dispatched gas vans, especially designed by SS engineers, to Russia. Called S-trucks, the vehicles looked like ordinary trucks. But inside they were designed so that the exhaust hose emptied poisonous carbon monoxide into the enclosed quarters at the back. Each truck could accommodate ninety persons. The setup killed the ninety victims within fifteen minutes.

Some of the Einsatzgruppen squads used the S-trucks exclusively for women and children. The vans were later used in other countries of Eastern Europe. In the first death camp of Chelmno, which opened near the Lodz ghetto in Poland in December 1941, the trucks were used to kill 360,000 Jews.

THE COMPLETE PLAN FOR THE FINAL SOLUTION TO THE JEWISH QUESTION

On July 31, 1941, a month after the Russian campaign had begun and while the Einsatzgruppen were busily at work, Goering passed a written order to Heydrich to prepare an organized plan for the "final solution" to the Jewish Question.

Five months later, Heydrich was ready to reveal his plan. Many events had taken place in the meantime. On December 7, 1941, Japan had bombed Pearl Harbor. The Americans declared war on Japan the very next day. Three days later, Germany and Italy challenged the United States. Global war had exploded. Now Germany faced enemies on two fronts.

Hitler's war on Jews had mushroomed, too. Already a half-million Russian Jews had fallen to Einsatzgruppen bullets. At the Chelmno death camp, S-trucks had been gassing Jews from the nearby Lodz ghetto daily for the past six weeks. Other camps in Poland were being hastily equipped with death machinery. On January 20, 1942, Heydrich called a meeting of all important Nazi officials at Wannsee, a town near Berlin. The Wannsee Conference agenda? A total

plan for exterminating the 11 million Jews of Europe. This figure included Jews in all of the Soviet Union and the British Isles, countries which the Nazis believed they were soon to control.

Heydrich revealed how this massive murder campaign was to be carried out. The Einsatzgruppen were to continue their slaughter of Russian Jews. However, it had been decided that shooting was too expensive and starvation too slow for doing away with the large number of the remaining Jews.

The Nazis had already tested another effective and efficient murder method as part of the Fuehrer's Euthanasia Institute ("mercy-killing institute") in Germany: huge gas chambers for the killing; crematoria for disposing of the remains. Existing machinery plus similar new equipment was being transferred and installed at camps in Poland located near the crowded ghettos. Once completed, the death houses were to dispose of not only ghettoized Jews but also of all others living in Europe. No Jew was to remain alive. Europe would be "combed from west to east" in order to be "Jew-free."

Naturally, so many millions could not be killed all at once. Heydrich revealed the plan for the "selections." First, Jews would be separated by sex, and then by ability to work. The weakest were to be murdered at once—the old, the sick, children under twelve, many women.

Those able to work were to be shipped to the East to be used in hard labor such as road building. No attempts would be made to keep this work force alive and healthy. They were to be driven to the limits of their endurance and placed on starvation diets. Many, of course, would die off.

What if some slaves survived this ordeal? Heydrich emphasized that the "hard core" few were to be kept alive only until the death machinery "caught up" with its huge reservoir of victims. Then they too were to follow the death route to the camps.

The whole Nazi murder operation was to be carried out in secrecy, of course. All SS-involved personnel had taken a military oath of secrecy. And whenever the Final Solution was mentioned in written orders, polite expressions such as "final action," or "final evacuation" were to be the euphemisms (code words) for murder.

HITLER'S EUTHANASIA PROGRAM, CODE NAME T4

Hitler's murder program included not only "inferior races" like Jews and Gypsies. At least 100,000—possibly as many as 300,000—of his own countrymen were executed, too. Historical records dealing with Hitler's "mercy killings" of asocials, or "undesirable Germans," are not complete for an accurate count. But we do know that Hitler's obsession with the creation of a master race made him order the murders of many Germans who he felt might "contaminate" the super-Aryan race of the future.

Who were these "misfits" that Hitler exterminated? People with hunched backs or other physical deformities. Mentally ill patients. Mongoloid and other mentally deficient children and adults. Carriers of diseases. Even criminals with long records. Why them? Hitler reasoned that habitual criminals had "bad blood," too.

At first, loyal SS doctors and nurses gave the euthanasia victims injections of poison. Then SS engineers designed giant-sized gas chambers. These were made to look like shower rooms so as not to alarm those about to be executed. After much trial and experimentation, the Euthanasia Institute personnel decided on carbon monoxide as the killer gas.

Victims' families generally received government telegrams announcing the deaths of their kin due to "natural causes," "pneumonia," or "heart attack."

The T4 program ended in 1941 when a public outcry persuaded Hitler to call it off. However, neither the knowledge gained, the equipment designed, nor the personnel involved in this program went to waste. All were soon transferred lock, stock, and barrel to Poland for Hitler's Final Solution Program.

Discussion Question: How did the doctors involved in the T4 program violate the Hippocratic oath?

THE DEATH CAMPS

Between 1941 and 1942, expertly trained SS engineers and architects were busily designing and setting up the death machinery in six major death camps in Poland: Treblinka, Chelmno, Sobibor, Maidanek, Auschwitz-Birkenau, and Belzec. By the time they were finished, these killing centers were capable of doing murder in an assembly-line fashion. Gassing was the main murder method in these large camps. Many minor camps scattered throughout Poland had also been given the order to kill Jews. Without gas chambers, these camps employed SS killers with guns instead.

A death camp was not a concentration camp. It had no facilities or barracks to house prisoners, only gas chambers to kill. However, two of the death camps were combination death-concentration camps: Auschwitz and Maidanek. At these two, 10 percent of all new arrivals were selected for forced labor in nearby plants.

Selection for death or for work was done as soon as the cattle trains pulled up to the camps. On the loading platform, a camp officer sized up each arrival. With a flick of the thumb, each person was directed to join either the small group to the officer's right or a larger group to the officer's left.

Those sent to the right were to be slave laborers housed and worked only so long as their strength held out. Then another selection process would thin out their ranks to make room for new, stronger workers. Men and women laborers were stationed in separate quarters of the camps.

Those sent left were marched directly to the gas chambers, where men on duty stood ready and waiting.

At the other four death camps, the entire trainloads went straight to their deaths. If the human cargo numbered more than a death camp's equipment could handle at one time, the first victims were herded out to the gas chambers while the others were locked in either the cattle cars or crude sheds to await their turn.

Auschwitz was the largest camp of all. It was intended to handle not only Jews in the Polish ghettos but also those deported from all over Europe. The other five camps were mainly designed for Jews from the Polish ghettos.

NAZIS TRICK JEWS INTO GAS CHAMBERS

Most of the death camp victims walked willingly into the gas chambers simply because they had no idea they were about to die. Nazi trickery had deceived them from the time they boarded the cattle trains to the moment the gas chamber doors slammed behind them.

The Nazi killing operation had one priority: efficiency. The plan was to kill as many people in as short a time as possible with no resistance or delay. Consequently, the Nazis bent over backward to keep their victims calm and unaware of their true fate.

Their big game began with deportation to the death camps. Telling Jews they were to be "resettled in the East for labor," the SS passed out work permits, reminded all to bring along tools and work clothing, and suggested that money be exchanged for foreign currency before travel to save the time and trouble of doing it

later in their new homes.

Many Jews who willingly boarded Eichmann's trains remembered the postcards that they had received from relatives who had gone before them. Their cards had reassured, "We are well. Everything is fine here. We have food and work." Little did the new travelers know that the cards had been written at gunpoint.

The SS also used food as bait to board the trains. To the starving Jews in the Polish ghettos, they offered bread and jelly to eat along the way. To those whose hunger was unbearable, that alone was enough inspiration to go.

Upon arrival at the camp, those too ill or too weak to walk were told to board waiting Red Cross trucks that would take them to a rest camp. In reality, the trucks headed straightaway to the gas chambers. At Auschwitz, the sign at the main gate, WORK MEANS FREEDOM, was a big lie, too. And when families being separated during selection began to panic, the guards eased their fears by promising they would be reunited after the "baths and delousing."

Baths? Delousing? After days on end without soap and water in the trains and the never-ending torment of body lice from the infested railroad cars, nothing could have sounded better to the weary travelers.

To keep their victims' spirits up, SS chiefs in some of the camps ordered the camp orchestra, often made up of the finest Jewish musicians in Europe, to play cheerful music to accompany the crowds on their walk to the "baths."

Sure enough, the walkers soon stopped before a large modern-looking building on which a sign reading BATHS was posted. The building really housed both the gas chamber and the crematoria.

The game went on and on. Once inside, Jews were sometimes given towels and soap. They were told to tie their shoes together, to arrange their clothing neatly, and to remember the spot where their belongings were located in order to avoid confusion in finding them after bathing.

THE MOST NOTORIOUS NAZI CAMPS

When the doors of the gas chambers swung open, a look upward usually calmed the nervous Jews' fears. Showerheads—really gas jets—completed the picture of the Nazi trickery.

It was not until the doors slammed shut and the lights blinked out that the big game was over. Mad scrambling and dreadful screaming always began when the trapped Jews detected the first traces of gas. But the tumult died down within ten minutes or so. Scanning the scene within from an outside peephole, the SS on duty then gave a signal for the giant exhaust fans to start up. The fans were part of the game, too. They pulled out the remaining telltale fumes to clear the air for the next incoming group.

Wearing gas masks, men on duty dragged the bodies to waiting elevators that carried the corpses to the crematoria on the lower level. But before the bodies were fed into the furnaces, other workers along the death assembly-line searched the victims' mouths and yanked out gold teeth and fillings. This gold would later be melted down and reshaped into bars to enrich the Reichsbank.

Called **Sonderkommando**, the camp prisoners forced to do all this dirty work in the crematoria and gas chambers were usually Poles or Jews. After three or four months of such duty, they too were put to death, for the Nazis wanted no living witnesses to their crimes.

Nazi lies, combined with modern death machinery, worked all too well. At Auschwitz, where four giant-sized chambers were designed to hold 2,000 people at once, the camp commander, Rudolf Hess, had also hit upon a new and deadly gas called **Zyklon B**. Normally used as a strong disinfectant, Zyklon B, a bluish crystalline substance, produced a highly toxic gas strong enough to snuff out 2,000 lives in five or six minutes. To keep up with the disposal of so many bodies, Hess ordered the four crematoria to operate round the clock.

Utilizing such efficiency, Auschwitz began to "process" 12,000 Jews every single day. This meant that 12,000 human beings were killed, their bodies reduced to ashes, and their belongings (shoes, eyeglasses, tools, clothing, jewelry, money, toys, suitcases, baby carriages) all sorted and shipped to collection centers within twenty-four hours!

Discussion Question: How does their trickery make the Nazis seem even more evil?

DEPORTATION TO THE DEATH CAMPS IN POLAND

An Organized System

In charge of moving Jews to the killing centers in Poland were Chief Engineer Adolf Eichmann and his special units of SS. Their job was not a simple one. Much groundwork had to be covered before the trains could roll. Jews had to be identified. Their property had to be registered for easy transferral to new Nazi owners. Part of confiscated Jewish wealth to be deposited in the Reichsbank had to be reserved for payment to railways to cover the enormous cost of this mass transportation—even though the passenger fares were one-way tickets to death. Finally, all captives had to be rounded up for transport.

To simplify the process, Eichmann and his men moved into one country at a time. Generally, Jews who were not citizens of that particular country were deported first. (Many of these unfortunate people were refugees who had fled from the Nazis in earlier years.) Then the native Jewish community followed.

Two factors determined how smoothly and easily the Eichmann teams could get their jobs done: (1) the degree of control the Nazis had over the government of the occupied country, and (2) the way local populations felt about their Jews.

Jews in Greater Germany and Poland Go First

Naturally, the Nazis had the tightest control of the government and local population in the Greater Reich: Germany, Austria, and Czechoslovakian territories. Western Poland and the Government General were in the tight Nazi grip, too. Jews there had already been identified and their property Aryanized. Millions of Jews, already gathered and locked up in either the Polish ghettos or labor camps, were just a short distance away from the death camps.

Consequently, Jews from these areas were whisked away to their deaths very quickly and without much local interference. By the fall of 1943, the Polish ghettos were empty. Three million Polish Jews were dead—nearly all of Polish Jewry. Only a handful survived in labor camps where their services were still needed. Likewise, 90 percent of Jews in the Greater Reich were quickly "processed" according to Nazi law.

Jews in Nazi-Occupied Europe Are Next

The Nazis allowed the countries of occupied Europe varying degrees of self-government. In some instances, those with the most "freedom" cooperated the least in handing over their Jewish citizens to the Eichmann teams.

In the Western European countries especially, the local populations actively interfered with the deportation process. Many, hating the Nazi invaders and regarding Jews as their persecuted countrymen, came to the rescue of Jewish neighbors and friends. In fact, organized underground resistance movements developed to thwart everything the Germans did. But despite brave and heroic rescue efforts, Eichmann and his SS managed to get most of their job done in the end.

The brave Dutch, who steadfastly supported their Jews, were able to save only one fourth of their Jewish population. Under tight scrutiny of Nazi guard, and with few hiding places in this little, flat, wide-open country, 105,000 Dutch Jews were deported to the East.

The people of Belgium managed to hold on to only 40 percent of their Jews. And although the Norwegians helped half their Jews to escape to neutral Sweden, the other half ended up in Eichmann's transports.

Two thirds of French Jews managed to survive the Holocaust. France during the war was divided into three sectors: one controlled by the French Vichy government, and the other two occupied by German and Italian forces. In the Italian jurisdiction, Jews were safe. Kindhearted Frenchmen protected and sheltered many Jews in the other two zones. From there, nevertheless, 90,000 Jews were rounded up and sent to their deaths.

As German forces invaded and occupied most of Greece and Yugoslavia, Jews quickly became victims of the Final Solution. Over 80 percent of Greek Jews and 60 percent of those living in Yugoslavia perished.

For the 8,000 Jews of Denmark, the story had a happier ending. When the Danes heard the rumor that Jews were to be deported, they sneaked more than 90 percent of their Jews across the waters to neutral Sweden. Eichmann's SS seized about 500. The rest were saved.

And thanks to the courage and compassion of Merlika Kruja, prime minister of the tiny country of Albania, not one member of the 350 Jewish families living there fell victim to the death camps. This diplomat's daughter Angela, now living in Pittsburgh, Pennsylvania, clearly remembers her father's role in rescuing Jews not only from the Final Solution but also from the early years of the Holocaust. She recalls:

When Hitler began to persecute Jews in Austria and Germany, my father opened the borders of Albania to let 350 Jewish families in. We were then under Italian occupation, and the Italian vice king, Savino, was willing to look the other way.

A few years later, when Germans occupied our country, the German ambassador approached my father and said, "We have information that you have hundreds of Jewish families here. We want them.

Pretending ignorance, my father said, "I don't know what you are talking about, but I will check on it. Come back in two weeks, and I shall have an answer for you."

Kruja moved quickly. With the help of his attorney general (who is now Angela's husband), he created fake passports identifying the Jews as Albanian Christians and shipped them off to new homes in the free world.

Angela recalls, "When the two weeks were up, my father said to the Germans, 'Your information was all false. No Jews are here. You can search for yourself!'"

Discussion Question: Why were the Jews' rescuers truly heroes?

Jews in Axis Countries

The European countries that formed the Axis, or allied powers of Germany in World War II, were Italy, Hungary, Bulgaria, Finland, and Rumania. But just because these countries had formed a military alliance with Germany did not mean they all agreed with Nazi policies toward Jews. Therefore, whenever the Germans asked the Axis powers to deport their Jews, some complied and others did not.

Three factors made it possible for Germany's allies to act independently on the Jewish Question: (1) They were not under the occupation or scrutiny of hostile German soldiers or the military police, (2) they were able to manage their own government affairs, and (3) they had control over their own Jewish citizens.

Neither Italy nor Hungary was willing to let its Jews go until German force finally occupied their countries. Nor had Italian dictator Benito Mussolini or Hungarian ruler Admiral Miklos Horthy fully cooperated in passing anti-Jewish laws in their lands before that. To keep the Germans happy, both leaders had passed only watered-down versions.

In fact, the Italians resisted not only giving up Jews from their own country but also Jews living in any of the territories Italy occupied. Throughout the war, the Italian soldiers played a cat-and-mouse game with the Nazi Jew-hunters. Jews knew this. Therefore, when Italian forces occupied territories in France, Greece, Croatia, and Albania, many Jews fled to these sectors and placed themselves under Italian protection. It was when German troops came into Italy in the fall of 1943 that Eichmann and his SS deportation masters took over. They deported 8,000 of the 40,000 Italian Jews to the death camps of Poland.

Hungarian Jews were the last to be deported to the death camps. While Horthy had complied in deporting his "foreign" Jews, native Jews had remained at home until the very end of the war. With the German armies fast losing the war, and with the Allies repeatedly threatening them with punishments for their war crimes, it seemed the Hungarian Jews were safe.

But when German forces occupied Hungary in March 1944, Eichmann's units followed close behind. He quickly began to round up and deport the Hungarian Jews to the death camps. Several world leaders, including American President Franklin D. Roosevelt, loudly voiced their protests. Cries were heard for the Allies to bomb the gas chambers of Auschwitz or even the railroads that led to them.

Even Eichmann himself had come up with a plan to save not only the Hungarian Jews but also 1 million Jews in all of Nazi-occupied territory. Through Joel Brand, a Jewish representative from Budapest, Eichmann offered to sell the Allies a million Jews for supplies: coffee, cocoa, tea, and 10,000 trucks.

But the bombs did not fall on the railroad lines. No one accepted Eichmann's offer. Instead, the slaughter of Hungarian Jews continued at such speed, the gas chambers of Auschwitz could not keep up. Then Nazi killers began to shoot the Hungarian deportees. And they beat to death countless Jewish children.

By the time the combined protests of world leaders finally persuaded the Hungarian government to halt the deportations, six weeks had passed. Three fourths—or 400,000—of the Hungarian Jewish population was dead.

Another of Germany's allies who stood up for her Jews was Bulgaria. Bulgarians had willingly let go of "foreign" Jews living in their country. But when it came to deporting native Jews, the government, Church, and citizenry said "No!" That simple refusal saved 50,000 Jewish lives.

Finland, too, just by outright refusal, saved her 2,000 Jewish citizens.

The 600,000 Jews of Rumania were another story. A local war against them raged here without any Nazi persuasion. In a revolution to bring about a one-party system in Rumania, the Iron Guard, a fascist group, had also instigated massive pogroms in order to crush Jewish influence in the Rumanian economy. Many thousands of Jews had been massacred in this civil war.

Ion Antonescu, the Rumanian dictator who emerged, had no love for Jews either. Early in 1941, he began to expel them left and right from northern Rumania. He pushed thousands right into the path of the Einsatzgruppen. Some of the Iron Guard even pitched in and helped the killing squads to do their work.

By late 1941, Antonescu had shoved at least 250,000 Jews out of the country and onto a reservation in Transnistria in the Ukraine. Conditions in Transnistria were horrible. Driven to desperation, starving Jewish families began to eat cattle food and became paralyzed from it.

Diseases, unheated barracks, and forced labor made the death toll climb. Even the Nazis criticized the Rumanians for their unorganized system of Jew-handling. "Let us do it," the SS begged Antonescu.

The Rumanian dictator didn't listen. More interested in moneymaking schemes, he decided to ransom his Jews instead. For a fee per head, his Jews were allowed to emigrate to freedom. But few purses or borders opened up to Antonescu's Jewish hostages.

In 1944 Antonescu finally bowed to the Allies, who had threatened punishment for war crimes. He released the Jews from Transnistria. But by this time, barely 70,000 of the original quarter-million remained. In all, half of Rumania's Jews were dead.

THE DEATH CAMPS AND THEIR VICTIMS

The death camp of Auschwitz remained open the longest. In October 1944, when victorious Russian troops began to approach the camp, Chief Hess tried to get rid of the evidence of Nazi crimes by destroying most of the camp records and by ordering camp prisoners to tear down the gas chambers and crematoria. Other SS commanders of the death camps had done the same. For this reason, the exact number of murdered victims will never be known.

However, the Allies did confiscate many records. From these, it has been determined that at least 1.1–1.3 million people were killed in the six major death camps. More than half died at Auschwitz. The victims were gassed, shot, or died from overwork, starvation, or medical experiments.

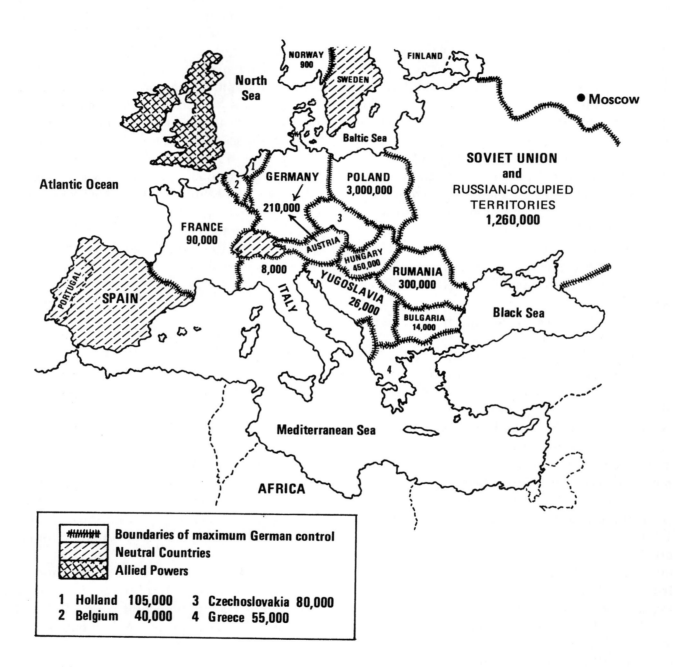

JEWISH VICTIMS OF THE HOLOCAUST

ESTIMATED NUMBER OF JEWS KILLED IN THE FINAL SOLUTION

COUNTRY	ESTIMATED PRE-FINAL SOLUTION POPULATION	ESTIMATED JEWISH POPULATION ANNIHILATED	
		Number	Percent
Poland	3,300,000	3,000,000	90
Baltic Countries	253,000	228,000	90
Germany/Austria	240,000	210,000	90
Protectorates	90,000	80,000	89
Czecholovakia	90,000	75,000	83
Greece	70,000	54,000	77
The Netherlands	140,000	105,000	75
Hungary	650,000	450,000	70
SSR White Russia	375,000	245,000	65
SSR Ukraine*	1,500,000	900,000	60
Belgium	65,000	40,000	60
Yugoslavia	43,000	26,000	60
Rumania	600,000	300,000	50
Norway	1,800	900	50
France	350,000	90,000	26
Bulgaria	64,000	14,000	22
Italy	40,000	8,000	20
Luxembourg	5,000	1,000	20
Russia (RSFSR)*	975,000	107,000	11
Denmark	8,000	—	—
Finland	2,000	—	—
Total	8,861,800	5,933,900	67

* The Germans did not occupy all the territory of this republic

Most but not all the 7 million were Jews. Included in that number were at least 200,000 Gypsies, hundreds of thousands of Russian prisoners of war, and thousands of political prisoners, Catholic and Protestant church leaders, Jehovah's Witnesses, Freemasons, Poles, and others.

Medical Experiments

The Nazis murdered thousands of their concentration camp prisoners through medical experiments. At certain camps SS doctors used prisoners as human guinea pigs. Often their experiments did not benefit medical science but merely satisfied sick curiosities.

For example, some studies were supposedly to promote the speedy procreation of the master race. How could Aryan mothers be made to bear not one but two, three, or even four superior babies at once? To discover the "secret" behind multiple births, experiments were carried out on twins and triplets at Auschwitz. Twins were gathered from all over Europe and sent to this death camp. Upon arrival, they were carefully examined and then dissected and studied further after they had been killed in the gas chambers.

Auschwitz also became the destination and testing grounds for dwarfs and giants. SS doctors studied them so that the future master race would be free from such "afflictions."

Other hideous experiments to test human endurance caused the experimental victims indescribable suffering. Thousands died in agony. How long could a man survive on seawater? How soon would he die lying nude in the snow or submerged in ice water? At what point did eardrums or lungs burst under pressure? To learn such "scientific data," highly educated SS doctors carefully observed, timed, and recorded the victims' reactions up to the very moment of their deaths.

After the war ended, many SS doctors stood trial for their crimes against these helpless people.

Chapter Nine Review

REVIEWING KEY POINTS

Exercise 1

1. In the German invasion of Russian territories, how did the role of the Einsatzgruppen differ from that of regular German troops?

2. Many say, "Those people who murdered all the millions of Jews during the Holocaust had to be insane!" Discuss why that statement is not really true.

3. How did anti-Semitism among the local populations in Russian territories work against Jewish victims during the Nazi invasion?

4. When and on whom were Nazi experiments with gas chambers and killer gases first used?

5. Discuss the full plans for the Final Solution revealed at the Wannsee Conference.

6. Discuss how Nazi trickery was used as part of the "efficiency plan" of the Final Solution.

7. Describe the daily "processing record" at Auschwitz.

8. Why were the millions of Jews in the ghettos of Poland the first to die?

9. How did the SS organize the deportation of hundreds of thousands of European Jews?

10. What factors determined how successful the SS were in their deportation of Jews?

11. Why were Germany's allies able to act independently on the Jewish question?

12. If so many Rumanian Jews were given the chance to emigrate to freedom during the war, why didn't more go?

13. How many people died in the Nazi gas chambers? Besides Jews, who were the other victims?

14. Why was the deportation of Hungarian Jews particularly tragic?

Exercise 2
Working a Crossword Puzzle

All of the terms used in the puzzle are explained in the preceding chapter.

ACROSS

1. The SS used _____ to lure Jews into the gas chambers without resistance.
2. _____ , or the total extermination of the Jewish people was Hitler's goal.
11. The killing squads who moved about in Russian territories were called the _____ .
13. Heydrich revealed the total plan for the Final Solution to all Nazi chiefs at a conference in _____ .
14. _____ _____ Jewish men, women, and children were murdered in the Holocaust.
15. World War II lasted _____ years.
17. The Final Solution began with Hitler's invasion of _____ in 1941.
18. S-trucks, or _____ _____ were gas chambers on wheels.
19. Eichmann and his SS moved into one country at a time to _____ Jews to Poland.
21. All the death camps were located in _____ .
23. Adolf _____ delivered all Jews to Poland via cattle trains.
24. Most Jewish victims of the Holocaust died in _____ _____ .
27. Rumanians, not Nazis, shot 60,000 Jews in _____ .
29. This country saved its 2,000 Jewish citizens by refusing to cooperate with the Germans.
30. Deported Jews were told they were being " _____ in the East for labor."
31. This country hid 8,000 Jews from Eichmann's Jew-hunters.
32. The prime minister of _____ saved 350 Jewish families by providing fake passports.
34. SS camp doctors used Jews and others as human guinea pigs in medical _____ .
35. Fifty thousand Jews in _____ were saved because the local people refused to let them be deported.
36. During "selections," all who were directed to the _____ went straight to the gas chambers.

DOWN

1. The Einsatzgruppen had _____ thousand members.
3. _____ was the first death camp to be opened.
4. In Hitler's _____ Institute, "unfit" Germans were killed.
5. Local support to Jewish victims came mostly from the populations in _____ Europe.
6. _____ _____ were the last victims to be deported to the death camps in Poland.
7. The _____ _____ to the Jewish Question was death to all Jews.
8. The largest Jewish massacres in Russian territories occurred in _____ .
9. The name of the gas-producing substance used first at Auschwitz was _____ .
10. The largest of all the death camps was _____ .
12. The process of choosing Jews for forced labor or the gas chambers was called _____ .
16. One death camp that was also a labor camp was _____ .
20. The Rumanian dictator forced Jews onto a reservation in where _____ thousands died from starvation and exposure.
22. Hitler classified all Germans with physical and mental handicaps or criminal records as _____ .
25. In Hitler's Final Solution, no Jew in Europe was to remain _____ .
26. Second in command under Hitler in the Final Solution was _____ .
28. Although they were Germany's allies, the _____ protected Jews in the areas they occupied.
30. During "selections," those who went to the _____ were reserved for labor.
33. European Jews were transported to the death camps in _____ cars.

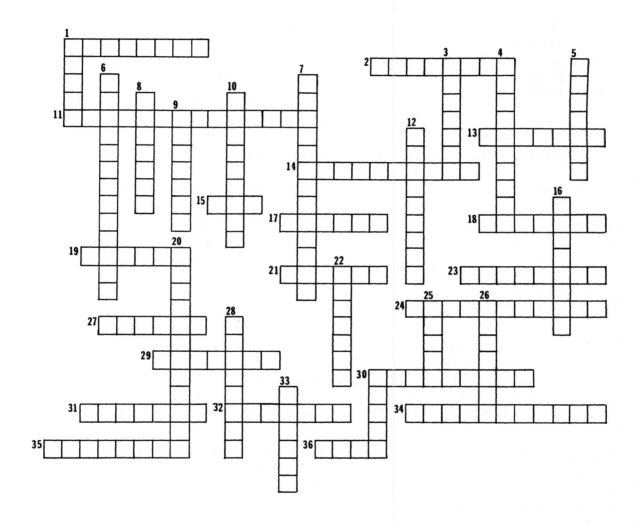

Exercise 3
Recognizing True and False Statements

Directions: Number your paper from 1–20. Some of the statements about the Holocaust are true and others are false. If the statement is true, write +; if it is false, write 0 beside the corresponding number on your paper.

1. From the start of his political career, Hitler had definitely planned to exterminate Jews.

2. More people should have given *Mein Kampf* serious consideration because Hitler spelled out his exact war moves in it.

3. The Final Solution pertained to only Jews in continental Europe.

4. Jewish Bolsheviks controlled the Communist party in Russia.

5. The Einsatzgruppen killed hundreds of thousands of Polish Jews because part of Poland was in Russian hands.

6. The Einsatzgruppen were hardened criminals.

7. Himmler believed that S-trucks were a more "humane" way of killing people.

8. Selections were made because the gas chambers could not deal with so many victims at once.

9. Nazis murdered tens of thousands of Germans.

10. The death camps were located in Germany.

11. A death camp was a special type of concentration camp.

12. The gas chambers of Auschwitz killed people from all over Europe.

13. Nazis treated Jews like animals.

14. Distance from the gas chambers had something to do with how soon the victims died.

15. The degree to which Nazis controlled a government determined how successful their deportations of Jews were.

16. The Axis Powers—Germany's allies—had no choice but to cooperate with the Nazis in their final solution.

17. Hungarian Jews could have been saved.

Exercise 3 (continued)

18. Only Jews died in Nazi gas chambers.

19. Highly educated and cultured people designed the death machinery for the Final Solution.

20. The Holocaust stands as one of the most documented events of history.

GIVING REPORTS

Topics to Research

1. Raoul Wallenberg, a non-Jew who played a role in rescuing Hungarian Jews from deportation. Read in the *New York Times* magazine, March 30, 1980, "The Search for Sweden's Raoul Wallenberg, The Lost Hero of the Holocaust."

2. Which world powers voiced protests against the deportation of Hungarian Jews? What did they say? Also tell why their protests didn't stop the deportations. Good source: *Why Six Million Died*, by Arthur Morse.

3. What was the response of Danish King Christian X when Nazi officials approached him about deporting Denmark's Jews?

4. More about the SS Einsatzgruppen. Good source: *Licensed Mass Murders*, by Henry V. Dicks, which has many case studies.

5. Life of the Sonderkommando (inmates who worked in the gas chambers and crematoria). Good source: *Eichmann's Inferno: Auschwitz*, by Dr. Miklos Nyiszli (the experiences of this Jewish doctor/author Sonderkommando at Auschwitz); or *Eyewitness Auschwitz*, by Philip Muller, an excellent book.

6. Why did the Allies turn down Joel Brand's offer from Eichmann to exchange Jewish prisoners for goods? Good source: *The Holocaust*, by Nora Levin.

7. More about Rumanian Jews during the Holocaust. Include how much Antonescu charged to free a Jew, how many Rumanian Jews managed to emigrate during the war, and what conditions were like in Transnistria.

8. More on Hitler's concept of "Jewish Bolshevism." Good source: *Mein Kampf*, by Adolf Hitler. Look in the index under Marxism.

9. Nazi medical experiments. Good source: *Doctors of Infamy*, by Alexander Mitscherlich.

Topics to Research (continued)

10. Why more countries did not accept Jews who were trying to flee the Nazis.

11. Analyze the history and character of the countries that tried to protect their Jews in spite of Hitler's orders.

12. Research Jewish life and the Jewish community in the Axis countries today.

Books to Review

1. *The Survivor: An Anatomy of Life in the Death Camps*, by Des Pres.

2. *Rescue in Denmark*, by Harold Flender, the account of the rescue of Denmark's Jews.

3. *Playing for Time*, by Fania Fanelow, a survivor of the Auschwitz camp orchestra.

4. *Babi Yar: A Documentary Novel*, by Kuzetov Anatoli, portrays a view of the Russian massacre through the eyes of a Russian youth.

5. *Manya's Story*, by Bettyanne Grey, the story of a young Russian couple who survive terrible pogroms during the Bolshevik Revolution of 1917.

6. *Memoirs of Italian Politics in Albania*, by Francesco di San Savino, the former Italian vice king of Albania during World War II. On pages 188–189, Savino memorializes the bravery and courage of the former Albanian Prime Minister Kruja in rescuing Albanian Jews from the Holocaust. Get an Italian translator to read the passage in English for you.

7. *Swastika Over Paris: The Fate of the Jews in France*, by Jeremy Josephs.

8. *The Shawl*, by Cynthia Ozick, two short pieces of fiction about a mother who loses her child to the hands of Nazi camp guards.

9. *Maus*, Volumes I and II, by Art Spiegelman, a cartoonist, who represents Jews as mice and Nazis as cats. Through cartoons, he tells the story of his parents in Auschwitz in the first volume and their journey to America in the second volume.

10. *The Death Train*, by Luba K. Gurdus, the story of the author and her family who spent much time on or near trains in their attempts to avoid the camps.

11. *Seed of Sarah*, by Judith Issacson, a memoir of an adolescent girl's middle-class life in Hungary and her experiences in a ghetto and in concentration camps.

12. *Nazi-Doctors: Medical Killings and the Psychology of Genocide*, by Robert J. Lifton, an examination of how doctors allowed themselves to participate in the Final Solution.

MAKING PROJECTS

Poster Ideas

1. Make a map of Europe indicating the areas Hitler wanted to reserve for more living space for Germans.

2. Reproduce the poem "Babi Yar," by Yevgeny Yevtushenko.

3. Picture the inside of a cattle car. Show people of all ages within.

4. Picture condemned Jews standing outside the gas chamber and crematoria. Show the BATHS sign posted on the building.

5. Make a collage of your impressions of the Final Solution.

6. List all the camps and the number of victims who died in each.

A Model Idea

Make a model of a death camp.

PUTTING ON A PLAY

Present one or several scenes from *Incident at Vichy*, by Arthur Miller, a play set in occupied France, which portrays how Jewish victims refused to believe what was really happening to them.

AUDIOVISUAL AID SUGGESTIONS FOR CHAPTER NINE

1. Rent *Act of Faith*, a 28-minute black-and-white film of how the Danes rescued their Jewish citizens from deportation to the gas chambers. **ADL**

2. Fourteen photographs of the successful rescue effort of the Danes to block the deportation of Denmark's Jews. **SSSS**

3. Rent *Night and Fog*, a 31-minute black-and-white film about the death camps and Final Solution. Teachers should preview the film first and prepare students for what they will see. A powerful film. **ADL**

4. Rent *Genocide*, a 52-minute color film portraying the Holocaust from 1920–1945. **ADL**

5. View *Susan*, a 58-minute video about the experiences of a young survivor of Dr. Mengele's medical experiments. **KSU**

6. View *Shoah*, a 10-hour comprehensive video of the Holocaust, which includes interviews with people on all sides as well as visits to camps, towns, and railways. (This video can be shown in parts and is available in most libraries and video stores.)

7. View *Kitty: A Return to Auschwitz*, a 90-minute videotape about Kitty Felix Hart, who as a teenager had been imprisoned in Auschwitz, and who returned to visit Auschwitz more than thirty years after her release, accompanied by her son. She relates many details about life there. **SSSS**

8. View *The Wannsee Conference*, an 85-minute color video that dramatizes the conference where the Final Solution was discussed (German with English subtitles). **SSSS**

✡ CHAPTER TEN

Jewish Resistance

JEWISH VICTIMS OF THE HOLOCAUST

Like Sheep to the Slaughter?

Some uninformed people believe Jews went to their deaths like sheep before the butcher. Even a few learned historians who wrote the first books on the Holocaust had that opinion. For their sources of information, however, those writers used the only records available at the war's end—documents written by Nazis who regarded Jews as less than human. Since then, thousands of newer and more reliable accounts of the Holocaust have been setting the record straight. Books based on non-German documents, diaries, and notes left behind by the victims, and the living testimonies of Holocaust survivors and other witnesses all prove one thing: Jews resisted their captors in many, many ways.

Why So Many Victims?

The majority of Holocaust victims had no idea they were to be put to death. Russian Jews, rounded up and murdered on the spot, were given no time to think or resist. Jews locked up in the ghettos and camps knew nothing about the Russian massacres. How could they? And when the deportations for "resettlement in the East" began, Nazi lies about work and food snared them into the trap of the gas chambers. By the time the first hints of the truth leaked out, millions were already dead. It was only when Jews learned the true fate Hitler planned for them that they decided to take up arms against the Nazis. Until then, many factors stopped them from fighting openly.

No Open Resistance in the Beginning

Most importantly, the victims had no arms. What were bare fists against machine guns and grenades?

Furthermore, Jews wanted to protect their families. Remember, not just fathers but mothers, children, aged grandparents, and other family members were being taken into Nazi custody. Uppermost in everyone's mind was how to keep loved ones from being hurt. If just one Jew rebelled, terrible reprisals fell on his family and the entire Jewish community. How many times did Nazis have to shoot down a hundred innocent people to prove they meant business?

In some cases, religious convictions held them back. Many strict Orthodox Jews viewed violence as an unholy act, even against a cruel enemy. To the end, they remained martyrs; they gave up their lives to honor God's name.

Hitler's starvation and forced labor policy also curbed Jewish desire to resist. As their bodies grew shrunken and weak from hunger and overwork, most victims began to concentrate not on a losing battle but on merely staying alive. As survivor Leah Gottisman says, "How could I think about fighting? Hunger was all I ever thought about. I was hungry, hungry, hungry. Hungry enough to put even a stone in my mouth."

Almost total lack of outside help was another big factor in holding Jews down. With no outside support to count on, escape was highly risky. Says John F., who spent most of his slave-labor years in six German camps:

Escape? Where to? We had no friends nearby. No place to go. We were isolated in a foreign country. We didn't speak the language. And no matter where we were, we couldn't escape who we were. The Germans called us **musselmen,** *or the living dead. We were one third the size of other people in the street . . . shrunken . . . emaciated . . . sunken eyes . . . our heads shaven bald. We wore wooden shoes and striped pajamas. We were sick. Who would be willing to help us? Escape? How could we even think of it?*

Not even the European resistance movements that fought to free lands from Nazi control offered much help to Jewish captives. Why? When Jews needed help most desperately, these underground movements were just getting started. In addition, Jews didn't qualify for their help. The European underground was organized along **national** lines, with each government in exile receiving weapons and aid from resistance headquarters in either Moscow or London. Jewish victims had neither a nation nor a government in exile to be their spokesman. They were being persecuted as Jews, not as Poles or Czechs or Austrians. To appeal to local resistance groups became the Jews' only alternative. But as it turned out, these nationals were reluctant to give up arms or to lend support.

Cut off completely from the outside world and unaware of their true destiny, most Jewish victims resisted their enemies in the early years, but only in passive ways. Two hopes gave them the courage to hold on: (1) the hope that Germans would lose the war, and (2) the hope that they would survive long enough for the Allied victory to free them.

Discussion Question: Do you think such hopes were out of the question or within reason?

PASSIVE RESISTANCE

Defying Nazi Orders

Without using force, Jews defied their enemies in many, many ways. Ghettoized Jews, forced to live like pack rats in filthy, overcrowded conditions, still kept their human dignity. Determined to carry on life as usual, they entertained one another, ignored orders to ban schooling and religious services, and rolled forbidden newspapers off their secret printing presses every day.

Jewish resistance often occurred right under the noses of unsuspecting Nazi bosses. Al Lewin tells of a funny incident:

For about three months, I was a butler for a German army officer. I had to clean his quarters and pick up his meals from his cook, Otto. One day I told Otto that the officer was having a girlfriend visitor for about two weeks and would be needing two portions per meal for as long as she stayed. The extra meal was really for me. "She" stayed for three months! And I had grown stronger and healthier every day. But one evening the officer, who was dissatisfied with his dinner, approached the cook. When Otto loudly complained about always having to stretch the food

*for two, the puzzled officer exclaimed,
"Two? What girlfriend?"*

And that was the end of that.

Discussion Question: How did the ghetto Jews' resistance require as much courage as (or more courage than) shooting a gun?

Smuggling and Sabotage

No ghetto or concentration camp was without a Jewish resistance group who worked to smuggle in food and supplies and to sabotage the Nazis in every way they could. Survivors tell of how slave laborers "fought back" with sabotage in German factories. Al Lewin recalls:

In 1942, I was ordered to report for forced labor in a munitions factory in Berlin. I was allowed to live at home, but I worked a twelve-hour daily shift and was paid thirty-five cents an hour for setting up the punch presses for making bullets. A few of us Jewish workers got together to make the bullets "scrap." I set up the machines so that one side of the bullets ended up thicker than the other. These defective bullets passed inspection because my friends rigged the inspection machines. We got away with it for six months until a trainload of these bullets was returned to the factory from the Russian front. They wouldn't fit the machine guns! Shortly afterward, our whole department was shipped to Auschwitz.

Mark Stern tells of his sabotage efforts while working in an airplane factory when he was a prisoner in the Flossenberg concentration camp:

My job was to inspect the riveting of the sheet metal on airplane wings. Another prisoner from the camp came to me and said he had connections on the outside [underground] who would supply larger rivets than those presently being used. These larger rivets would cause a defect in the wings and ultimately make the planes crash. I followed their suggestion and signed the inspection slips, which allowed the faulty airplane wings to pass through.

A month later, the SS took me in for questioning. They beat me a hundred lashes with a whip, but I never revealed the truth.

Hiding Out

Hiding out to escape Nazi capture was another means of passive resistance. Thousands of Jews did this successfully. They hid in every place imaginable: attics, closets, cellars, barns. But seldom were they able to escape capture without the help of good and courageous non-Jewish friends. For this reason, hiding out was more common in the countries of Western Europe, where anti-Semitism was not so strong and Jews were considered an important part of the community.

But brave people protected and sheltered Jews in Eastern Europe, too. Isadore Iwler tells an incredible story of survival that would not have been possible without the help of a Polish friend.

In June of 1942, the Einsatzgruppen came crashing into my hometown of Sanok in southwestern Poland, which was then under Russian occupation. They stormed into our home, gunned down my mother and father right before our eyes, ordered my two brothers and me to bury our parents, and then dragged us off to labor in the camp of Zasloff.

We later escaped when the Germans began to make selections for the death camps. One brother managed to hide out in a barn with some other Jews. My other brother and I made our way back to our family barn and made contact with a Pole who had grown up with us and had worked on my father's farm for many years. He and two other Poles delivered bread to us for eight months.

In the meantime, we had buried ourselves deep in a huge pile of wheat chaff in the barn where we made a sort of nest for hiding out. One day the SS came to search not only this place but also the barn where our other brother hid.

After this, we three took to the woods. There we dug a hole in the earth, shored up the sides with logs, camouflaged the exterior with brush, and lived there from June 1943 to September 1944! To survive, we stole whatever vegetables and fruits we could from nearby farms. We never ate meat. [Even now, kosher meats were all these religious Jews would touch.] Another brave Pole plus our original helper delivered us bread during all this time.

Mr. Iwler has never forgotten the help his boyhood Polish friend gave him. Over the years, he has sent this friend little "Care packages" of thanks.

Discussion Questions: Do you think you could have withstood the hardships of trying to keep alive as Isadore Iwler did? Would you have had the courage to hide and protect a Jewish fugitive during these times?

Posing As Non-Jews in the Outside World

A few Jews were able to pose as non-Jews in the outside community. However, many factors prohibited this type of resistance: Jews were well known by their neighbors, holdouts were often turned in, the person had to have an Aryan appearance, the person had to sever all contact with friends and family, false papers were needed to prove one's non-Jewish background, and governments kept records of all citizens, which included their religious affiliation.

Dora Iwler is an example of one who managed to conceal her Jewish identity because she was able to meet several of the above criteria. Dora explains:

I had a good Christian friend whose sister had died many years before. Posing as that dead sister, I went to the Roman Catholic Church where the baptismal records were kept and managed to convince the priest to give me "my" baptismal record. Then I made my way to the big city of Lwow where, because of the large numbers of people and my predominantly Polish appearance, I became lost in the crowd.

Until the summer of 1944, I worked as a domestic helper in a Polish home. However, one day as I walked along the city streets, I was approached by three old neighbors who recognized me. "You're still around!" they marveled. A few days later, the Gestapo picked me up.

After several weeks, as the Russian troops approached the Lancki-Janower labor camp where I was being held, the Germans forced all of us prisoners on a death march. I managed to escape. That's why I'm alive today.

Dora became Isadore Iwler's bride after the war.

Discussion Question: How do the testimonies of the Iwlers prove that individuals will respond differently to the same situation?

ARMED RESISTANCE!

The Truth Becomes Known

By mid-1942, the Final Solution was no longer a secret. Nazis themselves and Jewish escapees from the death camps had spread the first rumors. Suspicious of the speedy deportations, ghetto Jews had also smuggled out their own spies to learn the real destination of the cattle trains.

The truth became known. Death to all Jews! Now angry Jews decided to fight. If they had to die, it would be on their own terms.

Jewish fighters emerged everywhere—in the ghettos, even in the death camps. Some escaped to become partisans, or guerilla fighters, in the outside world.

The Warsaw Ghetto Revolt

Armed revolts occurred in at least twenty ghettos of Eastern Europe. Warsaw ghetto prisoners were not only the first Jews to revolt but also the first civilians in all of Nazi-occupied Europe to stage an armed uprising against the Nazis.

By the time the ghetto dwellers took up arms, 90 percent of the half-million Warsaw Jews were already gone. Starvation and disease had killed at least 100,000. The rest had been deported to the death camps. The remaining 60,000 were the most able-bodied workers whom the SS always saved for last. Many were teenagers.

The heart of Warsaw's fighters consisted of two main fighting forces of men and women: the 600-member Jewish Fighting Organization, under the leadership of twenty-four-year-old Mordechai Anielewicz, and the National Military Organization, composed of 400 fighters. However, as the battle progressed, all ghetto Jews were to join in the fighting.

They faced monumental problems. Very few of the fighters had had military training. Even worse, they had no arms. But what these young Jews lacked in equipment and training, they made up for in courage and determination.

Intense training sessions began. To store what little food and supplies they could get their hands on, they dug underground bunkers and passageways. Nor did they allow themselves to become discouraged when the local Polish resistance refused to give weapons to their emissaries who had stolen out of the ghetto. Returning almost empty-handed, the emissaries had only a few rusty guns and several rounds of dynamite and ammunition, which they had somehow managed to gather from other sources. But the Warsaw fighters didn't give up; they made their own Molotov cocktails, mines, and other weapons to trip Nazi feet.

When the SS entered the ghetto gates in January 1943 to round up another trainload of people for deportation, they were frightened out of their wits. Bombs, wild shooting, and mine explosions ripped into dozens of them. Twenty lay dying.

Even the Polish resistance was impressed when they learned about this episode. They still refused Anielewicz's invitation to join in the fight against their common Nazi enemy, but they did hand over a small supply of weapons. Emissaries of the Jewish fighters managed to pick up still another handful of supplies. Altogether, the Warsaw ghetto forces now had three machine guns, a few hundred guns, and a small supply of hand grenades.

They were certainly no match for the German forces who came down on them in full force on April 18, 1943. On Himmler's orders, 3,000 troops under the command of Jurgen Stroop descended on the ghetto. At the same time, tanks and other heavy artillery surrounded the walls of Warsaw. As reinforcements, 8,000 more German soldiers were stationed throughout the city of Warsaw. Himmler had promised Adolf Hitler a birthday present: the complete liquidation of the Warsaw ghetto within three days!

Hitler didn't get his present on time. After several days of savage fighting, Commander Stroop was flustered. German tanks had been splintered with bull's eye hits from Molotov cocktails. Mines exploded and machine-gun fire cut the German forces down every time they entered the ghetto. The puzzled Stroop couldn't figure out how the Jewish fighters were moving from place to place sight unseen. Nazi machine-gun sights had scrutinized the empty ghetto streets to no avail. Little did Stroop know that the ghetto fighters were traveling through the connected attics of the buildings.

Stroop's revenge turned black. He ordered new battle tactics: search dogs, airplane bombers, and fire. Now German bombers careened in and hurled their explosives at the ghetto buildings. Then Stroop ordered the systematic burning of the buildings block by block. Suspecting that Jews were taking shelter in underground sewers, his men unleashed gas and smoke bombs in the sewer systems. He was right. Choking and suffocating, Jews tried to hold on. Many who could not fit into the underground sewers or bunkers remained in the burning buildings to be consumed by fire rather than surrender to their Nazi tormentors. Those who jumped from the windows of burning buildings at the last minute became shooting targets for Nazi gunners.

On May 8, after twenty-one long days in this living hell, the Nazis surrounded the hideout of Jewish commander Mordechai Anielewicz and eighty other brave fighters. All eighty-one died in battle. By now the entire Warsaw ghetto was aflame. Yet the few Jewish fighters who remained refused to surrender. They fought on for another week!

By May 16, the ghetto was rubble. Over 15,000 Jews had died in battle. More than 50,000 had been captured and shipped off to death camps.

How many of their enemies did the Warsaw fighters kill? Although German documents say fewer than a hundred, more reliable sources put the figure at closer to a thousand.

The story of the brave Warsaw ghetto fighters did not end here. As late as the first week in July, snipers hiding out in the ghetto ruins were still killing German soldiers who passed by. Moreover, when the Polish underground waged their all-out attack on the Nazis in April 1944, a small number of survivors from the Warsaw ghetto resistance were among them!

Discussion Questions: Would you have the courage to resist the Nazis under these conditions? If you were a German soldier, do you think you'd feel justified in attacking the ghetto?

Armed Revolt in the Death Camps

Doomed Jews at the very doorstep of death revolted. All but a handful of the rebels were later overpowered and executed. Nevertheless, these brave people managed not only to wreck much property but also to kill some of their would-be murderers.

On August 2, 1943, two hundred prisoners rioted in Treblinka. They stole weapons, set the death camp on fire, and killed several guards before they were subdued. A dozen rioters escaped to freedom. The rest were captured and shot.

On October 6, 1944, twelve Jewish Sonder-kommando who worked in one of the gas chamber complexes of Auschwitz disabled the chamber with stolen explosives during a revolt, killed seventy of the SS guards, and tried unsuccessfully to escape. Although all were killed by the S.S. during the evacuation, they had done a thorough job on the death machinery in their building. After this, Auschwitz had only three gas chambers in operation.

In October 1943, some Jewish prisoners in Sobibor were a bit luckier. When several hundred of them stampeded out of the camp to rush to the safety of the woods, they trampled some guards to death and killed others with stolen guns and hatchets. Although most were later rounded up and shot, two hundred escaped. Many joined partisan units to continue their fight against the Nazis. In the meantime, the angry Sobibor inmates had created so much damage during the fracas, Himmler had to order the shutdown of the death camp two days later. Jews in the death row of Sobibor had indeed scored a victory.

Discussion Questions: Jewish prisoners on death row had no real hope of victory when they revolted. So why did they bother fighting? Would you have fought back?

JEWISH PARTISANS

Introduction

Not only did imprisoned Jews in camps and ghettos take up arms against their enemies. At least 100,000 Jewish men, women, and children became guerrilla fighters in the outside world. They either joined the underground movements that formed in nearly all countries of occupied Europe, or else they formed their own Jewish units. At least half these brave fighters lost their lives to the Nazis.

All-Jewish Partisan Units

It was mainly in Eastern Europe that Jews formed their own guerrilla units. Many were

those who had had the time and luck to flee before the Nazis captured them. Others were escapees from the ghettos and camps.

When Hitler's killer squads went crashing into Russian territories in 1941, thousands of Jews behind the front lines managed to get away. They took to the thick forests, swamps, and mountains of western Poland, Lithuania, Estonia, Latvia, White Russia, and the Ukraine. They grouped together to form family camps. Some camp members concentrated on making a home in the wilds, while others formed fighting units who committed themselves to three tasks: guarding the camp, rescuing as many other defenseless Jews as they could, and seeking revenge on the Nazis through guerrilla warfare.

Their problems were many. For an urban people with little or no knowledge of outdoor survival techniques, living in the open forests presented severe hardships. Moreover, nature and the Germans were not their only enemies.

At the beginning of the war, millions of Ukrainians and other Russian citizens had hailed the German invaders as liberators from the oppression of their communist rulers. Some local peasants here were also Jew-haters. Consequently, they not only helped in Nazi Jew-hunts but also tattled on Jews hiding out.

Jewish partisans could not even trust some of the Nazi-hating local gentry. While they, too, had formed partisan units of their own and lived right alongside Jewish campers in the woods, it was not uncommon for fanatics to shoot Jews outright. Thus anti-Semitism sometimes overruled the desire to overcome a common enemy.

Partisans from Polish Camps and Ghettos Face Even More Hazards

Escapees from the ghettos and camps of central Poland had to deal with several hardships even before they were able to join the partisan units in the forests. Successful escape was not the least of their worries. Unlike their Russian brothers, who had had military training and had held on to their old army weapons, most Polish Jews were unarmed and untrained. Where could they get guns that were already in short supply? Furthermore, they had to make it safely to the cover of far-off forests of western Poland without being caught or turned in.

And one large obstacle discouraged escape from the ghettos in the first place. The SS penalty for escape was death to the escapee's entire family in the ghetto. As a result, many who fervently wanted to become partisans would not risk leaving the ghettos until the deportations had taken most family members away or until their ghetto uprisings had been put down. By then it was too late, for many potential fighters had themselves perished. All these factors held back many young Polish Jews who might otherwise have added to the number of guerrilla fighters in the outside world.

Discussion Question: Would you and your family be able to withstand the hardships of living in the forests?

Jews in International Underground Movements

In all the countries of occupied Europe including Poland and Russia, Jews joined local resistance units. Sometimes they made their Jewishness known, and sometimes they kept their religion to themselves. In either case, bold and capable Jewish fighters became leaders of these groups. After the war, thousands of heroic Jewish partisans were decorated for bravery.

International and local units were not so much concerned with the rescue of Jews as they were with espionage and sabotage of the German war effort. However, they and their Jewish members often gave a helping hand to Holocaust victims whenever they could.

Jewish Soldiers in World War II

More than a million and a half Jewish Allied soldiers fought the Nazis face-to-face on the battlefields of World War II.

More than 30,000 Palestinian Jews, 10 percent of them women, fought in the British armed forces. One small unit of Palestinian Jews in the British forces fought the Nazis not as soldiers under the British flag but as Jews under their own Zionist flag bearing the yellow Star of David. Called the Jewish Brigade, this group was composed of 240 men and women parachutists.

Palestinian Jews had wanted to start their own Jewish war against the Nazis right from the beginning of the war. However, their British rulers had refused to allow a Jewish army on the grounds that Jews had no nation of their own. After many delays, the dogged persistence of Jewish fighters paid off. In the fall of 1944, the British relented and allowed them to have their own fighting unit.

The Jewish Brigade combined killing Nazis with rescuing Allied prisoners of war.

Chapter Ten Review

REVIEWING KEY POINTS

Exercise 1

1. Discuss why most Holocaust victims were unaware that they were to die.

2. Give several reasons why most Jews in the ghettos refrained from fighting in the beginning.

3. Give two reasons why the European resistance movements were not much help to the Jewish victims.

4. Discuss the many passive ways in which Jews resisted the Nazis.

5. At what point did Jews decide to fight back openly?

6. When did the local Polish resistance decide to give a few weapons to the Warsaw Jewish fighters?

7. Discuss the battle tactics that Nazi Stroop used against Warsaw Jews.

8. What two hopes gave imprisoned Jews the will to hold on?

9. Give two reasons why some citizens in Russian territories sometimes lent a hand to Nazi Jew-hunters.

10. Did Jews go to their deaths like sheep to the slaughter?

CHECKING YOURSELF

Exercise 2
Giving Reasons

Directions: Each incomplete statement in Part A explains something about the resistance of Jewish victims. Part B lists the reasons that complete the statements. Number your paper from 1–15. Next to the appropriate number, write the letter of the reason which best completes each statement. Each reason is used only once.

PART A—Incomplete Statements

1. The reason a few early authors of the Holocaust say that Jews went to their deaths like cowards is that

2. Hundreds of thousands of Russian Jews did not resist their murderers because

3. Most gas chamber victims died without protest because

4. During the early years of the Holocaust, most Jews refrained from open fighting because

5. Escape from the ghettos and camps was highly risky because

6. One reason why local underground movements were usually reluctant to give Jews weapons was that

7. Jewish resistance was not obvious in the beginning because

8. Jewish workers hampered the German war effort because

9. Hiding from Nazi Jew-hunters was more common in Western Europe because

10. Jews posing as non-Jews in the outside community were not usually successful because

11. Jews decided to battle their Nazi enemies late in 1942 because

12. Warsaw Jewish fighters were at a tremendous disadvantage because

13. An escapee from a Polish camp or ghetto in the Government General who wanted to join a partisan unit faced even more hardships than a Russian Jewish partisan because

Exercise 2 (continued)

14. Many young Jewish partisans stayed on to fight the Nazis from the ghettos because

15. Jews in the ghettos and camps struggled to keep alive because

PART B—Reasons

a. they believed the Allies would eventually rescue them.

b. they had to make their way safely to the cover of far-off forests and swamps in western Poland.

c. they were in short supply.

d. more non-Jews there were willing to take the risk of protecting Jewish neighbors.

e. they carried out sabotage in the German war factories.

f. they carried out their defiance under cover.

g. few in the outside world were willing to help.

h. they didn't want their families to be hurt.

i. they had no time to resist.

j. they used Nazi descriptions for their sources of information about Jewish behavior.

k. they had practically no weapons, no supplies, no outside support, and little military experience.

l. they knew then that death was their fate.

m. even if they could pass as non-Jews, they had to have proper identification papers from the government.

n. they didn't want to abandon their families to join partisan units in the forests.

o. they had been tricked.

Exercise 3
Matching Terms with Definitions

Directions: Number your paper from 1–10. Match each term in Column I with the word or phrase from Column II that best explains it. Write the letter of each correct answer on your paper next to the appropriate number.

COLUMN I		COLUMN II	
1.	Jewish Fighting Organization	A.	damage done by enemies who want to hamper a nation's war effort
2.	Mordechai Anielewicz	B.	the young commander of the Warsaw Jewish fighters
3.	Warsaw Jews	C.	they would not allow Palestinian Jews to form a Jewish army to battle the Nazis until 1944
4.	sabotage	D.	a unit of Palestinian Jewish fighters
5.	partisans	E.	German word meaning "the living dead," which Nazis called their prisoners
6.	Jewish Brigade	F.	the first European civilians to revolt against the Nazis
7.	British	G.	the death camp that was wrecked by doomed Jewish prisoners
8.	musselmen	H.	guerrilla fighters
9.	passive resistance	I.	the largest group of Warsaw Jewish fighters
10.	Sobibor	J.	defying without force

GIVING REPORTS

Topics to Research

1. The resistance activities of Jewish prisoners in individual camps and ghettos. Good source: *They Fought Back, The Story of Resistance in Europe*, edited by Yuri Suhl, has many interesting accounts.

2. How long did the professional armies of Holland, Poland, France, and Belgium hold out against the Nazi armies? Now compare these figures to the number of days Jewish Warsaw fighters resisted the Nazis. What does your research prove about the Warsaw fighters?

3. More on the Warsaw ghetto uprising. Good sources: *Uprising in the Warsaw Ghetto*, by Ber Mark, and *Hunter and Hunted*, by Gera Korman.

4. More about Mordechai Anielewicz, the leader of the Warsaw ghetto fighters.

5. What do the letters of Mordechai Anielewicz reveal about him? the situation of the Warsaw fighters? the attitude of the Warsaw fighters? Good source: *Uprising in the Warsaw Ghetto*, by Ber Mark, pages 54, 127, 156.

6. Hannah Senesh, a brave Palestinian teenager who lost her life fighting against the Nazis. Good source: *Heroes and Heroines*, by Jan Strong; *The Summer That Bled*, by Anthony Masters.

7. More about Jewish partisans. Good sources: *The Jewish Resistance: the History of Jewish Partisans in Lithuania and White Russia During the Nazi Occupation*, by Lester Eckman; *Not As a Lamb: The Jews Against Hitler*, by Lucien Steinberg.

8. Enzo Sereni, leader of Palestinian paratroopers who landed behind enemy lines in Europe to establish contact with Jewish victims. Good source: *The Emissary*, by Ruth Bondy.

9. Itzik Wittenberg, leader of the Jewish resistance of the Vilna ghetto.

10. More on Emmanuel Ringelblum and his Warsaw archives. Good source: *Notes from the Warsaw Ghetto*, by E. Ringelblum.

11. More on people who hid Jews or who helped Jews to hide.

Books to Review

1. *Uncle Mishna's Partisans*, by Yuri Suhl, based on the lives of a real group of Jewish resistance fighters in the Ukraine.

2. *Motele*, by Gertrude Samuels, a historical novel of the Jewish partisans in Russia and Poland.

3. *Anne Frank: The Diary of a Young Girl*, written by a Jewish girl in hiding with her family in Holland.

4. *Joseph and Me: In the Days of the Holocaust*, by Judy Hoffman, a true story of the author and her brother who hid from the Nazis in occupied Holland.

5. *The Upstairs Room*, by Johanna Reiss, true story of two Dutch girls in hiding from the Nazis.

Books to Review (continued)

6. *The Journey Back*, by Johanna Reiss, the sequel to *The Upstairs Room*.

7. *The Cigarette Sellers of Three Crosses Square*, by Joseph Ziemian, a true story of how a group of Jewish children escape from the Warsaw ghetto and survive in the Nazi-occupied city of Warsaw.

8. *Twenty and Ten*, by Claire Bishop, a novel of non-Jewish children who hide and protect ten Jewish children in occupied France.

9. *On the Other Side of the Gate*, by Yuri Suhl, a novel based on the real-life smuggling of an eighteen-month-old Jewish baby out of the Warsaw ghetto.

10. *Other People's Houses*, by Lore Segal, a true account of how an Austrian Jewish girl and her family took refuge in English homes to escape Nazi capture.

11. *The Gates of the Forest*, by Elie Wiesel, a novel of how a Hungarian Jew becomes a partisan.

12. *A Bag of Marbles*, by Joseph Joff, an autobiography that reveals how French Jews hid out in the Alps to escape Nazi capture.

13. *The Holocaust: A History of Courage and Resistance*, by Bea Stadtler, concentrates on the main events of the Holocaust and portrays the lives and roles of many heroes and heroines who resisted the Nazis.

14. *Child of the Holocaust*, by Jack Kuper, tells how a Jewish boy posed as a Christian during the Nazi era.

15. *The Wall*, by John Hersey, historical novel about the Warsaw ghetto revolt.

16. *Angry Harvest*, by Herman Field, tells how a Jewish girl hides with a Polish family.

17. *Children of the Resistance*, by Lore Cowan, relates how brave children in occupied Europe resisted the Nazis.

18. *Children with a Star: Jewish Youth in Nazi Europe*, by Deborah Dwork, dealing with the situation for Jewish children during the Holocaust, including their hiding.

19. *Anne Frank Remembered*, by Miep Gies, who had worked for Anne's father and who helped the family while they were in hiding.

20. *Rescuers: Portraits of Moral Courage in the Holocaust*, by Gay Block and Malka Drucker, a book giving the stories of forty-nine rescuers of Jews from the Nazis.

Books to Review (continued)

21. *The Diary of Anne Frank: The Critical Edition*, edited by David Barnouw and Gerrold Van Der Stroom, containing the version popularly known, which had been edited by her father, her original entries, and the diary as she had edited it in the Secret Annex.

MAKING PROJECTS

Poster Ideas

1. Picture the battle of Warsaw in January or in April of 1943.

2. Picture a Jewish partisan camp in the forests of western Poland or Russia.

Model Ideas

1. Using modeling clay, make a figure of a Jewish resistance fighter.

2. Find a picture of the Zionist (Israeli) flag used by the Jewish Brigade. Make one of your own from pieces of colored cloth sewn together or from colored paper.

CONDUCTING AN EXPERIMENT

To test your own feelings and reactions, role-play or discuss the following situation:

Two men armed with machine guns burst into your home and threaten to kill all the members of your family if just one of you makes an unnecessary move or does not do what you are told. You have no real idea what the men plan to do with you. You are always under guard. Several days pass. Your food supply begins to dwindle. Some of your family members get sick. What would you do? What would your feelings be? What would you hope for?

Assume that after several days, you somehow find out the men plan to kill all of you. How would you react then?

After you have brainstormed this situation with your class, discuss how you have just proven that the Jewish victims in Nazi prisons responded not in a "Jewish" way but in a typically human way.

PUTTING ON A PLAY

Choose a scene to act out from *The Diary of Anne Frank*, a play by Frances Goodrich and Albert Hackett based on the actual diary of Anne Frank, a Jewish girl hiding from the Nazis in occupied Holland.

AUDIOVISUAL AID SUGGESTIONS FOR CHAPTER TEN

1. Rent the 30-minute black-and-white film *The Legacy of Anne Frank*, an on-the-spot visit to the hiding place of Anne Frank and her family in Amsterdam, Holland. **ADL**

2. Filmstrip and cassette *Warsaw Ghetto: Holocaust and Resistance*, portrays the formation of and life in Warsaw but concentrates on resistance, both passive and armed. **JLC**

3. Filmstrip and cassette *Jewish Ghetto Fighters and Partisans*, describes actual incidents of armed resistance against the Nazis. **JEP**

4. View *Weapons of the Spirit*, a 38-minute color documentary about Le Chambon-sur-Lignon, a small village in France whose residents hid 5,000 Jews. **ZV**

5. View *The Other Side of Faith*, a 27-minute color documentary filmed in Poland, about a sixteen-year-old Catholic girl who hid thirteen Jews for two and a half years. **FVF**

6. View *Flames in the Ashes*, a 90-minute black-and-white documentary, featuring resistance fighters who reveal their experiences. **EM**

7. Watch *Au Revoir Les Enfants*, a 103-minute color film about the friendship that develops at a private boarding school between a Catholic boy and a Jewish boy given shelter by the headmaster. **SSSS**

8. View *The Courage to Care*, a 28-minute documentary in color and black-and-white, about ordinary people who helped victims of the Holocaust and who did not give in to the Nazis. **ZV**

✡ CHAPTER ELEVEN

The Aftermath

WORLD WAR II ENDS

When Hitler's frozen army surrendered to the Soviets in Stalingrad during the frigid winter of 1943, it was the beginning of the end of Hitler's winning streak in the war. After that, German forces began to feel the squeeze on all sides. As the Russians put the German troops on the run to the east, a new and second front opened up to Germany's west. On June 6, 1944, D-Day arrived: The Allies had successfully landed at Normandy in France. In the meantime, they had gained a foothold to the south, too, ripping North Africa out of German hands early in 1943 and invading Italy in September of that year. V-E Day finally arrived on May 8, 1945. On that day, the Germans unconditionally surrendered.

Afterward, Germany was divided into four zones, occupied by Russia, the United States, Great Britain, and France. The Allied Control Commission, composed of representatives from the four powers, became the temporary but supreme governing body of conquered Germany. It began the gigantic task of erasing Nazism from every institution in the land and restoring a more stable government to the Germans.

Eventually, because of Russia's unwillingness to cooperate with the others in unifying Germany, the German nation came to be a divided country again. The American, French, and English zones emerged to become West Germany, a democratic state, while the Soviet-controlled zone became known as East Germany, a

communist satellite.

Discussion Question: Why couldn't Nazism be erased from Germany overnight?

THE HOLOCAUST ENDS

Genocide Speeds Up as Germans Lose the War

As Hitler's armies plunged deeper and deeper into defeat, Hitler's war on Jews accelerated at a faster and more furious pace. In the spring of 1943, four months after the German defeat at Stalingrad, Himmler ordered the total liquidation of all the ghettos in Poland. So by the time the Russians occupied Polish soil, Polish Jewry was already dead. The few slave laborers who had remained in the labor camps of the Government General and whose services were still needed had been quickly transferred to labor camps in Germany.

Nazis Attempt to Cover War Crimes

With the Allies invading more and more German territory, the Nazi chiefs became panicky. Knowing full well the consequences of their actions, they tried to cover up all evidence of their war crimes. They burned records, tried to destroy gas chambers, and either shot many remaining prisoners in their concentration camps or else forced the inmates to march alongside them as they retreated. Most often these were death marches, for prisoners were shot as soon as their strength gave out.

But the Nazis didn't kill all their prisoners. Nor did they destroy all the incriminating evidence. Sometimes the SS camp guards were in such a hurry to get away, they left their camps wide open and unguarded. They did everything in their power to escape capture. Some disguised their appearances and sneaked off to hide on other continents. Others, like Hitler, Goebbels, and Himmler, committed suicide.

The Allies Liberate the Nazi Camps

When the Allies liberated the camps, they were shocked and horrified at what they saw. Thousands of unburied bodies covered the open ground. Some camps, like Bergen-Belsen were so contaminated with diseases, they had to be burned down immediately. Surviving prisoners were living skeletons, often too dazed and too weak to understand they were truly free now.

Immediately, the Allies ordered food and medicine. But for many thousands of prisoners, this help had come too late. Their bodies far beyond repair, they died in spite of good care. According to Leah and Sam Gottisman, Mark Stem, and other survivors who watched it happen, many starving survivors actually died from overeating. It was as if their shrunken and wasted bodies had forgotten how to digest food.

The Allies set to work helping the survivors to establish their lives again. Restoring their weakened bodies was just one of many problems. Now penniless, homeless, and without family, the remnants of the Nazi Holocaust faced a long and difficult road ahead.

Discussion Question: Assuming you were a Jewish survivor, why would there be little joy in liberation?

HITLER'S SUICIDE

On April 29, 1945, Adolf Hitler married Eva Braun, his mistress of thirteen years, in an underground bunker of the Chancellory Building in Berlin. Hours later, the newlyweds decided to carry out a premarital suicide pact. First, Hitler destroyed his dog, Blondi, by poisoning. Then Adolf Hitler shot himself. His bride of barely a day took poison.

Following the Fuehrer's last wishes, SS attending guards carried the bodies of the couple up to the Chancellory garden, drenched them with gasoline, and set them afire.

The evil Fuehrer was gone. His death was as bizarre and violent as his life. And he had remained consistent to the very end. In his last will and testament, he said history would prove that not he but the Jews had caused the war. He called Jews the "poisoners of all nations" and asked his followers to continue the fight to destroy them.

RESULTS OF THE NEW ORDER

Before they were finally stopped, the Nazis managed to make a good deal of headway in the creation of Hitler's so-called New Order. This new era of Nazi-controlled Europe had turned the continent into a giant graveyard. At the same time, Japan, Germany's Axis ally, had extended the war into Asia and many islands of the Pacific. By the time World War II had ended, over 45 million people lay dead. At least 17 million soldiers and 18 million civilians living in combat zones had lost their lives. The Nazi gangsters had murdered an additional 11 million unarmed and defenseless people. And more than 35 million had been wounded in the midst of warfare.

Hitler's men had exploited all the countries under their thumb: robbing banks, seizing gold to enrich the Reichsbank, grabbing billions of dollars worth of grain, natural resources, art treasures, even food supplies. That they caused severe shortages and hardships to the native peoples bothered the "Aryan masters" not at all.

They exploited the conquered peoples, too. Seven and one-half million Europeans had come to know the awful existence of Nazi slavery. Without warning, they had been dragged off the streets, separated from their families, and thrown into cattle cars to be herded into German factories, mines, fields, and homes. Besides Jews, Russians, Czechs, Poles, Serbs, Croats, Dutch, French, and Italians became victims of the Nazi slave drivers. They were beaten, underfed, underclothed, and—if they complained—hanged or shot.

At least 2 million prisoners of war had also been forced into slavery even though the international laws of war set up at the Geneva and Hague Conventions had strictly forbidden this practice. Here as elsewhere, Hitler had made his own rules.

Hundreds of thousands of Europeans became the victims of yet another contemptible Nazi crime. The heartless SS thugs actually kidnapped ten- to fourteen-year-old children to be slaves for the Reich. For example, from Poland alone, most of the 200,000 children who were carted off to Germany were never seen again by their families.

THE MURDER VICTIMS

Although the true count will never be known, Hitler's henchmen murdered approximately 11 million people. The death camps of Poland were not the only sites of their senseless slaughter. Thousands upon thousands of prisoners were executed, starved, overworked, and tortured in Dachau, Mauthausen, Buchenwald, and more than a dozen other notorious Nazi prisons located in Germany and other occupied lands.

Christian victims included French, Dutch, Germans, Russians, Poles, Austrians, Yugoslavians, Czechs, Belgians. At least a half million of these people lost their lives because they dared raise their voices in protest or because they differed in political philosophy. Many had been communists, Social Democrats, Freemasons, Catholic priests and nuns, Protestant clergy, or Jehovah's Witnesses.

Added tens of thousands of innocent people were slaughtered as a result of Nazi policy regarding "crimes" against their own; for every Nazi official threatened or killed, one hundred hostages paid with their lives. Moreover, the Hitlerites always deliberately chose hostages who were well-known, highly respected people in their communities.

The SS killers dished out their most brutal treatment to groups they regarded as inferior or subhuman. In terms of numbers of murdered victims, next in line to Jews were the Slavic peoples. Among them, Russians, Poles, and Yugoslavians fared the worst.

The SS murdered Russians by the millions. Of the more than 5.5 million Russian prisoners of war held captive, only one million survived. Hundreds of thousands had been shot outright. Untold numbers, whom the Nazis had deliberately abandoned in the wilderness without food or shelter during the winter of 1941, died from overexposure and starvation. Many also perished from overwork and starvation in Nazi prisons. In addition, the SS Einsatzgruppen gunned down thousands of innocent Russians simply because they were community or political leaders or experts in science or other fields.

Two million Poles were slaughtered by the Nazis. Among the dead were thousands of homeless Poles who had frozen to death because SS landlords had evicted them from their homes in the dead of winter in 1939. The SS also machine-gunned tens of thousands of Polish intellectuals, priests, community leaders, government officials, or any other Poles with more than an elementary-school education, for they wanted only uneducated slaves at their beck and call. In addition, many thousands of Poles fell victim to the inhuman treatment in Nazi concentration camps.

The SS made an effort to make Europe not only Jew-free but Gypsy-free as well. Under Nazi law, a person was defined as a Gypsy and earmarked for death even if he or she had only two great-great-grandparents who were Gypsies. Of the 700,000 Gypsies living in all of Nazi-occupied Europe 200,000 were executed. Gypsies shared in the same tortures reserved for Jews: the Einsatzgruppen, the gas chambers, the ghettos, and the medical experiments.

No group, however, was held in lower esteem than the Jews. To Nazis, Jews were poison, animals, scum. Because of this, Hitler had declared a special war on them.

Discussion Questions: In your opinion, did Hitler as a world leader contribute anything to mankind? to Germany?

JEWS ARE THE MOST PERSECUTED GROUP OF ALL

Jews were the most persecuted of all Nazi victims. Of this there can be no doubt. First, no other group suffered as high a percentage of deaths as this tiny group of people. More than 65 percent of continental European Jewry was wiped out. That was six of every nine people. Besides that, one of every four victims had been a child under fourteen. The Nazis murdered 1.5 million Jewish children.

Moreover, punishing Jews was required by Nazi law. The Nuremberg Laws, the yellow star, the ghettos, the Final Solution—all of these were laws. In other words, it was civic duty in the Nazi state first to discriminate against and then to kill Jews. Any citizen of Nazi-occupied lands who protected Jews violated these laws and thereby risked severe penalties, including death.

The mass murder of Jews was done according to a well-thought-out, highly organized plan. Details were handled by a special office for Jewish affairs staffed by the highest Nazi officers. The SS searched for Jews, confiscated their property, and provided a transportation system to cart them to death houses especially designed to kill them.

Remember, too, Hitler's determination that no Jew was to remain alive. The entire Jewish people was to be made extinct.

In addition, Nazis exploited Jews down to their very skin and bones. After robbing them of all earthly possessions, they drained all their strength in slave labor and even utilized their dead bodies. Human skin adorned many a Nazi chief's living room in the form of a lampshade.

Another difference between Jews and other victims of the Holocaust concerned the surviving members of their families. While bereaved Europeans faced many hardships in rebuilding their lives and in adjusting to life without their loved ones, they were able to begin anew once the Germans were defeated. This was not so for the handful of Jewish survivors of the Holocaust. For many, their ordeal was still not over.

Their long searches for relatives were fruitless; most found no one. Old friends were gone, too. With Hitler's destruction of 30,000 Jewish communities, there was little of home left. Moreover, old neighbors did not always welcome the Jews back. Nor were their possessions left in safekeeping with others or their homes and other property always willingly returned to them.

For example, when Jews returned to their hometown of Kielce in Poland to reclaim their property, a pogrom broke out. On July 4, 1946, over a full year after the Nazi Holocaust had ended, forty-one Jewish survivors were murdered! Afterward, a chain of bloody pogroms erupted throughout Poland. To incite the mob violence, Jew-haters had persuaded a child to say he had been abused in a Jewish ritual bloodletting ceremony.

So it is well worth remembering that persecution of European Jews neither began nor ended with Hitler's New Order. The Holocaust was a continuation of a long history of Jewish persecution in Europe.

The greatest tragedy is that millions of Jews could have been saved but weren't. Other Nazi victims who died during the course of the war had had little opportunity to save themselves. But Hitler's war on Jews began six long years before World War II ever started. There had been plenty of time and opportunity to rescue Jews from their Nazi tormentors. But most people in a position to help merely stood by and did nothing. That is the real tragedy of the Holocaust. It was not just a Nazi crime, but a major crime of human indifference to others' suffering.

Discussion Question: Do you think the Holocaust could have occurred without the background of long-standing European anti-Semitism? Discuss why or why not.

WHO IS RESPONSIBLE FOR THE HOLOCAUST?

Genocide Is Not Hitler's Crime Alone

Adolf Hitler could not and did not murder 6 million people by himself. He and his party chiefs may have masterminded the crimes and given the orders. But others carried out the actual killings. Were these followers personally responsible, too? Did they have to obey the orders of superiors, which involved criminal acts? Did they have a choice? We shall deal with Nazi war crim-

inals and the issue of **moral choice versus obedience to authority** in the next chapter.

Nor was genocide strictly a German crime. Naturally, most of the guilt for the Holocaust lies on the shoulders of the Nazi leaders and killers who planned and executed the killings of Europe's Jews and others. However, not every German was a Nazi, and not every Nazi was a German. Thousands of other anti-Semitic Europeans collaborated in the Final Solution. So the guilt crosses nationality lines.

All the responsibility for the Jewish slaughter does not necessarily stand with the actual perpetrators of the crime. Some of it rests with the onlookers—the Nazi-hating citizens and governments of the world who could have saved millions of Jewish lives but didn't. Did the majority of these bystanders remain uninvolved because they were unaware of what was happening?

DID THE WORLD KNOW WHAT WAS HAPPENING TO JEWS?

The Free World

Citizens and governments in the free world knew. Newsreels and newspapers had kept them up-to-date on every detail of the Holocaust—from the moment it started in Germany in 1933 until war broke out in 1939. Even after that, the European underground and Allied espionage kept the free world posted on all Nazi atrocities. It was not long after the invasion of Russia that the Einsatzgruppen's actions were reported, for these killers had made no attempt to hide their massacres. Moreover, it was as early as the summer of 1942 that the Allies had positive proof of Hitler's order to exterminate Jews.

The Germans

The German people knew. They heard the

Nuremberg Laws proclaimed, watched the boycotts of Jewish business, saw the fires and violence of Kristallnacht explode in their midst. They watched Jews disappear from their country. And millions of Germans had family members who were loyal Nazis.

Did they know about the death camps in Poland? It is very possible that many Germans did not know about this. The Nazi government did not broadcast its dirty work.

The Civilians of Occupied Europe

Governments and citizens of occupied Europe knew. Nazi invaders always ordered governments to enforce their anti-Jewish laws and to turn over Jewish citizens. Jews wearing yellow stars did not go unnoticed. Nor did the disappearance of a Jewish classmate or shop owner. And when the SS arrived at midnight to round up Jewish neighbors and pounded loudly on their doors, the walls of nearby apartments and homes did not shut out the sound. Perhaps people heard rumors of the death camps, perhaps not. But if they lived in the vicinity of the death houses, it was impossible not to smell the burning flesh from the crematory smokestacks for miles around.

Railroad officials, the civilians who were at the very heart of the deportation process, also knew. Yes, Eichmann and his SS teams organized the mass movement of millions to the ghettos and death camps. But it was civilian railroad personnel who steered the cars along the tracks to Auschwitz and the other camps. It was they, too, who counted all those heads of women, children, and men who boarded their trains so that they later could collect the transport costs from the SS. And when Jews boarded their trains from far-off points like France or Bulgaria or Greece, how many officials in how many towns and cities had to coordinate their schedules in order to clear the tracks for direct passage to Poland?

Discussion Questions: Should we become involved if the human rights of others are being violated? If you witnessed a mugging or violent encounter, would you try to help the victim? If you were a bystander during the Holocaust, what would you have done?

HOW MUCH HELP DID BYSTANDERS OFFER JEWISH VICTIMS?

The Germans

What about the masses of German people? Although they were well aware of the anti-Semitic course of their government and witnessed the persecution of Jews firsthand, most remained silent bystanders.

However, while it is true that Hitler enjoyed widespread support and even worship of the German people, there were also millions of Germans who hated Hitler and all he stood for. It is worth remembering too, that he never did receive a majority of popular votes in any election. Among the dissenters were Catholic and Protestant clergy, Social Democrats, communists, and many others.

Some Germans formed anti-Nazi resistance groups. Several people attempted to assassinate Adolf Hitler. There were also German soldiers and army officers who voiced their disapproval of SS atrocities against Jews. Al Lewin remembers one who tried to help him:

A friend of mine escaped from camp once. The SS questioned me about it. When I refused to tell them anything, they hung me by my ears. This was quite a painful ordeal. [After the war, Lewin had to have plastic surgery on his ears to correct the disfigurement caused by this torture.] *The German guard assigned to watch over me was basically a good man. To help me whenever the officers weren't around, he would let the ropes down enough so that my feet touched the floor and the pressure and pain on my ears was temporarily relieved. Then as soon as he heard the officers approach, he would hoist me back up again.*

However, in the atmosphere of Nazi terror and totalitarianism, all resistance had remained weak, for there was no tolerance of dissenters. The Stormtroopers and SS terrorized Germans, too. Concentration camps and tortures were open to all. In fact, the attempted assassins of the Fuehrer were executed in such a vile manner that others with the same inclination probably backed down. It is probable that most Germans who disapproved of Nazi persecution of Jews remained silent because they were afraid.

But even here in the heart of Nazidom, there were brave German people who risked their own lives to shelter Jews. Because of them, 5,000 German Jews survived the Holocaust.

Discussion Questions: If you were a German during this time, how would you have reacted to Nazi terror? to the Jewish dilemma?

The Civilians of Occupied Europe

It is true that local attitudes toward Jews sometimes made a difference in the way Nazis handled their "Jewish problem." If you recall, people like the Danes saved nearly all their Jewish citizens from deportations to the gas chambers. On the other hand, in other countries like Holland where local support for Jewish neighbors was just as strong, the Nazis managed to get rid of nearly the entire Jewish community anyway. So no hard-and-fast rules about the collective responsibility of Europeans can be made.

One must remember that the non-Jewish citizens of Europe lived under the constant threat of Nazi terror, too.

Generally speaking, the citizens of Poland and in all Russian territories put up the least resistance to Nazi treatment of Jews among them. The majority remained indifferent. A few even lent a hand to the Nazi Jew-hunters. Occasionally, local pogroms even accompanied Nazi terror. Moreover, it was in this climate of hatred against Jews that Hitler had decided to build the death camps and to send in the killing squads. But one must not forget that there were good and brave people in all these territories who did come to the rescue of Jewish neighbors and risked and lost their own lives because of it.

The strongest support of Jews came from citizens who lived in the other occupied countries of Western, Northern, and Southeastern Europe. Here thousands of Jewish lives were saved by people from all walks of life: government leaders, ordinary citizens, clergy, nuns, even children. Many of these heroes lost their own lives for their efforts.

Religious Leaders

Help came to thousands of Jewish victims from Protestant and Catholic clergy and nuns in many European countries including Germany, Greece, France, Holland, Bulgaria, and Hungary. From their pulpits they spoke out against Nazi atrocities. They sheltered Jewish children and adults in their homes and convents. By issuing fake baptismal records, they made Jews "instant" Christians and therefore immune to Nazi terror.

For their rescue efforts, many thousands of religious men and women paid with their own lives.

However, none of the world's religious leaders took a firm stand against Nazi atrocities involving Jews. There were many worldwide appeals to the Vatican and to Pope Pius XII to publicly excommunicate Nazis who were Catholics and to call a halt to Jewish persecution. But here, too, an official policy of silence was maintained. Knowing that thousands of Nazi-defying priests had already paid with their lives, and fearing that brutal retaliation would fall on more clergy and lay Church leaders, the Pope decided to seek aid for Jews through quieter methods. He sent out instructions to Vatican representatives and clergy in all of occupied Europe to try to persuade governments to stop the deportations and to rescue Jewish victims whenever possible. The response to papal instructions saved thousands of Jewish lives.

Discussion Questions:	In your opinion, were people of occupied Europe less responsible for the Holocaust than people in the free world? Why?

The Free World

In the best position to stem the Nazi genocide were the nations of the free world. They had all the necessary ingredients: the means, the influence, the power, and all the facts about the Holocaust down to the tiniest detail. However, meaningful government action did not come for many years.

Here is the free world's record during the Holocaust:

1933–1938

When German Jews were stripped of civil rights, suffered the pogrom of Kristallnacht, and were imprisoned or forcibly expelled from Germany and Nazi-controlled Austria and Czechoslovakia, all the free world did was to scold Hitler.

The League of Nations did form a Committee to Handle Refugee Problems, but it solved nothing, for it lacked support, funds, and necessary visas. The Evian Conference slammed the doors of thirty-one nations shut to the Jewish refugees. And the British White Paper barred their entry to Palestine, home of their ancestors.

1939–1944

When American and English citizens read news reports of Nazi atrocities in the camps and ghettos and about the killer squads and death camps in Poland, some formed small protest groups. They sent letters and petitions to their government leaders. Rallies and magazine articles appeared here and there. All asked, "What kind of democracies are we? Do something! Lift the Allied blockade of food and supplies to Jewish and other Nazi victims in enemy lands! Bomb the gas chambers! Trade Jews for enemy prisoners of war! Open our doors and let Jews in!"

In December 1942, the Allies warned the Hitlerites of punishment for their extermination of Jewry.

Four months later, on April 19, 1943, while Warsaw Jews were battling the Nazis for their lives, British and American leaders called an Allied meeting in Bermuda to discuss the Jewish refugee problem. The Bermuda Conference amounted to nothing. The United States refused to change its immigration laws. The British refused to tear up the White Paper. The Russians refused to admit there was any special Jewish problem. They said many people besides Jews suffered Nazi persecution.

No discussion of exchanging war prisoners for Jews came up. The Allies shunned bombing the gas chambers or railroad lines that led to them, citing "too many technical difficulties" or "danger in delaying the war effort." No one argued that if earlier Allied planes had easily been able to bomb war factories just a stone's throw from Auschwitz, why couldn't they now hit the railroad ties?

The Allies' final answer to the Jewish dilemma? "Our victory will free them. No special military effort can be made specifically for Jewish victims."

From January 1944 On

Finally, on January 22, 1944, United States President Roosevelt did something. He formed the War Refugee Board. By now, the death camps had been working round the clock for dozens of months. The Einsatzgruppen had long since done their job in Russian territories. Four million Jews were already dead. But Roosevelt's War Refugee Board was better late than never. Through its brave rescue efforts and the contributions and support of a Jewish organization called the American Joint Distribution Committee (JDC), hundreds of thousands of Jewish victims were snatched away from the poison gas and ovens.

Why Did the Free World Wait So Long to Act?

1. In the beginning, many political pressure groups and government leaders chose not to become politically involved with another nation's internal affairs. This hands-off policy was maintained even at the expense of innocent lives.

2. Many people feared involvement in another war. Even when Hitler began to seize land in Europe and openly violated the Versailles Treaty, the war-weary democracies let him have his way. "No more war!" cried many Americans. "Let Europe settle their own problems from now on!" Afraid that interference in the Jewish dilemma would antagonize Hitler, these protestors preferred to let him and the Jewish victims alone.

3. When reports of Nazi atrocities against Jews hit the newspapers, many readers believed they were highly exaggerated.

Those who insisted they couldn't be true called them "typical war stories." Even some news reporters themselves wrote the articles with an air of skepticism.

4. Anti-Semitism ruled some heads and hearts. People who disliked Jews shouted, "If we make a special effort to rescue Jews, then Hitler is right; we *are* fighting a 'Jewish war.' Many Europeans are suffering from Nazi persecution. Not just Jews!" These anti-Semitic pressure groups were not without influence in political and diplomatic matters.

Discussion Question: Do you feel that the United States has an obligation to step into a foreign country to protect human rights?

Were Jews Responsible for Their Own Destruction?

Hitler had always accused "international Jewry" of controlling the world. If anything, the exact opposite was true. Without a country to receive them, a government to represent them, or an army to protect them, Jews were in fact powerless. That is precisely why 6 million went to their deaths.

Jews living outside Nazi-occupied Europe had no power to stop the Nazi slaughter either. Though all shuddered at their governments' inaction to stop the tide of Jewish persecution and questioned the Allies' claim that special efforts to divert arms or military action toward Jewish victims would hamper the war effort, many were even too embarrassed to speak out. They didn't want to appear disloyal. They didn't want to add to Hitler's accusation of a "Jewish war."

However, there were many Jewish organizations throughout the world who actively came to their brothers' support. Those such as the World Zionists, the World Jewish Congress, and the American Joint Distribution Committee did everything in their power to transfer food, money, supplies, and medicine to Jews in Nazi-occupied lands.

Palestinian Jews carried out dramatic rescue efforts. Establishing two offices in Geneva, Switzerland, and Istanbul, Turkey, both neutral countries in the war, these rescuers not only maintained contact and sent in lifesaving supplies but also freed Jews from Nazi territories through illegal immigration and underground escape ventures on secret ships. One group that succeeded in smuggling over 30,000 European Jewish children into Palestine was Youth Aliyah.

However, all these groups soon had their hands tied by government red tape. Once the United States entered the war in 1941, an Allied blockade cut out all further shipments of goods and money and even blocked communication with Nazi-occupied territories. The Allies worried that such aid might fall into enemy hands. That was the end of all contact between the persecuted Jews and their brothers until after the war was over.

How Did the Trapped Victims Respond to the Holocaust?

First, they tried to hold on. But they were stripped of everything they had. They tried desperately to emigrate. But few would have them. They tried to hide. There were few hiding places. They cried for help. But no one answered their call. Then the trapped Jews fought back. And they lost. In the words of Emmanuel Ringelblum, the noted Warsaw ghetto historian, theirs was a "struggle between a fly and an elephant."

Chapter Eleven Review

REVIEWING KEY POINTS

Exercise 1

1. Why did the Nazis try to destroy records and to escape capture at the end of the war?

2. How was Hitler's death in keeping with his life?

3. In your own words, briefly describe Hitler's New Order of 1939–1945.

4. How were the 11 million people whom the Nazis murdered any different from the rest of the 35 million war casualties?

5. All Europeans under Nazi rule suffered, but give several reasons why Jews stand out as the most persecuted Nazi victims of all.

6. Why is the Holocaust called "a major crime of human indifference"?

7. Discuss why the Holocaust neither began nor ended with Hitler's New Order.

8. Why was the free world in the best position to help the Jewish victims?

9. How did the Allies propose to free the Jewish victims from Nazi torture?

10. Discuss why the free world waited so long to go to the rescue of the Jewish victims. Point out how many victims were already dead by the time Roosevelt set up the Refugee Board.

11. Discuss how the responsibility for the Holocaust lay beyond Hitler and Nazi party chiefs.

CHECKING YOURSELF

Exercise 2
Working a Crossword Puzzle

Directions: All the terms used in this puzzle are explained in Chapter Eleven.

ACROSS

1. Hitler committed _____ at the end of the war.
2. The section of Germany controlled by American, British, and French after the war.
4. After World War II the _____ _____ _____ took over the government of Germany.
8. In 1942 the Allies met in _____ to discuss the Jewish refugee crisis.
12. The _____ _____ was in the best position to help the Jewish victims.
13. Initials of the group that worked with the Refugee Board to free Jews in 1944.
15. Mrs. Adolf Hitler: _____ _____ .
16. Hitler wanted to exterminate _____ , too.
17. June 6, 1944, when the Allies landed in Normandy, France, is called _____ .
18. The day the Germans unconditionally surrendered is known as _____ .
19. Next to the Jews and the Gypsies, the _____ suffered the most from Nazi hatred.
20. _____ Germany, the name of the Russian-controlled zone.
21. Six million Jewish women, children, and men were destroyed during the Nazi _____ .
22. _____ against Jews had existed in Europe centuries before the Holocaust occurred.

DOWN

1. In 1943 German armies surrendered to the Russians in the city of _____ .
2. In 1944 Roosevelt formed the _____ _____ _____ to rescue Jews from the Holocaust.
3. The Germans violated nearly all the rules of war established at the _____ Convention.
5. Persecution of Jews was required by Nazi _____ .
6. Nazis murdered 1.5 million Jewish _____ .
7. Millions of Jews could have been _____ from the Holocaust.
9. The Allies refused to _____ the railroad lines leading to Auschwitz.
10. Altogether, the Nazis murdered _____ million unarmed, defenseless people.
11. Hitler's Third Reich lasted _____ years.
14. Before his death, Hitler blamed _____ for causing World War II.

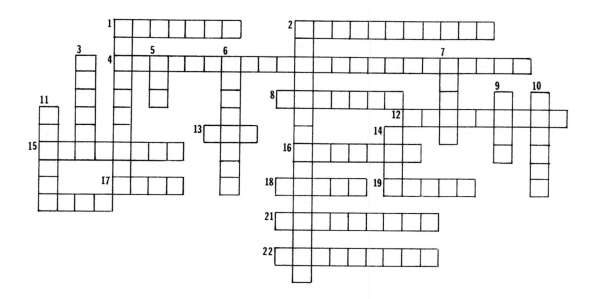

GIVING REPORTS

Topics to Research

1. The assassination of SD Chief Reinhard Heydrich in Czechoslovakia in May 1942, and Hitler's response, the total destruction of the town of Lidice. Good sources: *The Rise and Fall of the Third Reich*, by William Shirer; or *Target: Heydrich*, by Ivanov Miraslav.

2. The total assets of the Reichsbank after it had been filled with gold and other wealth from Jews and other conquered peoples. Also find out if these treasures were ever returned after the war.

3. The role of the International Red Cross in the rescue of Jewish victims.

4. More on the role of the American government in the rescue of Jewish victims. Good source: *While Six Million Died*, by Arthur Morse.

5. The cost of World War II in dollars, the war debts that resulted, and the extent of destruction of Europe's cities.

6. The anti-Nazi activities of the White Rose, a group of German students led by Hans and Sophie Scholl. Good sources: *Students Against Tyranny*, by Inge Scholl; or Chapter 6 in *To Kill the Devil*, by Herbert Malloy Mason.

7. How many Europeans in occupied Europe helped Jewish victims? Good source: *Their Brothers' Keepers: The Heroes and Heroines Who Helped the Oppressed Escape Nazi Terror*, by Philip Friedman, a documented account of non-Jews who came to the rescue of Jewish victims.

8. Hitler's physical and mental condition at the end of the war. Good source: *The Last Days of Hitler*, by H.R. Trevor-Roper.

9. The many plots and attempts to assassinate Hitler by Nazi-hating Germans such as Field Marshall Erwin Rommel (The Desert Fox), Count Claus von Stauffenberg, Helmuth von Moltke, and Hans von Donanyi. Good source: *To Kill the Devil*, by Herbert M. Mason.

10. The many efforts of Monsignor Angelo Roncalli to save Jews from death. (Roncalli later became Pope John XXIII.)

11. German minister Martin Niemoller and the Confessional Church, who defied the Nazis and protested anti-Jewish treatment.

12. German Protestant minister Heinrich Gruber's efforts to help Jews, and his punishment.

Topics to Research (continued)

13. The fascinating story of Kurt Gerstein, a conscience-stricken SS man whose job it was to deliver Zyklon B to the death camps and who took notes on the Final Solution with the intention of revealing the horrible Nazi crimes to the world. Find out what happened to him and his notes at the end of the war. Good source: *The Holocaust*, by Nora Levin.

14. The Garden of Righteous Gentiles, located at Yad Vashem (Israel's memorial to the 6 million Jewish dead), which commemorates the efforts of non-Jews to save Jewish victims of the Holocaust. Good source: Martin Gilbert's *The Holocaust*.

15. Yad Vashem, Israel's memorial to Holocaust victims.

16. More about Hitler's final hours. Good sources: *Hitler*, by Joachim Fest; *The Last Days of Hitler*, by H.R. Trevor-Roper.

17. Youth Aliyah and Aliyah Bet, the Palestinian underground rescue operation that smuggled tens of thousands of Jewish victims into Palestine. Good sources: *The Last Escape*, by Ruth Kluger and Peggy Mann; also *The Holocaust, A History of Courage and Resistance*, by Bea Stadtler.

18. Joop Westerwill, a Dutch teacher who rescued many Jews.

19. The role of President Roosevelt's War Refugee Board in rescuing Jews from deportation. Good source: *While Six Million Died*, by Arthur Morse.

20. The Mossad, a Palestinian underground rescue group that helped European Jews to escape capture.

21. Eva Braun and Geli Raubal, the two women in Hitler's life.

22. The nuns of St. Catherine Church in Vilna, Poland, their role in helping Jewish victims, and their capture and punishment.

23. Zegota, the Council for Aid to Jews, an underground rescue group of Poles who helped Jews.

24. Other stories of individual Jews who hid out to escape Nazi capture.

Books to Review

1. *The Assisi Underground: The Priests Who Rescued Jews*, by Alexander Ramati, a true story of how Italian Franciscans sheltered and protected hundreds of Jews.

2. *Ceremony of Innocence*, by James Formann, a novel based on the true story of the White Rose, an organization of German students who opposed Hitler.

3. *On the Other Side*, by Mathilde Wolff Monckeberg, a diary written by a German woman who hated Hitler.

4. *Out of the Fire*, by Ernst Papanek, a man who saved thousands of Jewish children from the Holocaust.

5. *In the Face of Danger*, by Kay Mara, a story of how two Hitler Youth members hide and protect two Jewish girls in an attic.

6. *The Eighth Sin*, by Stefan Kanfer, portrays the fate of the Gypsies under Hitler.

7. *I Was There*, by H.P. Richter, reveals how two young Nazis become disillusioned with Hitlerism.

8. *The Evil That Men Do: The Story of the Nazis*, by Arnold P. Rubin, a history of the Holocaust that concentrates on the choices made by the victims, the Nazis, the collaborators, and the bystanders.

9. *From Ice Set Free: The Story of Otto Kiep*, by Bruce Clements, tells of the resistance and ultimate hanging of Kiep, a Nazi-hating German.

10. *A Prisoner and Yet . . .* , by Corrie ten Boom, reveals how the author and her family were imprisoned and enslaved by the Nazis for helping refugees.

11. *Diary of a Nightmare*, by Ursula von Kardorff, the diary written during the Nazi era by a Nazi-hating young German woman.

12. *The Altruistic Personality: Rescuers of Jews in Nazi Germany*, by Samuel P. Oliner and Pear M. Oliner, from a scientific analysis of over 700 interviews with rescuers and non-rescuers of Jews in the Holocaust.

13. *Conscience and Courage*, by Eva Fogelman, a look at rescuers of Jews during the Holocaust.

MAKING PROJECTS

Poster Ideas

1. List the rules of war pertaining to war prisoners as defined by the Geneva and Hague conventions. Then indicate how the Nazis violated all of them.

2. Picture a bombed-out European city at the war's end. Label your scene "Hitler's New Order."

3. List the number of civilians, country by country, who were killed in World War II.

4. Follow the same procedure as in number 3 except use statistics showing the number of soldiers killed.

5. Using the results of the New Order revealed in this chapter, indicate them on your poster. Use pictures from magazines to represent each idea.

6. Make a collage of your impression of the aftermath of the Holocaust and the New Order.

7. Picture a secret ship carrying Jewish refugees to Palestine.

8. Picture a Holocaust survivor with a yellow star on his or her prison uniform. Label it "Hitler's Most Persecuted Victim."

9. Picture what you think a Nazi concentration camp looked like when the Allies discovered it.

PUTTING ON A PLAY

Present one or several scenes from one of the following plays:

1. *The Deputy*, by Ralph Rolfhochhuth, which deals with the response of the Roman Catholic Church to the Holocaust.

2. *Doctor Korczak and the Children*, by Erwin Sylvannus, which concentrates on the responsibility of the German people for the Holocaust.

AUDIOVISUAL AIDS FOR CHAPTER ELEVEN

1. Rent *Hangman*, a 12-minute color film based on Maurice Ogden's poem portraying the individual's moral responsibility for others' welfare. **ADL**

2. Rent *Avenue of the Just*, a 58-minute documentary that deals with questions of conscience and morality and of why some bystanders during the Holocaust reacted compassionately toward Jewish victims while others remained indifferent. **ADL**

3. Rent *Memorial*, a 17-minute color film that reveals resistance efforts of non-Jewish teenagers, clergy, and other citizens. **ADL**

4. Three-minute color film loop *Liberation of the Concentration Camps*, includes on-the-spot newsreel coverage of the liberation of the camps and prisoners. **SSSS**

5. The record "The Holocaust" gives an overview of the events and aftermath through an interview with Yuri Suhl, a noted Jewish author and lecturer. **CM**

6. View *Opening the Gates of Hell*, a 45-minute documentary in color and black-and-white, that gives interviews, photos, and footage of what American liberators of the Nazi concentration camps found. **EM**

✡ CHAPTER TWELVE

Postwar Response to the Holocaust

Introduction

After the war, the revelation of all the hard facts about the Holocaust played upon the conscience of the world. Shock and horror and sympathy for the Jewish victims and the surviving members of their families moved governments and private citizens around the world to take steps to prove their sorrow over the Jewish tragedy.

THE NATIONAL JEWISH STATE OF ISRAEL IS FORMED

From the word **Zion**, the Hebrew word for Israel, are derived the words **Zionist** and **Zionism**. Zionists are people, both Jews and non-Jews, who strived to create a national home for the Jewish people in Palestine. Zionism, their movement, began in 1897 and was led by Theodor Herzl, a Viennese lawyer-journalist who became convinced that as long as Jews were a minority group, they would be persecuted. He concluded that to escape anti-Semitism, Jews had to have a country and government of their own. His book, *The Jewish State*, based on this idea, attracted attention around the world.

On August 29, 1897, Herzl called a worldwide meeting in Basel, Switzerland, of all Jewish leaders interested in striving for Jewish independence. At this First Zionist Congress, 200 Jews established the World Zionist Organization and pledged to buy property and set up a Jewish nation in their ancient homeland in Palestine through lawful means. Fifty years after the meeting, the Jewish state of Israel would be born out of the tragedy of the Holocaust.

Discussion Question: Do you agree with Herzl?

British Agree with Zionists but Arabs Balk

The British, who seized Palestine from Turkish rulers during World War I, agreed with the Zionists. On November 2, 1917, the British government issued the Balfour Declaration, which supported "the establishment of a national home for the Jewish people in Palestine." The League of Nations also accepted this declaration in July 1922, when it officially made Palestine the mandate of Britain, for it recognized the traditional ties that world Jewry had to that land.

Arabs living in Palestine were furious, however. They argued, "We, the vast majority of the population, have lived in Palestine for hundreds of years. It is ours!" At the same time, Jews stubbornly defended their position. "God promised us this land, and we have lived here for more than 4,000 years!" Severe fighting broke out.

To settle the argument, the British government decided to give in to the Arab majority. In 1922, it assigned three fourths of Palestine, all the area east of the Jordan River, to the Arabs.

However, still living in the tiny area sectioned off to Jews were over a million Arabs. Neither Jews nor Arabs were happy with this arrangement.

As time went on, tens of thousands of Jewish refugees poured into their tiny Promised Land to escape persecutions first in Eastern Europe and then in Nazi Germany. As this influx of Jewish immigrants grew, so did Arab hostility. Sporadic Arab attacks on Jewish communities mushroomed into full-scale revolts.

British Appease Arabs with White Paper of 1939

By 1938, as conditions in Germany became impossible for Jews, the Arab-Jewish situation in Palestine grew more and more tense. World war was also in the air. Fearing the Arabs might turn against them, the British moved to appease them. Out came the British White Paper of 1939, which slowed down Jewish immigration into Palestine to a mere trickle.

To the Palestinian Zionists, lives were more important than laws. They began to smuggle the desperate victims across European borders and past the Arab and British patrols that guarded the borders and shores of Palestine.

However, World War II not only brought these rescue efforts to a standstill but also locked the Jewish victims firmly in the Nazis' grip.

Holocaust Survivors and Palestinian Jews Ignore the White Paper

Not even when the war ended did the British open Palestine to the thousands of Jewish survivors of the Holocaust who wanted to leave Europe. The barrier of the White Paper still stood. The Palestinian Zionists didn't let that stop them. Once again their smuggling operations began. Jewish survivors, mostly Eastern European Jews, sneaked across forbidden waters and slipped beyond British and Arab lookouts into Palestine.

Once again, violence erupted between the incoming refugees and the Arabs and British officials who were trying to keep them out. Finally, Britain gave up trying to settle the Arab-Jewish argument. In 1947 they turned the problem over to the General Assembly of the United Nations and announced they were giving up their mandate.

By now the world reaction to the Jewish survivors who were trying to steal their way into Palestine, their promised homeland, was very sympathetic. People everywhere had come to realize that the Holocaust might never have claimed so many millions of innocent victims had the gates of Palestine been open to them in the first place.

Discussion Questions: Why do you think so many Eastern European survivors wanted to leave Europe? In their position, how would you feel?

The United Nations Approves the Formation of Israel

In November 1947, the General Assembly recommended that Palestine be divided into two parts: one state for Jews and one for Arabs. On November 29, 1948, the United Nations voted and approved this partition of Palestine. The Zionists were pleased. The Arabs were not.

The State of Israel was born on May 14, 1948.

NAZI WAR CRIMINALS ARE PUNISHED

Allied Warnings of Nazi Punishment

Long before the war ended, the Nazis knew they would be punished for their crimes against Jews and other conquered peoples of Europe.

From 1941 on, the Allies and the European governments in exile issued several warnings of legal punishments. At the Moscow Conference of October 1943, Roosevelt, Stalin, and Churchill, with the support of thirty-three nations, vowed to make the Nazis pay for their horrible deeds. The Allies threatened, too, that German war criminals would be tried in courts by representatives of the countries against whom they had committed their crimes.

A United Nations Committee for the Investigation of War Crimes also began to gather evidence against the Nazis during the last two years of the war.

Discussion Question: Why do you think the Nazis continued on with their crimes?

The Nuremberg Trials

Six weeks after the war had ended, the Allied powers met in London, signed an agreement to prosecute Nazi war criminals, and set up a court called the International Military Tribunal. This tribunal, made up of eight judges, two each from the United States, Britain, France, and the Soviet Union, began the tremendous task of gathering evidence and preparing a case against the Nazis.

The amount of evidence against them was mind-boggling. Besides the living testimonies of many, many witnesses and victims, Nazi documents captured by the Allies at the end of the war were enough to fill 1,500 two-ton trucks!

The first trial, held at the Palace of Justice in Nuremberg, Germany, lasted for ten months—from November 1945 to October 1946. Twenty-one of the twenty-four Nazi leaders indicted stood trial. The whereabouts of Martin Bormann, Hitler's deputy, was uncertain; Gustav Halbach, head of Krupp Steel Works, was too ill Labor Front, had committed suicide in his jail cell.

To prevent further suicides, the authorities placed all Nazi prisoners under twenty-four hour guard. Despite this precaution, Hermann Goering, Hitler's air force chief, somehow managed to commit suicide by taking poison.

The defendants were tried for (1) participating in a conspiracy to wage war; (2) crimes against peace, or waging war; (3) war crimes, or breaking international laws of war such as mistreating war prisoners and submitting captives to forced labor; (4) crimes against humanity, or genocide, deportations, and other atrocities.

There was no question as to the guilt of the accused. Most tried, however, to absolve themselves of personal responsibility for the crimes by saying they had been following orders of superior officers. This argument held little weight with the Nuremberg judges.

Of the twenty-one Nazi war criminals tried, three were acquitted, seven were sentenced to prison terms, and the rest were sentenced to death by hanging. On October 16, 1946, the condemned prisoners were hanged at the Nuremberg jail. Those given prison terms were sent to Spandau Prison in Berlin.

Several organizations had also been put on trial. Among those found guilty and condemned as criminal organizations were the SS, the SD, and the Gestapo. Among the acquitted were the general staff and high command of the German armed forces.

Between 1947 and 1949, another series of war trials was held at Nuremberg. Here, before tribunals set up by the Allied Control Commission, were tried 185 Nazi officers of lower rank, SS doctors who had performed gross medical experiments, German industrialists who had used slave laborers, and Nazi judges whose former decisions had been warped by Nazi philosophy. Twenty-four of these war criminals were sentenced to death, and of the 117 others who received prison sentences, twenty were imprisoned for life.

Thereafter, many military courts throughout Europe continued to pass judgment on other Nazi war criminals and made them pay for their crimes accordingly. Though many Nazi war criminals are no longer alive today, the hunt for them still goes on.

Discussion Questions: Even though they were following orders, were the Nazis still guilty, in your opinion? Is a person more obligated to follow the dictates of his conscience or the orders of a superior?

The Genocide Convention

In December 1948, the United Nations took further steps to prevent future Holocausts. At this Genocide Convention, the U.N. members defined genocide, made it a crime under international law, and promised to hold accountable any government guilty of it.

Germans Pay Reparations

After the war ended, Jewish survivors were ill, homeless, penniless, and without family. Yet they made no demands that the German government pay for the crimes against them. The only help surviving Jews asked for and received was funds for the basic necessities of food, medicine, and shelter. Relegated by the Allies, the monies came from German funds and were paid to individuals or to Jewish agencies representing those who had emigrated from Europe after the war.

Eventually, Germany paid back Jewish survivors who requested payment for property seized by the Nazis. This was done mainly in the American zone of Germany.

In addition, in 1952, Konrad Adenauer, the chancellor of West Germany, proposed to make reparations to Israel, now the home of world Jewry, for Jewish properties seized by the Nazis. A treaty was drawn up, and under its terms Germany was to pay Israel the sum of approxi-mately one billion dollars over a period of the next twelve years. This move was widely supported by the majority of German people.

However, East Germany, under Soviet rule, refused to pay all debts to Jews.

Discussion Question: The Soviet refusal to pay debts to Jews indicated what type of attitude toward the survivors?

Roman Catholic Church Moves to Erase Religious Anti-Semitism

In 1964 the Roman Catholic Church made a strong effort to erase religious anti-Semitism. That year, Roman Catholic bishops from throughout the world convened in Rome and discussed anti-Semitism at length. Their Declaration of Non-Christian Religions stressed the common bond between Christianity and Judaism. It also made a conscience-binding rule for all Christians to follow: Christians are forbidden to teach or promote the idea that Jews of today or of ancient times are cursed for or guilty of the crucifixion of Christ. The bishops also declared hatred and persecution of Jews to be deplorable.

Discussion Question: Do you think religious anti-Semitism still exists today?

Nazi War Criminals Still at Large Are Hunted Down

Over 100,000 Are Never Caught

Another tragic aspect of the Holocaust is that the vast majority of Nazi war criminals have never been brought to justice. Knowing exactly what was coming to them if they lost the war, they ran for cover when the war ended. Of those who successfully escaped, many used secret escape routes set up by Odessa, the organization of former members of the SS.

Of approximately 150,000 Nazi war criminals, only about 30,000 have ever been brought to trial. Of the rest, thousands have died off without ever having to answer for their crimes. And between 15,000 and 20,000 went on to live as free individuals. On this wanted list are not just Nazis themselves but European collaborators who helped to point out and round up Jews for the German occupiers. All of these war criminals live hidden behind false names and appearances throughout Europe, South America, the Near East, and the United States.

Nazi War Criminals Are in America Today

Some sources say at least 200 or 300 former Nazis live in the United States. All are illegal residents because United States immigration laws strictly forbid the entry of persons with criminal records. For this reason, Nazi war criminals—if they are discovered—are eligible for deportation to stand trial in Germany or other foreign lands.

What is our government doing about the war criminals living in our country? In 1977 President Jimmy Carter appointed a special law team to investigate and prosecute convicted Nazi war criminals living in the United States. And in March 1979, the United States government took additional steps to intensify the search. More funds, more investigators, and the transfer of the Nazi-criminal search team from the United States Immigration and Naturalization Service (INS) to the Criminal Division of the United States Justice Department promises to push more of the Nazi war criminals into the public eye.

However, there is one loophole through which the war criminals can still escape. No American citizen may have his citizenship stripped away or be deported unless there is "clear, unequivocal, and convincing evidence

that he has committed a crime. That is the problem: The war crimes occurred decades ago. As more and more time passes and witnesses die off, proof against the Nazi war criminals is harder and harder to come by.

Even though considerable evidence does surface, it is not always enough to incriminate those under suspicion of war crimes. For example, one case that received much publicity concerns John Demjanjuk, a retired American autoworker who was accused of being the infamous Nazi concentration camp guard Ivan the Terrible. In response to these charges, U.S. authorities stripped him of his American citizenship in 1981 for allegedly hiding his Nazi past when he emigrated to the United States after the war.

Israeli officials extradited Demjanjuk to Israel to stand trial. The former autoworker's attorneys responded by waging a seven-year battle. The controversy finally ended when the Israeli Supreme Court overturned his conviction on the grounds of reasonable doubt that he was Ivan the Terrible. The Supreme Court also rejected petitions that Demjanjuk be tried for other possible war crimes.

Demjanjuk returned to the United States in 1993, following his release. Since then, he has continued the fight to regain his U.S. citizenship.

The West German Statute of Limitations Is Removed

In 1979 the United States government also moved to encourage the West Germans to keep up their search for Nazi war criminals. The United States took this action because the West German **statute of limitations**, or law that limits the time a criminal can be arrested after his crime has been committed, was due to run out in January 1980. That meant that any Nazi in hiding could then come out in the open without fear of reprisal.

In March 1979, the United States government sent twenty-five representatives to Bonn,

West Germany, to try to influence the German government to extend their statute of limitations indefinitely. Other world powers chimed in with that request, too. In addition, something had occurred in Germany to help swing public opinion in the same direction: In 1978 the TV special *Holocaust* was presented on German television.

All these forces were effective persuaders. On July 3, 1979, the **Bundestag** voted to remove the statute of limitations on Nazi war criminals altogether. The upper House of Representatives also gave their approval on May 9, 1979. Now no living Nazi war criminal can ever be immune from prosecution.

> **Discussion Questions:** Do you believe statute of limitations laws should exist? Why or why not?

Nazi-Hunters Are Searching for War Criminals

Tony DeVito, USA Hunter

If Tony DeVito can help it, no Nazi hiding in the United States will go uncaptured. DeVito began his search for war criminals as an agent working for the United States Immigration and Naturalization Service (INS). His dedication to his job has paid off. Because of him, the first Nazi war criminal ever to be deported from the United States—a New York housewife named Hermine Ryan—stood trial in Germany in 1975 for having shared in the responsibility for the murders of a quarter of a million Jews in the death camp of Maidanek in Poland.

DeVito resigned his job in protest in 1974, however, when his files began to disappear mysteriously, and others in his department refused to cooperate with his efforts. From then on, he has been working on his own to pry as many Nazis out of their hiding places as possible.

But DeVito's protests did not go unheard. Congress reacted by conducting investigative hearings into the INS. And, as mentioned on the previous page, the Nazi search team has been transferred to the Criminal Division of the United States Justice Department.

Why has Tony DeVito dedicated his life to bringing Nazis to justice? He happened to pass through Dachau, a Nazi prison camp in Germany, several hours after it had been liberated by American soldiers. The sight of human suffering caused by the Nazis has never left him.

> **Discussion Question:** Why do you think people were uncooperative with DeVito or were stealing his files?

Simon Wiesenthal, Worldwide Hunter of Nazis

If any name makes the blood of a Nazi war criminal run cold, it is Simon Wiesenthal. This supersleuth, sometimes called the Jewish James Bond, has dedicated his life to searching for Nazi war criminals in all parts of the world and has successfully tracked down at least 1,100 of them.

A Holocaust survivor himself, Wiesenthal has been hunting Nazi desperadoes ever since 1945 when American soldiers liberated him and thirty-four other prisoners from Mauthausen, a Nazi camp in Austria. They were the only survivors of the original 149,000 inmates. To them and to the 11 million other Holocaust victims—both Jews and non-Jews—who did not survive, Wiesenthal feels he owes a debt. That debt is to make sure they are not forgotten. Bringing Nazi criminals to justice is his way of doing that.

Wiesenthal credits much of his success to others who volunteer their help. Donations keep the doors open to his headquarters, the Jewish Documentation Center in Vienna, Austria. Clues to evildoers in hiding come from many people throughout the world: friends, strangers, government officials. Even conscience-stricken former Nazis have provided leads to guilty comrades' hideouts. And Wiesenthal has come up with some prize catches indeed.

Wiesenthal Brings Adolf Eichmann to Trial

Adolf Eichmann, the chief engineer and deportation master of the Holocaust, reportedly once said, "I shall jump into my grave laughing because the fact that I have 5 million Jews on my conscience gives me extraordinary pleasure." Simon Wiesenthal managed to wipe the smile off Eichmann's face and send him to his grave a condemned killer.

Eichmann had tried very hard to elude capture. After the war, he escaped from an American prison camp and made his way to Argentina, where he took on the name Roberto Klements. There he lived a free man until 1959.

In the meantime, he had been joined by his three children and his wife, whom he again "married." Mr. and Mrs. Roberto Klements did not live happily ever after. Eventually Eichmann was spotted by a Holocaust eyewitness. That report and evidence that Mrs. Eichmann had gone to Argentina led Simon Wiesenthal to Eichmann's hideaway.

In 1960, based on Wiesenthal's findings plus the investigations of the Israeli government, Israeli agents were soon dispatched to the scene of Eichmann's new home. They managed to spirit him off past the noses of Argentinian border authorities and right into the hands of the very people he had tried to annihilate—the Jews.

The kidnapping of Eichmannn created a stir in the world. Many nations criticized Israel for it. They said the Israelis should have asked to have Eichmann extradited to Germany or Israel for trial. Argentina felt betrayed. And the controversy went on and on.

Israeli authorities apologized but contended that in the absence of an international court (the Nuremberg courts had been dissolved by now) and in view of the fact that Germany had not since asked for Eichmann to be extradited, it was the duty of all countries of the world to try criminals who had violated international laws. The matter was settled.

When Adolf Eichmann was brought to trial on April 11, 1961, he came face-to-face with some of his victims. As a safety precaution, the court authorities thought it best to place Eichmann in a bullet-proof booth in the crowded courtroom—lest one of his victims lose control at the sight of him.

"We can't get a fair trial here!" Eichmann's lawyers cried. "How can you blame him for **breaking** a law when the deportation of Jews **was** the [Nazi] law? The judges here are all prejudiced against our client."

Eichmann gave the court the same old excuse his cronies had given at the Nuremberg trials, "But, Your Honor, I was only doing my duty and following orders! I am not personally responsible." The judges disagreed. On May 31, 1962, Adolf Eichmann was hanged for his crimes against the Jewish people.

Discussion Question: Assuming you were a Holocaust survivor observing Eichmann's trial, how would you feel?

Wiesenthal Roots Out Other Notorious Criminals

Franz Stangl, SS Commandant of the Sobibor and Treblinka death camps who supervised the murder of over 1.2 million human beings, stood trial in West Germany in 1970. He was brought to justice largely because a former Nazi friend had betrayed his hiding place to Wiesenthal and because Wiesenthal had persisted in a three-year struggle to have Stangl deported from his haven in Brazil, where extradition and statute of limitations laws had protected him.

Also a former supervisor of Hitler's Euthanasia Institute, Stangl testified at his trial that after witnessing so many "mercy killings," he was able to view the execution of 5,000 people a day in the death camps as "all in a day's work."

Stangl served only a few months of his life sentence imprisonment, for he died of a heart attack in 1971.

Worldwide attention also shifted to Wiesenthal's expert undercover work when he rooted out Karl Silberbauer, the Gestapo officer who had arrested Anne Frank, her family, and friends in Amsterdam in 1944.

Another famous Nazi war criminal who eventually did come to trial was Klaus Barbie. Barbie, who was head of the Gestapo in Lyon, was known as the infamous Butcher of Lyon. He was convicted in 1987 of crimes against humanity. He died in 1991.

On Wiesenthal's Most-Wanted List

Wiesenthal knows he can't capture all of the tens of thousands of Nazis on his most-wanted list. However, there are several for whom he has particularly searched:

1. Dr. Josef Mengele, the evil doctor in charge of selections at Auschwitz, who not only sent millions to the gas chambers but also performed hideous medical experiments on thousands of Jewish and Gypsy children, had been living in Paraguay. Though much international pressure was applied on the Paraguayan government to extradite Mengele for trial, it has refused to do so. Maintaining that he has left the country, the government revoked Mengele's citizenship. Wiesenthal insisted, however, that Mengele was still living there in his jungle hideaway. However, in 1985 forensic experts positively identified bones exhumed from a Brazilian grave as being those of Mengele even though no recent dental records existed to make an absolutely certain identification. It is reported that Mengele had drowned in 1979.

2. Walter Rauff, the Nazi supervisor of the gas-van killing operation, lived in Chile, protected by that country's statute of limitations law, which forbids the arrest of any criminal fifteen years after the date of his crime. Rauff died in South America without ever having been brought to trial.

3. Martin Bormann, Hitler's former deputy and the second most powerful man in Germany after 1943, was tried and convicted **in absentia** at Nuremberg and sentenced to hanging. However, he never served his sentence. After the war, he escaped by making his way to Italy. A secret submarine then carried him to South America. To this day, no one knows for sure whether Martin Bormann is alive or dead. At least once a year since the war ended, he has been "spotted" in some part of the world. On the other hand, there are those who insist Bormann is dead. One man swears he shot and killed him. Another has claimed he buried Bormann's body. In any case, there is no proof either way.

Beate Klarsfeld, German Nazi-Hunter

Nazi-hunters come in the German variety, too. Following close behind Wiesenthal in the chase for Nazis is Beate Klarsfeld, a Christian born and bred in Berlin and the daughter of a former Wehrmacht soldier. Beate and her husband Serge, a French Jewish lawyer, devote full time to bringing Nazi war criminals to the fore.

Their immediate targets have been 300 Nazi war criminals once tried and convicted in the French court after the war for having deported 90,000 French Jews to the gas chambers but now living openly as free men in Germany. Old laws on the German books had protected these criminals from being either extradited to serve their sentences in France or retried in the German courts.

Largely because of the Klarsfelds' efforts and public demonstrations, the old Nazis are no longer protected by German laws. As of February 1975, a treaty signed by both the Germans and French now permits the German courts to try the war criminals again. In February 1980, the three top Nazi chiefs involved with the deportation of French Jews were brought to justice, convicted, and sentenced to prison terms. Serge Klarsfeld had prepared airtight cases against them.

The Klarsfelds don't limit their work to pinpointing and gathering evidence against the former Nazis. They have often confronted them face-to-face. Once they tried, unsuccessfully, to kidnap an old Nazi to bring him to trial. And in 1968 Beate slapped the chancellor of Germany, Kurt Kiesinger, right in the face as he walked through a large crowd in Berlin's Congress Hall! Why? To show the world that the Germans could and would not tolerate a German chancellor with a dark Nazi past.

In 1981, undercover work by Nazi-hunters like the Klarsfelds caused the world to focus on another important international leader with a suspected Nazi past: Kurt Waldheim, president of Austria, who had also served as secretary-general of the United Nations. For his former role as a Nazi officer, Waldheim was charged with having direct ties to Nazi atrocities. He was ostracized worldwide, and American authorities barred him from entering the United States.

NEO-NAZIS (NEW NAZIS) ARE MAKING THEIR PRESENCE KNOWN

Introduction

Not only are many Nazi war criminals alive and well, Nazism itself is not dead either. It has reared its ugly head in many countries of Western Europe, and North and South America.

However, it is neither an organized international movement nor an affiliation of old die-hard Nazis determined to carry on Hitler's work. There is no central leader, no national headquarters, no main platform. Rather, the Nazis of today are loosely scattered groups of hatemongers with one thing in common: They thrive on racism and bigotry.

American Neo-Nazis

Dating back to the 1950's, Nazis in the United States are splintered into several groups headed by different individuals. Total membership has never exceeded 2,000.

The largest functioning group is the NSPA, or National Socialist Party of America, headquartered in Chicago, Illinois. Their leader, Frank Collin, reminiscent of Adolf Hitler, sports a toothbrush mustache and slicks his hair straight back. Like his predecessor, Collin is a jobless, homeless racist who lives off party funds. However, the old Fuehrer would turn over in his grave if he knew the real background of this Nazi heir. Collin's Jewish father spent months in the Nazi prison camp of Dachau. Needless to say, he is not on speaking terms with his son.

The American Nazi dream is of a white empire untainted by blacks or Jews. Wearing their Stormtrooper uniforms and swastika armbands, American Nazis have screamed into watching TV cameras, "Six million more! Six million more! Send blacks back to Africa!" Occasionally, they have carried out acts of violence such as making threatening phone calls, vandalizing synagogues and other private property, and beating up Jews and blacks in the streets. A common and favorite Nazi poster shows three rabbis performing ritual murder on a Christian child.

Another Nazi group, the White Power Movement, has been busily distributing the ancient *Protocols of the Elders of Zion* all over the United States to "prove" Jews want to take over the world. They also are printing "evidence" that the Holocaust never happened at all!

American Nazis are no secret organization. The First Amendment to our Constitution, ratified in 1791, guarantees all Americans—including neo-Nazis—the right to free speech. The American Civil Liberties Union stands behind the right of any group in the United States to exist and to demonstrate, even when the ACLU disagrees with that group's views.

Discussion Question: Do you agree that neo-Nazis should have a right to exist and to demonstrate?

Nazism in Germany

The German constitution has strictly outlawed the Nazi party. Despite this and the Allies' attempt to denazify Germany after the war, traces of Hitlerism still linger on in Germany.

Some men who once wore the Nazi swastika on their sleeves and lapels are now members of the government and civil service. Right-wing neo-Nazi political groups such as the so-called German Democratic party have recently sprung up. And according to Chil Rakowski, an official of the Jewish Community Center in Munich, Germany:

Some old Nazi teachers, still in our schools, do little to teach our children tolerance. And little has been done to teach a lesson from the past. A German student does not study Third Reich history until he enters his final year in high school. And then it is only a twenty-hour course.

Who are the new Nazis of Germany? They are mostly young radicals supported by a few from Hitler's old school. They cry that Germany was not entirely to blame for World War II, that Nazi war criminals should be pardoned, and that the Holocaust is a big hoax cooked up by the Jews. What about the tons of Nazi records, films, and tapes that document the Holocaust? "All fake!" they cry.

Are the new Nazis all just talk? Not really. German police have uncovered secret caches of Nazi weapons. West German authorities suspect that the neo-Nazis have connections with the Arab terrorists who continually threaten the peace of Israel. And the Nazis' bombing near Munich at the Oktoberfest celebration in the fall of 1980 proves their capacity for hatred and violence. In the 1990's the neo-Nazis have continued to make their presence felt with various violent activities.

How much of a threat are the German neo-Nazis? Like their American counterparts, they represent an extremely small percentage of their nation's citizenry. For example, during a 1978 poll in which Germans were asked whether they would ever support another Adolf Hitler, 90 percent voted a definite "NO."

Yet, as a spokesman for the 30,000-member Jewish community in West Germany said when asked his opinion about the neo-Nazis, "Small snakes are poisonous, too!"

Discussion Question: Do you agree with the Jewish spokesman?

Chapter Twelve Review

REVIEWING KEY POINTS

Exercise 1

1. If the Jewish state of Israel had existed during the war, why might the Holocaust never have occurred?

2. When the British issued the White Paper of 1939, how did they go back on their promise to allow Jews a home in Israel?

3. How did Germans view paying reparations to Israel as an atonement for all the Jewish property "Aryanized" by the Nazis? How did they react to the televised drama of the Holocaust?

4. At the Nuremberg trials, why was there no doubt as to the guilt of the Nazi war criminals?

5. Were these Nazi criminals correct in testifying that they had followed the laws of their land and the orders of high government officials in persecuting Jews?

6. What is the loophole through which Nazi war criminals living in the United States can still escape?

7. When was the first Nazi war criminal deported from the United States to stand trial for war crimes?

8. What did President Carter do in 1979 to widen and intensify the search for old Nazis living in America?

9. Who was Simon Wiesenthal's "biggest catch"? What circumstances made his trial so dramatic?

10. In view of Hitler's New Order, why is it hard to accept that some people are actually promoting Nazism again?

CHECKING YOURSELF

Exercise 2
Matching People and Their Behavior

Directions: Number your paper from 1–10. Match the people in Column 1 to their responses in Column 2. Each response is used only once. Your answers will be letters.

COLUMN 1—People

1. Hitler, Goebbels, and Himmler
2. The Germans
3. The neo-Nazis
4. The United Nations
5. The Allies
6. Nazi war criminals
7. The Roman Catholic Church
8. Tony DeVito
9. Beate Klarsfeld
10. Simon Wiesenthal

COLUMN 2—How They Responded to the Holocaust After the War

A.   hunts old Nazis living in Germany.

B.   tracks down Nazi war criminals hiding throughout the world.

C.   searches for Nazi war criminals living in America.

D.   brought Nazi war criminals to justice in Nuremberg after the war.

E.   call the Holocaust a hoax and promote hatred toward Jews, blacks, and other minorities.

F.   evaded capture and went into hiding in many cases.

G.   paid Israel and Jewish survivors reparations for lost property.

H.   made genocide a crime under international law and approved the formation of the Jewish state of Israel.

I.   rejected the teaching that Jews were responsible or cursed for the crucifixion of Christ and declared hatred and persecution of Jews sinful.

J.   committed suicide.

GIVING REPORTS

Topics to Research

1. European Jewry before and after the Nazis. Good source: *American Jewish Yearbook*, Volume 63.

2. More about Zionism. Good source: *Next Year in Jerusalem*, by Robert Goldston.

3. The Genocide Convention of December 1948. Include the convention's definition of genocide. Give the position of the United States on the genocide question. What is our country's position on the issue today?

4. A synopsis of the movie *The Odessa File*.

5. Arthur R. Butz, a professor at Northwestern University who wrote *Fabrication of the Hoax*, a book based on the idea that the Holocaust never happened at all.

6. The attitude of German youth today regarding the Holocaust and Adolf Hitler.

7. The 1978 attempt by American Nazis to parade and demonstrate in Skokie, Illinois, a neighborhood including several hundred Holocaust survivors. Tell how Skokie Jews reacted.

8. The position of the Ku Klux Klan toward Jews. Include specifics of their anti-Jewish activities in America.

9. The neo-Nazi bombings and terrorist activities toward Jews of France during the fall of 1980.

10. The scope and influence of the neo-Nazis in England.

11. Frank Walus, Nazi war criminal rooted out of hiding in 1975 in Chicago, Illinois: the first United States citizen to lose citizenship for his role in Nazi war crimes.

12. Spandau Prison, the jail in Berlin reserved for Nazi war criminals.

13. Erich Erdstein, a Nazi-hunter in South America.

14. The BUND, a secret organization of Nazis in America during the World War II years.

15. The American Civil Liberties Union, its role and function in the United States and its position on the neo-Nazis.

16. The charges brought against Kurt Waldheim, former secretary-general of the United Nations and former president of Austria.

Topics to Research (continued)

17. The case of John Demjanjuk: his trial for alleged Nazi activities and his fight for U.S. citizenship.

18. Recent neo-Nazi activity in Germany and in the United States.

19. Holocaust denial, especially by Germans and by Americans.

20. Reactions and attitudes of children of Holocaust survivors and of children of Nazis.

21. The Holocaust Memorial Museum in Washington, DC: architecture and meaning.

22. Other Nazi war criminals who have been found.

Books to Review

1. *Nazi Hunter: Simon Wiesenthal*, by Iris Noble, is Wiesenthal's biography.

2. *Wherever They May Be*, by Beate Klarsfeld, the German Nazi-hunter, concerns Nazis in hiding.

3. *Justice in Jerusalem*, by Gideon Hausner, concerns the trial of Adolf Eichmann.

4. *House on Garibaldi Street*, by Harel Isser, portrays Eichmann's capture and arrest.

5. *The Bormann Brotherhood*, by William Stevenson, deals with escape and survival of Nazi war criminals.

6. *My Enemy, My Brother*, by James Forman, a novel of how a teenage survivor of a Nazi prison decides to find new life in Israel.

7. *Ben-Gurion: A Biography*, by Robert St. John, the life of Israel's first prime minister.

8. *Exodus*, by Leon Uris, a novel concerning the smuggling of Holocaust survivors into Palestine before the state of Israel was declared.

9. *Forged in Fury*, by Michael Elkins, retells how a group of Jewish resistance fighters continued their hunt for Nazis after the war ended.

10. *The Sunflower*, by Simon Wiesenthal, a tale of how a dying Nazi asks a Jew for forgiveness for his role in the Holocaust.

Books to Review (continued)

11. *Children of the Holocaust*, by Helen Epstein, based on interviews with children of Holocaust survivors in the United States, reveals how they responded to the Holocaust.

12. *The Holocaust: The Neo-Nazi Mythomania*, by Serge Klarsfeld (Beate's husband).

13. *New Lives: Survivors of the Holocaust Living in America*, by Dorothy Rabinowitz.

14. *The New Nazis of Germany*, by Wellington Long.

15. *The Avengers*, by Michael Bar-Zohar, concerns the **Israeli Brigade**, a group of Holocaust survivors also known as "The Avengers" who set out after World War II to capture or kill Nazis.

16. *The Hunt for Martin Bormann*, by Charles Whiting.

17. *Chaim Weizmann: Builder of a Nation*, by R. Baker, the biography of Weizmann, the first president of the new state of Israel, is an excellent source for the development of Zionism.

18. *Wanted! The Search for Nazis in America*, by Howard Blum.

19. *The Murderers Among Us*, by Simon Wiesenthal, concerns Nazi war criminals in hiding.

20. *Denying the Holocaust: The Growing Assault on Truth and Memory*, by Deborah E. Lipstadt, an account of an international movement of Holocaust denial, its growth, and its attempt to change truth.

21. *The Drowned and the Saved*, by Primo Levi, the author's thoughts on the meaning of the Nazi exterminations, forty years later.

22. *In Hitler's Shadow: West German Historians and the Attempt to Escape from the Nazi Past*, by Richard Evans, concerning attempts to lessen Germany's responsibility for the Holocaust.

23. *Hitler's Children: Sons and Daughters of Leaders of the Third Reich Talk About Their Fathers and Themselves*, by Gerald Posner.

Making Projects

Poster Ideas

1. List the main provisions of the Genocide Convention of 1948.

2. Make a map of the new nation of Israel.

3. Picture Adolf Eichmann in a bulletproof booth at his trial in Israel.

4. List the twenty-two Nazi war criminals tried at Nuremberg and their sentences.

Conducting Personal Interviews

To find out how Holocaust survivors feel today about their experiences with the Nazis, conduct a series of personal interviews. Are the survivors bitter, willing to forget or to forgive? Report your findings.

A Classroom Experiment

Role-play the Nuremberg trials. Choose students to portray the roles of judges, jury, prosecution and defense attorneys, and defendants. Defendants should range from highest Nazi officers to lowest-ranking camp guards.

Putting On a Play

Present one or several scenes from one of the following:

1. *The Investigation*, by Peter Weiss, a play based on Nazi war criminal trials held in Frankfurt, Germany. Much of the play dialogue is actual court testimony.

2. *The Man in the Glass Booth*, by Robert Shaw, a play centering on the theme of the postwar response of the Holocaust survivor.

AUDIOVISUAL AID SUGGESTIONS FOR CHAPTER TWELVE

1. For the issue of **personal moral choice versus obedience to authority:**

   a. Two filmstrips and a cassette, *I Had No Choice But to Obey: The Question of Personal Responsibility*, by Denoyer and Geppart. **SSSS**

   b. Rent *Joseph Schultz*, a 14-minute color film pertaining to an actual World War II incident in which a German soldier chooses to be shot rather than to do the shooting.

   c. Rent *Obedience: The Milgrim Experiment*, a 45-minute black-and-white film of a psychological experiment conducted at Yale University. **ADL**

2. Rent *Judgment at Mineola*, a 14-minute color film concerning the possible deportation of Boleslav Maikovskis, a Nazi war criminal discovered in hiding in Long Island, and his neighbors' reaction to his former Nazi record. **ADL**

3. Rent *California Reich*, a 60-minute color film depicting the Nazis in America, the members, their views, and their activities. **RBC**

4. Rent *Verdict for Tomorrow*, a 28-minute black-and-white film of the Eichmann trial. **ADL**

5. View *Skokie*, a 121-minute color video dramatizing the events of 1978 in Skokie, Illinois, when neo-Nazis wanted to march in an area where there are many Holocaust survivors. **AE**

6. View *Dark Lullabies*, an 82-minute color video made by a child of survivors about the effect of the Holocaust on postwar generations of Jews and Germans. **EM**

7. View CBS's *60 Minutes* segment "Sins of the Fathers" (April 14, 1991), showing a meeting between children of survivors and children of Nazis (available through the CBS network).

✡ CHAPTER THIRTEEN

Jews in Today's World

IS ANTI-SEMITISM STILL AROUND?

Between 1945 and the mid-1960's, anti-Semitism had nearly been swept under the carpet. The sad memory of the Holocaust had done that. People everywhere felt uncomfortable with anti-Jewish feelings.

But this is not true today. In varying degrees and for many reasons, anti-Jewish feelings exist in nearly every country where Jews live.

For one thing, the current generation—those born after World War II—feels little guilt about the Holocaust, mostly because they know very little about it. Moreover, because unscrupulous, power-hungry people are aware that the old stereotyped attitudes still linger on in narrow minds everywhere, they know that anti-Semitism is still an effective political weapon. And they are using it. Extremist right-wing (neo-Nazi) and left-wing (communist) political groups have been keeping it alive in the countries of the free world. In other lands, dictators are promoting it as government policy.

In 1994, for the first time, the United Nations Human Rights Commission went on record to condemn "anti-Semitism and related intolerance." While this resolution may make a difference in the lives of many people, those with extreme prejudices will not change their thinking overnight.

Where are anti-Jewish feelings and actions the strongest and most dangerous? They threaten in countries where economic and political upheaval exists. This is the traditional environment where anti-Semitism grows best.

Discussion Question: Are you aware that anti-Jewish feelings exist?

JEWS IN THE MIDEAST

Arabs Refuse to Recognize Israel As a Jewish State

Barely five minutes after the new nation of Israel came into being on May 14, 1948, it came under the siege of five surrounding Arab nations. Hundreds of thousands of Arabs living in the Jewish state of Israel abandoned their homes in the midst of the warfare and took refuge in neighboring Arab states. They were fully confident they would be able to return to their homes under new Arab rulers when the fighting was over. Those fleeing Palestinian Arabs were mistaken. By fall the little but mighty Israeli army had not only brought the armies of Lebanon, Iraq, Egypt, Syria, and Trans-Jordan (now Jordan) to defeat but also had seized much new Arab territory.

Israel had indeed won this War of Independence. But the Arabs would neither sign a peace treaty nor recognize the new Jewish state. They maintained that Palestine (now Israel) was theirs and vowed to drive the Israelis into the sea.

For the next thirty years, they tried to carry

out their threat. Arab-Israeli history became stained with bloodshed spilled in three more wars: the Sinai War of 1956, the Six-Day War of 1967, and the Yom Kippur War of 1973. In between these major conflicts, Arab terrorist attacks on Jewish communities and Israeli retaliatory actions occurred continuously.

Finally, in 1975, one Arab nation made a peace gesture. Egyptian President Anwar Sadat approached United States Secretary of State Henry Kissinger to be a mediator for peace talks between Egypt and Israel. After much bickering over peace terms, Sadat and Israeli Prime Minister Menachem Begin accepted United States President Jimmy Carter's invitation in 1977 to hold their conferences in the United States. In March of 1979, the Egyptians and Israelis finally signed a peace treaty.

At last, after three decades, one Arab nation recognized Israel as the Jewish state.

Israeli Jews Face Many Unsolved Problems

However, the problems of the Jewish nation are by no means over. The peace between Egypt and Israel rests on very shaky ground for several reasons:

1. Only Egypt has signed a peace treaty with Israel. The other Arab states are so opposed to it they have broken off diplomatic relations with their brother state of Egypt. However, the positions of the Arab states seem to be in flux, so it is difficult to predict what will ultimately happen.

2. The PLO, or Palestinian Liberation Organization, under the leadership of Yasir Arafat, threatened to war on Israel until it was given a part of Israel as its own independent state. The PLO is the most militant group of Palestinian Arabs (now referred to simply as **Palestinians**) who abandoned their homes in Israel during the War of Independence in 1948. (Many Arab residents of

Israel did not leave, however, and today there are more than a million Arab citizens of Israel).

Since that time, the Israelis have refused to allow the Palestinians back into Israel, and the surrounding Arab states have not welcomed them as citizens either. Consequently, the Palestinians have become the Israelis' bitterest enemies. Now numbering 4 million, they live scattered everywhere. At least 1 million, homeless and jobless, have been living in refugee camps set up and supported by the United Nations since 1948. The rest have dispersed to many parts of the world including the United States.

To call attention to their cause, the PLO, claiming to represent the majority of their people, carried out terrorist activities in Israel and in other countries. It hijacked planes, kidnapped hostages, planted bombs in public places, and shot up airports. During the 1972 Olympics, in Munich, Germany, a group of Palestinian terrorists murdered eleven Israeli athletes.

Some negotiations between Israel and the PLO have taken place. In 1993, the two groups signed a peace accord. However, this peace gesture has not stopped the fighting between the two groups, and the prospect of a lasting peace is still in question.

3. These Middle East problems have spilled over into world politics, threatening the peace and security of the world. The two biggest rivals and world powers, the United States and the former Soviet Union, have become involved. Russians have been supplying Arabs with arms and military advisers. Americans, alarmed by the possible spread of communism, have tried to soothe tempers on both sides but have come to the rescue of Israelis by supplying them with war planes. People everywhere have begun to worry that the conflicts in the Middle East might explode into another world war.

4. Arab oil has become a powerful weapon against Israel and her friends. For several months, during the 1970's, the Arabs refused to sell oil to Israel's supporters. Then they quadrupled the price. They also boycotted trade with any nations that dealt with Israel. The result in the United States, England, and other countries was a severe energy crisis, skyrocketing prices of oil and oil products, and weakening economies.

5. Outward support of Israel has begun to weaken under Arab-Soviet pressure. In November of 1975, eighty-nine governments represented in the United Nations (many of whom had voted the new Jewish nation into existence in May of 1948) took sides with the Arabs and the Russians in calling Zionism racism. The United Nations ultimately rescinded its position of calling Zionism racism in 1991.

6. The Arabs are using anti-Jewish prejudice as part of their war against Israel and the countries of the West who support Israel. During the 1960's and 1970's, the Arabs widely circulated that old forgery, the *Protocols of the Elders of Zion*, to "prove" that world Zionists are trying to take over all the governments on earth. Added to that old charge is propaganda borrowed by the Arabs from the Russians: Zionists are an international ring of conspirators in cahoots with United States Central Intelligence Agency agents and spies from Western Europe; Western democracies are an instrument of Jews who control the banks, the press, and everything else of any importance.

As a result of all these problems, the Jews of Israel once again find themselves enmeshed in twentieth-century international struggle. How international attitudes will affect Israel's future and the future of all the world's democracies remains to be seen.

Discussion Question: What does America have to do to avoid dependency on Arab oil and resulting high energy costs?

JEWS IN THE FORMER SOVIET UNION

Jews Still Used As Scapegoats

The most dangerous breeding ground of anti-Semitism is in the former Soviet Union. The anti-Jewish policies of the communist government that began soon after the Bolshevik Revolution in 1917 continue to this day.

Following in the footsteps of the old Russian czars, communist leaders used Jews as scapegoats for Russian problems in order to cover up for poor leadership and deficiencies in the Soviet system. Public trials were staged where Jews were tried and condemned for "crimes against the state." Many leading Jewish writers and intellectuals were executed. Russian propaganda then used the condemned Jews as an example of all that is evil in Soviet society.

Much Discrimination Against Jews

There are no anti-Jewish laws in Russia. However, Jews have faced much pointed discrimination. Like all citizens, they must carry a passport identifying their nationality. Theirs must be labeled "Jewish," not "Russian." Jews alone have been denied the cultural privileges which one hundred other ethnic groups living in Russia enjoy. While all the rest have had the right to use their own languages, to practice their own customs, and to maintain their own cultural institutions and schools, Jews have been discouraged from being Jewish in any way.

Through "forced assimilation," the authorities have tried to make "Jewishness" disappear. They have all but destroyed Jewish culture. All

Yiddish books, schools, and other institutions have vanished from the Russian scene. Today barely fifty synagogues are in operation throughout the former Soviet Union's vast territories. Only a dozen or so rabbis live in Russia, for Jewish seminaries were banned long ago. And the restriction on the manufacture of Jewish religious articles has eliminated all but the oldest and most tattered prayer shawls and prayer books.

As added incentive to drive young Jews away from their traditional beliefs, the atheist communist rulers reserved all important jobs and government positions for nonbelievers only. However, even nonreligious Jews suffer job discrimination. While some do hold responsible positions in science, technology, the professions, and the arts, there are fields denied to them altogether. These include top government and diplomatic posts, commanding positions in the armed forces, and teaching jobs in universities.

Arab-Israeli Wars Intensify Anti-Jewish Feelings

The Arab-Israeli wars have also triggered more intense and even violent anti-Semitism in Russia. In spite of expert Soviet military advice and modern weapons provided to the Arabs, the tiny Israeli nation somehow always managed to win the wars. So the Soviets took it out on their Russian-Jewish citizens.

To eventually eliminate Jews from professional positions, authorities sharply cut the number of Jewish students permitted to enter universities. Other Russian Jews were dismissed from their jobs. Here and there Jewish homes were turned upside down by nasty raiders, angry over Arab losses in the wars.

The old anti-Semitic propaganda standby also hit the Russian presses: the *Protocols of the Elders of Zion*. That and other anti-Jewish pamphlets and books were circulated in an effort to turn the public against their Jewish neighbors.

How did the Russians explain the Arab losses in the war? They said the three-headed bogeyman was the international Zionists, American secret agents, and spies from other democracies of the West who were out to subvert not only Russia but also the world.

Discussion Question: How was government mistreatment of Jews in the 1980's nearly the same as it was a century ago in Russia?

This intensified anti-Jewish campaign backfired against the communist policy of "Russianizing" Jews. Instead of taking pride in themselves as Russians, some angry young Jews began to take pride in their Jewishness for the first time. Spurred on by Russian antagonism, they bravely stood up to their government and asked why they were not allowed to leave Russia. World opinion chimed in with that question, too. Consequently, the former Soviet Union came under widespread criticism for its ill-treatment of Soviet Jewry.

In 1970 Russian authorities gave in to world pressures. They swung back the Iron Curtain to allow Jews and others out. During the decade after 1971, 170,000 Russian Jews received visas to freedom.

In the 1980's, more and more Jewish families left their Russian homeland to resettle elsewhere. However, for a short time in the very early 1990's, the plight of Jews in Russia seemed to improve. The former Soviet system appeared to disintegrate with the fall of communism. Perestroika motivated many Russian Jews to stay close to home in the hope they finally would have the freedom of enjoying Jewish cultural traditions openly.

However, a harsh and worsening economic situation in the early 1990's gave rise to extreme nationalism in Russia, placing hope for the freedom of living a Jewish life on shaky ground. Anti-Semitism has been on the increase ever since. And in 1993, the exodus of Russian Jews continued: Approximately 120,000 departed

Russian soil for new homes in many other parts of the world.

Pitfalls remain on the emigration path. A Soviet Jew applying for a visa may experience problems at work or be ostracized by neighbors. And once the visa is applied for, there is no guarantee that emigration will be allowed. Authorities have locked in thousands of Jews and other would-be émigrés because their jobs or other circumstances make them "too knowledgeable" about Russian affairs.

Of the 1 to 1.5 million Jews who still live in the former Soviet Union, many probably will decide to remain at home among family and friends, even in the face of so much discrimination. In Russia, it is never easy to pick up roots.

JEWS IN ARGENTINA

Anti-Semitism has also been running rampant in Argentina, whose Jewish community of 1.5 million is the largest in South America. Neo-Nazis, old Nazis living here incognito, radical fascists, and a large Arab community have all made their hatred known to the Jews around them. Firebombings of Jewish property, vandalizing of synagogues, and even murders have occurred in many recent waves of violence. While the military government of Argentina has taken steps to protect the Jewish community, it too has been under attack by extremist groups.

JEWS IN GERMANY

To learn firsthand about Jews who live in Germany today, the author of this book conducted interviews in West Germany in August 1980 with two important figures of the Jewish community there: Dr. Hanns Lamm, leader and spokesman for the entire West German community and president of the Jewish Community

Center in Munich; and his assistant, Mr. Chil Rakowski.

Question: Describe the attitudes of Jews in Germany today.

Mr. Rakowski: Jews had a past in Germany, but we have no future. Before the war, Jews played an important role in German affairs, but no more. We are not involved in politics at all. And though the majority of the 30,000 Jews in West Germany are stable economically, many have invested in foreign interests as a safety precaution. At the slightest hint of trouble, we are prepared to leave the country. We are currently experiencing an economic boom in West Germany today; however, we believe the future of our democracy rests on that. The problem here is that there are no deep ties or traditions to democracy. In the event of an economic crisis or collapse, we fear that fascism could take root again. The Jewish community will not wait around to see that happen.

Question: Are most of the Jews in Germany today descendants of the original prewar German Jewish community?

Dr. Lamm: No, the vast majority are Jews from Eastern Europe. For example, of the 5,000 Jews who live in Munich today, only about a hundred are a part of the original German-Jewish community.

Question: Why did Eastern European Jews come here?

Mr. Rakowski: Most came here to camps for displaced, homeless persons set up by the Allies after the war. Then they didn't leave for a variety of reasons. Most could not get visas. Many were too ill. When life was begun anew in the atmosphere of democracy and economic progress after the war, it was also easier to stay.

Question: Describe the Jewish community of West Germany.

Mr. Rakowski: We are mostly urban dwellers, not concentrated but interspersed among the Christian community. West Berlin, with 8,000 Jews and three synagogues, holds the largest Jewish population in West Germany. However, we are an extremely small minority group. Of the 400,000 "foreigners" who reside here, Jews, at 30,000, barely make up a half percent of the total German population.

Most Jews are shopkeepers, merchants involved in clothing, furs, jewelry, textiles. Some are involved with building. Many of those born here after the war have strong academic backgrounds and are professional people.

Question: What is the attitude of this generation of Germans about the Holocaust?

Mr. Rakowski: The majority refuse to talk about it. They say they had nothing to do with it; therefore they have no guilt. They always point out that Germany paid restitutions to Israel. And when questioned by Americans about the Holocaust, they say "Wasn't United States behavior in Vietnam just as bad?"

Question: What about anti-Semitism in Germany?

Dr. Lamm: Aside from neo-Nazi activity, it is not a burning issue here. In my eleven years as president of this community, never once has an anxious mother reported to me that a student or teacher chided her child with an anti-Semitic remark.

Mr. Rakowski: Anti-Semitism plays a very limited role. Throughout my entire education in West Germany, from the lower grades to college, never once was I taunted by an anti-Semitic remark or mistreated because I am Jewish.

Any anti-Semitism that exists is kept under the surface. It is obvious only in southern Germany and more in small towns and in the countryside among very conservative farmers.

Strong prejudice is currently being directed toward Germany's "guest workers," the Turkish, Greek, and Italian manual laborers who live and work in the factories of West Germany. In fact, government officials are very friendly to the Jewish community. They often go out of their way to be cooperative. You might say that **philo-Semitism** (much "love" or "fondness" toward Jews) exists here. And that makes us uncomfortable, too, because it proves that German-Jewish relationships are not normal.

Discussion Question: Do you agree that "being too nice" to a minority group may make them uncomfortable?

JEWS IN THE USA

<u>Jews Have Fared Best in America</u>

Outside Israel, nowhere in the world do Jews enjoy more freedom than in the United States of America. But this does not mean all Americans are free of negative feelings toward Jews.

Anti-Jewish prejudices arrived on American shores right along with our forefathers. Future generations learned their attitudes from the old. And the cycle of anti-Semitism has continued ever since.

Never, however, has American anti-Semitism taken the monstrous shape it took in Europe. Only on occasion has it exploded into violence. More often than not, non-Jewish Americans have vented their prejudices in economic and social spheres. They have excluded Jews from certain neighborhoods, private clubs, private schools and universities, and jobs. Jewish emigration to America during the Nazi stampede was also severely limited because many Americans held prejudices.

Even in these areas, though, anti-Semitism has continued to dwindle among Americans. The civil rights laws of the 1950's not only made discrimination unlawful but also convinced many people it was wrong. Consequently, more and more Jews are moving into once "exclusive" neighborhoods. Private country clubs and prep schools have more Jews on their rosters than ever before. And American Jews shine in every field of achievement.

Why have Jews fared better in America than in any other country? One big reason stems from President Franklin Delano Roosevelt's quotation, "All Americans are immigrants."

In America's multinational melting pot, where nationalism did not favor one particular ethnic group, Jewish differences did not single them out for suspicion or contempt. Nor has the Jewish inclination to cling to old customs and practices annoyed too many of their American neighbors, for often these neighbors have been

doing the same thing. Italians, Poles, Greeks, Japanese, Irish, and many others have continued to preserve their cultural heritages. And who can deny the popularity of international festivals on the American entertainment scene?

American Jews Have Concerns

Still, American Jews of today are worried. The Mideast crisis has heightened their awareness of growing anti-Semitism in the world. While the United States government and the majority of Americans have stood solidly behind Israel's fight to survive, the shortage and high cost of gasoline created by the Arab embargo have been real hardships.

American Jews question how the American economy and public opinion will fare in the event of another Arab freeze or price hike on oil. They wonder what might happen to the American economy if the Arabs withdraw their huge reserves of oil money from the banks of the West where it is now held.

They are concerned, too, about their friends and relatives in Israel, and they continue to pour in dollars of support for the small Jewish nation.

The anti-Semitic remarks by the neo-Nazis and members of the Communist Party USA also make them shudder.

Behind their fears is the troubling fact Jewish history has long taught them: In the event of severe economic or political upheaval, people need a scapegoat. The traditional and favorite scapegoat for such ills has been the Jews.

Chapter Thirteen Review

REVIEWING KEY POINTS

Exercise 1

1. Discuss why unscrupulous politicians have blamed Jews for economic and political problems for hundreds of years.

2. Who are the Palestinians, and what is their argument with the Israelis?

3. Discuss the many problems the Jews of Israel face today.

4. How do Soviet authorities use Jews as scapegoats for problems in Russian society?

5. Discuss the Soviet discriminatory practices toward Jewish citizens.

6. Why have Arab-Israeli wars affected Jews living in Russia?

7. What do German Jews see as the biggest threat to their security? What are they prepared to do just in case?

8. Go back to Chapter Seven and reread the section entitled "Jews in Modern Germany." Using the information about Jews in Germany from this chapter, compare their situations.

9. Although anti-Jewish feelings have persisted in America since Colonial times, American Jews have suffered less from persecution than Jews of Europe. Why?

10. What are the concerns of American Jews today?

11. Why is Argentina a hot spot of anti-Semitism today?

CHECKING YOURSELF

Exercise 2
Recognizing True and False Statements

Directions: Number your paper from 1–20. Some of the statements below are true and some are false. For a true statement, write +; for a false statement, write 0.

1. Most Russian Jews want to leave the Soviet Union to make new homes elsewhere.

2. There is less anti-Semitism in the United States now than ever before.

3. The Arab nations have violated their peace agreement with Israel.

4. The United States has supported Israel's right to exist.

5. Israel has the backing of all the countries of the United Nations that voted it into existence in 1948.

6. The Arab-Israeli struggle has turned into a contest between democracy and communism.

7. Argentina has the largest Jewish community in South America.

8. The government of Argentina, which has tried to protect Jewish citizens, is stable.

9. A large percentage of the Israeli population are Holocaust survivors or descendants of survivors.

10. There are many anti-Jewish laws in Russia.

11. In Russia, Jews have to call themselves Jewish but are not allowed to be "Jewish" in any way.

12. The Soviet Union is the most dangerous breeding ground of anti-Semitism.

13. Most Jews in Germany today came there from Eastern Europe after the war and never left.

14. Fascism, which includes both communism and Nazism, is hard on Jews.

15. American anti-Semitism has been expressed in social and economic areas more than in political matters.

16. German Jews today suffer from open German hostility.

Exercise 2 (continued)

17. Although anti-Semites have used Jews throughout history as the scapegoats for economic and political problems in their countries, that couldn't happen in this day and age.

18. American civil rights laws have made people obey but really haven't changed their thinking toward giving minorities equal rights.

19. In order to erase anti-Semitism and other prejudices toward minorities, we have to learn to respect and tolerate others' differences.

20. The Holocaust provides a lesson not only about the period from 1933–1945 but also about human behavior in the past, present, and future.

GIVING REPORTS

Topics to Research

1. The Communist Party USA and its anti-Jewish program.

2. Any one of the Arab-Israeli wars mentioned in this chapter.

3. The circumstances surrounding the PLO massacre of eleven Israeli athletes during the 1972 Olympics.

4. The case of Leo Frank, an innocent American Jew who was lynched for the murder of a girl in Atlanta, Georgia, in 1915. Good source: *America Is Also Jewish*, by Richard Goldhurst.

5. The contributions of American Jews. Good source: *Americans All*, by Oscar Leonard.

6. The role of American Jews in banking, the steel industry, insurance firms, the press. Good source: *New Republic*, December 1974. (Get this magazine in your local library.)

7. The current situation on the Palestinian issue in the Mideast.

8. How do Americans feel about the Ku Klux Klan? about the neo-Nazis? about the Communist Party USA?

9. Compare the Jewish population figures of Europe country by country before World War II and now. Good source for today's figures: *The World Almanac*.

10. Israel today. Include immigration, political parties, the people, the government, the culture, the lifestyle.

11. The Falashas of Ethiopia, a 30,000-member black Jewish community.

12. Emigration of Jews from Russia and other republics of the former Soviet Union.

13. The increased activity of neo-Nazis in the early 1990's.

14. The impact of the fall of communist governments in Eastern Europe and the former Soviet Union on Jews in those countries.

15. Anti-Semitism in the world today.

16. Current education of the Holocaust for the youth of Germany and of the United States.

17. The current status of Arab-Israeli relations.

Books to Review

1. *Here I Am a Jew in Today's Germany*, by Irving Halperin.

2. *Taking Root: Jewish Immigrants in America*, by Milton Meltzer.

3. *Gentleman's Agreement*, by Laura Hobson, a novel of how a Christian pretends to be a Jew so that he can experience anti-Semitism in America.

4. *Jews in Soviet Russia Since 1917*, by Lionel Kochan, a collection of articles on this subject.

5. *Israel, the Arabs, and the Middle East*, by Irving Howe and Carl Gershman.

6. *America Is Also Jewish*, by Richard Goldhurst, tells of Jewish immigrants and their contributions to American culture.

7. *Soviet Policy Toward Jews and Israel, 1917–1974*, by Lester Eckman.

8. *The Survivors: A Report on the Jews in Germany Today*, by Norbert Muhlen.

9. *Jews of Arab Lands in Modern Times*, by Norman A. Stillman.

10. *From Time Immemorial: The Origins of the Arab-Jewish Conflict Over Palestine*, by Joan Peters.

11. *Argentina and the Jews: A History of Jewish Immigration*, by Haim Avni.

12. *Against All Odds: How Survivors of the Holocaust Succeeded in America*, by William B. Helmreich.

KEEPING A SCRAPBOOK

Keep a current-events scrapbook on:

1. Developments in the Mideast that affect the nation of Israel. (Include newspaper cartoons.)

2. References made to the Holocaust.

3. The activities of neo-Nazis around the world.

4. Activities of the Ku Klux Klan in America.

AUDIOVISUAL AID SUGGESTIONS FOR CHAPTER THIRTEEN

1. Rent the 28-minute film *The Price of Silence*, which portrays anti-Semitism in Russia today. **JCS**

2. Rent *Let My People Go!*, a 54-minute black-and-white film, a historical survey of Jews from their beginnings in Palestine to the establishment of Israel in 1948, which emphasizes the Holocaust and the rise of modern Zionism. **FI**

APPENDIX

A BACKWARD LOOK AND A FORWARD LOOK

The study of the Holocaust and Jewish history has provided some important lessons that are well worth remembering:

1. Be aware that anti-Semitism and other deadly prejudices are just under the surface waiting to be fanned alive.

2. Know that politicians use scapegoats during times of trouble.

3. Be wary of demagogues, power-hungry leaders who stir up people by appealing to their prejudices.

4. Realize that uncontrolled power in the hands of a few can wipe out human rights.

5. Face up to the reality that prejudice can and has moved modern, civilized, highly educated people to extremes such as murdering innocent men, women, and children.

6. Realize how and why the Holocaust occurred and know that similar tragedies can happen again at any time, at any place, and to any minority group because they are basically small and defenseless.

7. Understand that morally we all should be our "brothers' keepers," and that to remain indifferent to others' suffering and mistreatment is wrong—just as wrong as committing the act of evil ourselves.

EXTENDED ACTIVITIES

1. Through research, reporting, and discussion compare the persecution of Jews in the Nazi Holocaust to

    a. The persecution of minority groups in America such as blacks, women, Asians, American Indians, and others.

    b. Genocides that have occurred in other parts of the world such as the slaughter of the Armenians by the Turks, the massacre at My Lai, Idi Amin's atrocities in Uganda, and others.

2. Write an editorial on

    a. Why the study of the Holocaust should be a part of everyone's education.

    b. Whether the Holocaust could happen again.

3. Make a set of murals or models depicting a theme from each chapter in this book.

4. Write a short story describing an episode during the Holocaust.

5. Write an essay on anti-Semitism.

6. Write a dramatization of one event of the Holocaust that sticks in your mind.

7. Make a list of words you have added to your vocabulary from studying this unit on the Holocaust.

8. Prepare a bulletin board depicting the Holocaust.

9. Make an illustrated time line showing the development of the Holocaust from the rise of Hitler to the establishment of Israel.

10. Write a poem about the Holocaust. Use words that appeal to the five senses of smell, taste, touch, hearing, and sight in order to give the reader a clear impression of what the Holocaust must have been like.

Audiovisual Aid Distributors

Symbol	Distributor's Name and Address	Symbol	Distributor's Name and Address
ADL	Anti-Defamation League 315 Lexington Avenue New York, NY 10016	EM	Ergo Media, Incorporated P.O. Box 2037 Teaneck, NJ 07666
AE	Academy Entertainment New York, NY 10003	FI	Films Incorporated 1144 Wilmette Avenue Wilmette, IL 60091
AVNA	Audiovisual Narrative Arts, Incorporated Box 9 Pleasantville, NY 10570	FVF	Film and Video Foundation 1800 K Street, N.W., Suite 1120 Washington, DC 20006
AVP	Ambrose Video Publishing 381 Park Avenue South New York, NY 10016	JCS	Jewish Chautauqua Society 838 Fifth Avenue New York, NY 10021
BJE	Bureau of Jewish Education 590 North Vermont Avenue Los Angeles, CA 90004	JEP	Jewish Education Press 426 West 58th Street New York, NY 10019
BLP	Ben-Lar Productions 22 East 17th Street New York, NY 10003	JLC	Jewish Labor Committee 25 East 78th Street New York, NY 10021
CM	Classroom Materials 93 Myrtle Drive Great Neck, NY 11021	JMS	Jewish Media Service 15 East 26th Street New York, NY 10010
CT	Contemporary Films 330 West 42nd Street New York, NY 10036	KSU	KSU Teleproductions Kent State University C-105, Music and Speech Building Kent, OH 44242
EHE	Embassy Home Entertainment 1901 Avenue of the Stars Los Angeles, CA 90067	LCA	Learning Corporation of America 1350 Avenue of the Americas New York, NY 10019

Symbol	Distributor's Name and Address	Symbol	Distributor's Name and Address
LF	Landmark Films Incorporated 3450 Slade Run Drive Falls Church, VA 22042	SSSS	Social Studies School Service 10000 Culver Boulevard, Department JO P.O. Box 802 Culver City, CA 90230
MSU	Michigan State University Audiovisual Department East Lansing, MI 48823	SWC	Simon Wiesenthal Center Yeshiva University of Los Angeles 9760 West Pico Boulevard Los Angeles, CA 90035
NDR	NDR International P.O. Box 68618 Indianapolis, IN 46268	ZV	Zenger Video 10200 Jefferson Boulevard, Room 902 P.O. Box 802 Culver City, CA 90232-0802
PBS	PBS Video 13220 Braddock Place Alexandria, VA 22314		
RBC	RBC Films 933 North LaBrea Avenue Los Angeles, CA 90038		

Answers to Chapter Reviews

THE INTRODUCTION

EXERCISE 1—Reviewing Key Points

1. (a) To rule the world, to enslave all conquered peoples, and to annihilate Europe's Jews.

   (b) His armies conquered almost all of Europe, enslaved millions, and killed two thirds of European Jewry.

2. Living in all parts of the world, Jews were a minority religious group. Persecuted for their religious beliefs and behaviors, they fled from place to place. Religious bias followed them everywhere.

3. Because Jews rejected the religious beliefs and deities of all others, fearful, superstitious non-Jews blamed them for every natural disaster or social ill.

4. (a) Religious anti-Semitism—hateful attitudes toward Judaism as a religion.

   (b) Political anti-Semitism—using Jews as scapegoats for political and economic problems in order to gain political power.

   (c) Racist anti-Semitism—calling Jews a physically and mentally inferior group of people.

EXERCISE 2—Matching

PART A		PART B	
1. B	6. A	1. F	6. G
2. H	7. G	2. C	7. D
3. C	8. D	3. E	8. J
4. J	9. I	4. I	9. H
5. F	10. E	5. B	10. A

CHAPTER ONE

EXERCISE 1—Reviewing Key Points

1. Class discussion

2. By becoming baptized, a Jew was fully accepted into the Christian community.

3. Out to "rescue" the Holy Land from Muslim nonbelievers, the Crusaders killed Jews—like the Muslims, non-Christians—along their path.

4. Laws forbade them to own property, to be farmers, or to be in any profession. These jobs were all that were left. The nobility made Jews their tax collectors.

5. They couldn't own land or slaves. They were experienced in trading and money matters.

6. Crusades, libels, blame for the black plague, the pogroms.

7. They were in debt to Jewish moneylenders. They wanted to confiscate Jewish money. Germany was not a nation but a scattered network of many areas, each governed by a different king.

8. The Renaissance broke down superstition. No longer the instrument of Church affairs, the state separated itself from Church policies; Church laws against Jews were no longer state laws. The Reformation led to religious tolerance of Judaism. The French Revolution brought Jewish emancipation.

9. They rejected Jewish emancipation as a "French idea."

10. They tried to become as "German" as possible in order to be accepted because they had so long been isolated.

EXERCISE 2—Matching Terms with Definitions

1. heretic	6. atheist	11. Muslim
2. Crusades	7. Judaism	12. stereotype
3. baptism	8. infidel	13. ghetto
4. Christianity	9. pagan	14. pogroms
5. blasphemy	10. polytheism	15. synagogue

EXERCISE 3—Finding Reasons

1. c   2. a   3. d   4. e   5. b

CHAPTER TWO

EXERCISE 1—Reviewing Key Points

1. Answers will vary.

2. Many Eastern Europeans who lived in the Austria-Hungarian Empire wanted their own independence and their own nations.

3. Germany. He believed Austrians who spoke German to be true Germans in every way.

4. He called Germans a master race; Eastern Europeans, a race fit for only slavery; Jews the most inferior humans.

5. He said German politicians—Jews and communists—had "stabbed Germany in the back" by forcing the winning German armies to stop fighting.

6. The nationalists and the communists.

7. Under that system, they had helped the kaiser to rule.

8. Answers will vary.

9. To "free" Germany from Jews.

EXERCISE 2—Crossword Puzzle

ACROSS

1. Joseph
5. monarchy
6. Ebert
9. Wilhelm
12. anti-Semitism
13. defeat
19. Reichwehr
21. Germany
22. Munich
23. Bolsheviks
25. Democrats
27. dodger
28. Ludendorff

DOWN

2. Austria–Hungary
3. socialism
4. free
7. racist
8. Vienna
10. Marx
11. German Workers
14. Communist
15. One
16. Hindenberg
17. republic
18. Schickelgruber
20. race
24. swastika
26. Lueger

CHAPTER THREE

EXERCISE 1—Reviewing Key Points

1. To overthrow the German democracy by destroying anti-Nazi political parties and by creating chaos to make Germans lose faith in their government's ability to keep order.

2. To take power legally by having Nazi delegates gain the majority of seats in the Reichstag.

3. The German economy improved; people had no complaints about their government.

4. A forgery that was supposedly the minutes of a worldwide meeting of Jewish elders conspiring to seize world power. Hitler had it reprinted and distributed copies to the public during his political campaigns.

5. The Gestapo, or secret police, arrested and imprisoned Jews and other Nazi "enemies." The SD, or security police, gathered intelligence information. The Einsatzgruppen, or political police, were killing squads who gunned down a million Jews in Poland and Russia. The Waften SS were military units that hunted down Jews throughout Europe.

6. No, other Europeans were also involved. Most were ordinary people.

7. In times of political and economic troubles.

8. The Great Depression of 1929.

EXERCISE 2—Giving Reasons

1. hi	6. i	11. d
2. a	7. b	12. n
3. e	8. m	13. o
4. f	9. j	14. g
5. l	10. k	15. c

EXERCISE 3—Defining Terms

1. Nazi swastika
2. "My Struggle"
3. living space

Exercise 3 (continued)

4. Nazi Germany
5. House of Representatives
6. Air Force (German)
7. Army (German)
8. Army (German)
9. Protective Guard (SS)
10. SS political police
11. the leader
12. Stormtroopers
13. a violent attempt to overthrow a government
14. German
15. German
16. a violent attempt to overthrow a government
17. the ideas of Adolf Hitler
18. a system to spread political ideas
19. Nazi secret police
20. Nazi security police

EXERCISE 4—Recognizing Information

1. a   2. d   3. d   4. d   5. b

CHAPTER FOUR

EXERCISE 1—Reviewing Key Points

1. 1,000 years (up to 1871); 47 years, 1871–1918; 15 years, 1918–1933.

2. They owned most of the land in Prussia, the largest German state; they were the commanders of the army; and they held the highest government positions.

3. Proud of their cultural heritage and their new nation, some Germans claimed Jews were not true Germans and should not be regarded as citizens.

4. Believers in this idea said German citizenship belonged only to "true German folk" those tied together by "blood" and ancient traditions and culture—not to Jews, whose "roots" and cultural heritage were different. That Jews had lived in Germany for hundreds of years did not matter.

5. Racists believed Jews who had "bad blood and bad genes" would "pollute" the blood of future German generations.

Exercise 1 (continued)

6. Because they saw anti-Semitism—popular among the masses—as an effective tool to use in getting votes.

7. They were losing their power to the cities and the factory laborers, and they blamed many of their problems on Jews, who they said controlled the cities and the labor unions.

8. They feared the competition of larger Jewish-owned department stores.

9. Class discussion.

10. Fourteen years (1919–1933).

11. The working classes. They were not a majority in the Reichstag and always had to form a coalition with other parties to run the government.

12. Communists and Nationalists. The communists wanted a communistic government like that in Russia; the Nationalists wanted a monarchy restored.

13. Inflation and depression.

14. After the depression of 1929.

15. Communists and Social Democrats.

EXERCISE 2—Recognizing Information

1. d	6. b	11. a
2. a	7. d	12. d
3. b	8. c	13. b
4. d	9. a	14. a
5. c	10. d	15. c

EXERCISE 3—Choosing the Correct Answer

1. a	6. c
2. b	7. b
3. a	8. a
4. c	9. b
5. b	10. b

CHAPTER FIVE

EXERCISE 1—Reviewing Key Points

1. They play upon the fears and prejudices of the people during troubled times; they use scapegoats; they promise cures for problems.

2. The communists.

3. That communists would take over Germany and make all wealth and private property the property of the state.

4. Jobs and bread for the workers, and decent earnings and no more debts for the middle classes.

5. He said the great German army did not lose the war but were "stabbed in the back" by German politicians.

6. He called Germans a master race, vowed to rebuild their powerful army and to make the German nation the leader of the world.

7. It was hampered by severe economic problems and the Social Democrats' inability to solve economic problems or to form a coalition to run the government.

8. They used him to destroy the communists and felt they would control him later.

9. The communists and the Social Democrats.

10. Others who feared a communist takeover if the Nazis were undermined talked him into naming Hitler chancellor.

11. He had the Reichstag set afire, blamed the communists, passed an emergency law to give the right to arrest "enemies" of the state, and jailed thousands of communists.

12. The Nationalists.

13. Their destruction was part of a bargain he made with the army commanders who promised in return to support him for president.

EXERCISE 2—Filling In the Dates

1. 1928
2. 1929
3. 1930
4. 1932

5. January 30, 1933
6. March 1933
7. June 30, 1933
8. August 2, 1934

EXERCISE 3—Matching Terms

1.	J	6.	C
2.	A	7.	F
3.	B	8.	D
4.	I	9.	G
5.	E	10.	H

CHAPTER SIX

EXERCISE I—Reviewing Key Points

1. Class discussion.

2. In preparing Germany for war, he called up millions to serve in the armed forces, to work in armaments factories, or to build highways for military transports.

3. Hitler knew the churches helped to lift the morale of the people.

4. Class discussion.

5. Class discussion.

6. He feared they might overthrow him, so he waited until all of Germany as well as the lower ranks of the armed forces were Nazified first.

7. Class discussion.

8. Ordinary prisons house criminals who have broken laws; Nazi prisons were run by criminals who imprisoned decent, law-abiding citizens accused of being "enemies" of the Nazi state.

9. Political enemies—communists, Social Democrats, and other rival political parties.

10. In 1938. They waited until Nazi propaganda and fear tactics had made pro-Jewish citizens too afraid to speak out or had persuaded others that persecution of Jews was right.

EXERCISE 2—True And False

1. 0	6. 0	11. 0
2. 0	7. +	12. 0
3. +	8. 0	13. +
4. 0	9. +	14. +
5. +	10. +	15. 0

EXERCISE 3—Completing Statements

1. autobahns
2. Dachau
3. concentration camp
4. Nazi Labor Front
5. Goebbels
6. Hitler Youth
7. transit camps
8. KZ
9. New Greater Germany
10. death camps
11. New Order
12. Third Reich
13. Kapos
14. terror
15. Gestapo
16. labor camps

CHAPTER SEVEN

EXERCISE 1—Reviewing Key Points

1. The exact date when Hitler gave the order to exterminate all of European Jews.

2. Class discussion.

3. Germans with Jewish ancestry.

4. Class discussion.

5. By annexing Austria, his homeland, the Sudetenland of Czechoslovakia, and other German-speaking areas to Germany, he created an all German-speaking state called the New Greater Germany. He seized Poland and reserved western Poland for added living space for Germans. Poland had the largest Jewish population in Europe.

6. Money for travel, a visa, and proof to a host country that he or she would not be a burden; that is, an emigrant either had to be able to be self-supporting or else relatives had to vouch for his or her care.

7. Class discussion.

Exercise I (continued)

8. Non-Jewish Germans who hated Nazis; Austrian Jews; Czechoslovakian Jews; Polish Jews; Rumanian Jews; Hungarian Jews. When immigration quotas of receiving countries quickly filled up, there was no place for them to go.

9. Class discussion.

10. 3.3 million Polish Jews compared to 525,000 German Jews.

EXERCISE 2—Matching Dates

1. D   2. C   3. B   4. E   5. A

EXERCISE 3—Filling In the Spaces

1. 100,000   6. depression
2. One   7. economy
3. 80,000   8. government
4. thousands   9. big business
5. 1 percent   10. assimilated

EXERCISE 4—Crossword Puzzle

ACROSS

1. Aryanization   21. kosher
5. Poland   22. Nuremberg
9. FDR   24. Eichmann
12. Austria   25. Nazis
13. mischlinge   26. Jews
16. Soviet   27. Munich
18. *St. Louis*   28. Gestapo
19. expelled   30. Two

DOWN

2. refugee crisis   14. First Solution
3. star   15. civil-service
4. quota   17. book burning
6. Sudetenland   18. *Sturma*
7. Evian Conference   20. White Paper
8. Palestine   23. boycott
10. Kristallnacht   24. emigrate
11. Juden   29. two

CHAPTER EIGHT

EXERCISE 1—Reviewing Key Points

1. Eastern Europe was where the vast majority of European Jews lived.

2. Yes, Polish nationalism was working against Polish Jews. Many Poles felt Jews should not be citizens of the new nation.

3. Jews were to be imprisoned in ghettos and camps only until Hitler could find a final answer to clearing Jews out of Europe altogether.

4. Western Poland was incorporated into Germany as added living space for Germans. Poles and Jews were forced to go to the Government General.

5. Class discussion.

6. They were put to forced labor in mines and factories, and other areas of the war effort and then exterminated.

7. Nearly all Jews, except for several thousand who had been transferred to labor camps for necessary labor, were dead. They either had died from starvation and overwork or had been murdered in the gas chambers.

8. They knew Jews were less likely to resist orders given by their own people. By using fear and violence, they forced Jews to be their spokesmen.

9. Denmark, Norway, Belgium, Luxembourg, Holland, France, Greece, Yugoslavia, Hungary, Bulgaria, and Rumania came under German occupation. Nazi laws against Jews were imposed in all these countries.

10. Local populations here supported their Jewish citizens. Some even resisted the anti-Jewish laws.

EXERCISE 2—Citing Differences

2. spoke their own language of Yiddish

3. sent many of their children to their own private Yiddish schools

4. had their own style of dress

5. most clung to the traditional Orthodox Judaism

6. few converted to Christianity

7. kept their own names

Exercise 2 (continued)

8. rarely intermarried with Christians

9. lived in their own Jewish communities

10. many accepted Zionism, a move to create an all-Jewish state in Palestine, as the only answer to anti-Semitism

EXERCISE 3—Making the Correct Choice

1. a	6. a	11. c	16. b	21. b
2. b	7. a	12. a	17. a	22. a
3. a	8. a	13. c	18. c	23. b
4. c	9. b	14. b	19. c	24. c
5. c	10. a	15. a	20. c	25. c
				26. a

CHAPTER NINE

EXERCISE 1—Reviewing Key Points

1. They were to shoot unarmed civilians—Jews and other "political enemies."

2. The Einsatzgruppen were a group of "average" people.

3. Some helped Nazis to hunt down Jews.

4. As part of Hitler's Euthanasia Institute, Nazis murdered tens (or hundreds) of thousands of "undesirable" Germans in Nazi Germany between 1933–1941.

5. Class discussion.

6. Class discussion.

7. Every single day, 12,000 Jews were killed and cremated, and their belongings were sorted and distributed.

8. They were closest to the gas chamber; Nazis had tight control of the government.

9. Eichmann and his teams moved into one country at a time, deported "foreign" Jews first, then the rest.

10. How much control Nazis had of a government, and the degree of local interference or cooperation in the deportation process.

Exercise 1 (continued)

11. Nazis did not occupy their countries nor did they control their governments.

12. Not many countries were willing to receive the refugees.

13. Seven million. Many thousands of Gypsies, Russian POW's, political prisoners, Christian clergy and lay leaders, Jehovah's Witnesses, Freemasons, Poles, and others.

14. They were the last to be deported, the war was almost over, and they could have been saved.

EXERCISE 2—Crossword Puzzle

ACROSS

1. trickery
2. genocide
11. Einsatzgruppen
13. Wannsee
14. six million
15. six
17. Russia
18. gas vans
19. deport
21. Poland
23. Eichmann
24. gas chambers
27. Odessa
29. Finland
30. resettled
31. Denmark
32. Albania
34. experiments
35. Bulgaria
36. left

DOWN

1. three
3. Chelmno
4. Euthanasia
5. Western
6. Hungarian Jews
7. Final Solution
8. Babi Yar
9. Zyklon B
10. Auschwitz
12. selection
16. Maidanek
20. Transnistria
22. asocial
25. alive
26. Himmler
28. Italians
30. right
33. cattle

EXERCISE 3—True And False

1. 0	8. +	15. +
2. +	9. +	16. 0
3. 0	10. 0	17. +
4. 0	11. 0	18. 0
5. +	12. +	19. +
6. 0	13. +	20. +
7. +	14. +	

CHAPTER TEN

EXERCISE 1—Reviewing Key Points

1. Class discussion.

2. They wanted to protect their families; they had no weapons; they had no outside support; they were weak and sick.

3. When Jews needed help the most, they were not well organized; and because resistance groups were nationalistic, Jewish victims didn't qualify for their help.

4. Class discussion.

5. When they learned that death was their true fate.

6. After the Warsaw fighters attacked the Nazis the first time in January 1943.

7. Class discussion.

8. Hope that Nazis would lose the war and that an Allied victory would free them.

9. First, they welcomed the Germans as liberators from hated communist rulers; and second, some were also anti-Semitic.

10. No, they resisted the Nazis in many ways.

EXERCISE 2—Giving Reasons

1. J	6. C	11. L
2. I	7. F	12. K
3. O	8. E	13. B
4. H	9. D	14. N
5. G	10. M	15. A

EXERCISE 3—Matching Terms

1. I	3. F	5. H	7. C	9. J
2. B	4. A	6. D	8. E	10. G

CHAPTER ELEVEN

EXERCISE 1—Reviewing Key Points

1. To hide evidence of their crimes.

2. It was violent and bizarre. He still blamed Jews for his failures.

3. Answers will vary.

4. The 11 million murdered victims were unarmed civilians and were not living in combat zones.

5. Two thirds of Europe's Jewish population was murdered, Nazis made special laws against them, organized their mass murder, even killed 1.5 million of their children.

6. Many people knew about the Nazi persecution of Jews but did little or nothing to help them.

7. Class discussion.

8. The free world countries were not living under the harsh Nazi rulers, and they had the power to stop them.

9. Through an Allied victory.

10. Class discussion.

11. Class discussion.

EXERCISE 2—Crossword Puzzle

ACROSS

1. suicide
2. West Germany
4. Allied Control Commission
8. Bermuda
12. free world
13. JDC
15. Eva Braun
16. Gypsies
17. D-Day
18. V-E Day
19. Slavs
20. East
21. Holocaust
22. prejudice

DOWN

1. Stalingrad
2. War Refugee Board
3. Geneva
5. law
6. children
7. saved
9. bomb
10. eleven
11. twelve
14. Jews

CHAPTER TWELVE

EXERCISE 1—Reviewing Key Points

1. Jewish refugees, trying to escape Nazi terror, would have had a place to emigrate to safety.

2. The White Paper not only strictly limited Jewish immigration into Palestine for four years but also was to bar Jewish immigration altogether after five years.

3. They widely supported payment. They were very sympathetic to the televised drama.

4. Tens of thousands of records proved they were guilty.

5. Yes.

6. Clear evidence of their crimes must be given before they can be deported. Many witnesses of their crimes are now dead.

7. 1975.

8. Relegated more funds and more investigators and lawyers to search for criminals and made the Nazi search team part of the Criminal Division of the United States Justice Department.

9. Adolf Eichmann. He was tried in Israel in the presence of many of his victims.

10. Hitler and his Nazis were master destroyers. They contributed nothing to the world—only evil and bloodshed.

EXERCISE 2—Matching People

1. J	6. F
2. G	7. I
3. E	8. C
4. H	9. A
5. D	10. B

CHAPTER THIRTEEN

EXERCISE 1—Reviewing Key Points

1. Class discussion.

2. They are Arabs who fled Israel during the War of Independence in 1948. Israel will not allow them to return. The Palestinians want a part of Israel as their own homeland.

3. Class discussion.

4. They arrest them for crimes against the state, stage public trials, then use them as the cause of all evils in Russian society.

5. Class discussion.

6. Russia has aided the Arabs in the wars by supplying weapons and military advice, but Israel has won the wars. As a result, Soviet anger was directed toward Russian-Jewish citizens.

7. An economic crisis. They are prepared to leave the country.

8. Class discussion.

9. Nationalism in America has not favored one particular ethnic group and thus has not singled out Jews as different.

10. They worry about the safety and security of friends and relatives in Israel and about the reaction of the American public and the effect on the economy in case of another Arab oil freeze. They worry that such calamities may trigger anti-Semitism here and abroad.

11. Many fascists, old Nazis, and neo-Nazis who live there have attacked Jewish communities.

EXERCISE 2—True and False

1. 0	6. +	11. +	16. 0
2. +	7. +	12. +	17. 0
3. 0	8. 0	13. +	18. 0
4. +	9. +	14. +	19. +
5. 0	10. 0	15. +	20. +

Bibliography

Bauer, Yehuda. *The Holocaust in Historical Perspective*. Seattle: University of Washington Press, 1978.

Bauer, Yehuda, and Nili Keren. *A History of the Holocaust*. New York: Franklin Watts, 1982.

Berenbaum, Michael. *The World Must Know: A History of the Holocaust as Told in the United States Holocaust Memorial Museum*. Boston: Little Brown, 1993.

_____, ed. *A Mosaic of Victims: Non-Jews Persecuted and Murdered by the Nazis*. New York: New York University Press, 1990.

Dawidowicz, Lucy. *A Holocaust Reader*. New York: Behrman, 1976.

_____. *The War Against the Jews*. New York: Holt, Rinehart & Winston, 1975.

Drew, Margaret A. *Annotated Bibliography*. Washington, DC: United States Holocaust Memorial Museum.

Facing History and Ourselves: Audiovisual Resources. Brookline, MA: Facing History and Ourselves.

Ferencz, Benjamin. *Less Than Slaves*. Cambridge: Harvard University Press, 1979.

Fisher, Julius. *Transnistria: The Forgotten Cemetery*. South Brunswick: T. Yoseloff, 1969.

Gilbert, Martin. *The Holocaust*. Israel: Jerusalem Post, 1978.

_____. *The Macmillan Atlas of the Holocaust*. New York: DaCapo Press, 1984.

Hilberg, Raul. *The Destruction of the European Jews*. Chicago: Quadrangle, 1971.

_____. *Documents of Destruction*. Chicago: Quadrangle, 1971.

_____. *Perpetrators, Victims, Bystanders: The Jewish Catastrophe, 1933–1945*. New York: HarperCollins, 1992.

The Holocaust (booklet). Jerusalem: Yad Vashem, 1977.

The Holocaust, A Teacher Resource (booklet). Philadelphia: The School District of Philadelphia, 1977.

Holocaust: Israel Pocket Library. Jerusalem: Keter, 1974. (Compiled from material originally published in the *Encyclopedia Judaica.*)

Kaplan, Chaim A. *The Warsaw Diary of Chaim A. Kaplan.* New York: Collier Books, 1965.

Korman, Gerd, ed. *Hunter and Hunted: Human History of the Holocaust.* New York: Viking Press, 1973.

Lansmann, Claude. *Shoah: An Oral History of the Holocaust.* New York: Pantheon, 1987.

Levin, Nora. *The Holocaust: The Destruction of European Jewry 1933–1945.* Harper & Row, 1968.

Marrus, Michael. *The Holocaust in History.* New York: New American Library/Dutton, 1989.

Meltzer, Milton. *Never to Forget, the Jews of the Holocaust.* New York: Harper & Row, 1976.

Mokotoff, Gary, and Sallyann A. Sack. *Where Once We Walked: A Guide to the Jewish Communities Destroyed in the Holocaust.* Teaneck, NJ: Avotaynu, 1991.

Muffs, Judith Herschlag, and Dennis B. Klein, eds. *The Holocaust in Books and Films: A Selected Annotated List.* International Center for Holocaust Studies, Anti-Defamation League of B'nai B'rith. New York, Hippocrene Books, 1986.

Newman, Judith S. *In the Hell of Auschwitz.* New York: Exposition Press, 1963.

Nyiszli, Miklos. *Eichmann's Inferno: Auschwitz.* Greenwich: Fawcett, 1960.

Pilch, Judah. *The Jewish Catastrophe in Europe.* New York: American Association for Jewish Education, 1968.

Poliakov, Leon. *Harvest of Hate.* Westport: Greenwood Press, 1954.

Read, Anthony, and David Fisher. *Kristallnacht: The Tragedy of the Nazi Night of Terror.* New York: Random House, 1989.

Rubin, Arnold. *The Evil That Men Do.* New York: Messner, 1978.

Sabol, Macia. *Annotated Videography.* Washington, DC: United States Holocaust Memorial Museum.

Trunk, Isaiah. *Judenrat.* New York: Macmillan, 1972.

Tushnet, Leonard. *The Pavement of Hell.* New York: Martin's Press, 1972.

Yahil, Leni. *The Fate of European Jewry, 1932–1945.* New York: Oxford, 1990.

DEPORTATION, EMIGRATION, AND RESCUE
DURING THE HOLOCAUST

Avriel, Ehud. *Open the Gates!* New York: Atheneum, 1975.

Bauer, Yehuda. *Flight and Rescue: Brichah.* New York: Random House, 1970.

Chary, Frederick. *The Hungarian Jews and the Final Solution.* Pittsburgh: Pittsburgh University Press, 1972.

Druks, Herbert. "Western Complacency During the Holocaust" (sound recording). Danbury: Grolier Educational Corporation, 1978.

Fein, Helen. *Accounting for Genocide.* New York: Free Press, 1979.

Feingold, Henry: *The Politics of Rescue; The Roosevelt Administration and the Holocaust.* Brunswick: Rutgers University Press, 1970.

Friedman, Philip. *Their Brothers' Keepers.* New York: Crown, 1978.

Friedman, Saul. *No Haven for the Oppressed.* Detroit: Wayne State University Press, 1973.

Goldberger, Leo, ed. *The Rescue of Danish Jews: Moral Courage Under Stress.* New York: New York University Press, 1987.

Gutman, Yisrael, ed. *Rescue Attempts During the Holocaust.* Jerusalem: Yad Vashem, 1977.

Lavai, Jeno. *Hungarian Jews and the Papacy.* London: Sands, 1968.

Morse, Arthur. *While Six Million Died.* New York: Hart, 1968.

Rittner, Carol and Sondra Meyers, eds. *The Courage to Care: Rescuers of Jews During the Holocaust.* New York: New York University Press, 1989.

Stadtler, Bea. *The Holocaust*. New York: Behrman, 1968.

JEWISH RESISTANCE DURING THE HOLOCAUST

Ainsztein, Reuben, *Jewish Resistance in Nazi-Occupied Eastern Europe*. New York: Barnes & Noble, 1974.

Barkai, Meyer. *The Fighting Ghettos*. Philadelphia: J.B. Lippincott, 1962.

Bauer, Yehuda. *The Jewish Emergence from Powerlessness*. Toronto: University of Toronto Press, 1979.

Garlinski, Josef. *Fighting Auschwitz*. New York: Fawcett, 1976.

Hersey, John. *The Wall*. New York: Doubleday, 1968.

Krasowski, Shmuel. *The War of the Doomed: Jewish Armed Resistance in Poland, 1942–1944*. New York: Holmes & Meier, 1984.

Kren, George. *The Holocaust and the Crisis of Human Behavior*. New York: Holmes & Meier, 1979.

Langbein, Hermann. *Against All Hope: Resistance in Nazi Concentration Camps, 1938–1945,* trans. Henry Zohn. New York: Paragon House, 1993.

Mark, Ber. *Uprising in the Warsaw Ghetto*. New York: Schocken, 1975.

Steinberg, Lucien. *Not As a Lamb*. Fainborough, England: Saxon House, 1974.

Suhl, Yuri. *They Fought Back*. New York: Schocken, 1975.

Trunk, Isaiah. *Jewish Responses to Nazi Persecution*. New York: Stein & Day, 1978.

RAMIFICATIONS OF THE HOLOCAUST

Aymar, Brandt, and Edward Sagarin. *Laws and Trials That Created History*. New York: Crown, 1974.

Blum, Howard. *Wanted! The Search for Nazis in America*. New York: Quadrangle, 1977.

Conot, Robert E. *Justice at Nuremberg*. New York: Carroll and Graf, 1984.

Gribble, Leonard. *Justice?* New York: Abelard-Schuman, 1970.

Klarsfeld, Beate. *Wherever They May Be!* New York: Vanguard Press, 1975.

McKown, Robin. *7 Famous Trials.* New York: Crown, 1974.

Murphy, Brendan. *The Butcher of Lyon.* New York: Empire Books, 1983.

Pearlman, Moshe. *The Capture and Trial of Adolf Eichmann.* London: Weidenfeld, 1961.

Ryan, Allan A., Jr. *Quiet Neighbors: Prosecuting Nazi War Criminals in America.* New York: Harcourt Brace Jovanovich, 1984.

Stevenson, William. *The Bormann Brotherhood.* New York: Harcourt Brace, 1973.

Wiesenthal, Simon. "Nazi Hunter" (sound recording). New York: Grolier Educational Corporation, 1977.

HITLER AND NAZI GERMANY

Arendt, Hanna. *Origins of Totalitarianism.* New York: Harcourt Brace & World, 1966.

Barnett, Corelli, ed. *Hitler's Generals.* New York: Quill/William Morrow, 1989.

Bullock, Alan. *Hitler, A Study in Tyranny.* New York: Harper & Row, 1962.

Conway, John S. *The Nazi Persecution of the Churches.* New York: Basic Books, 1968.

Devaney, John. *Hitler.* New York: G.P. Putnam's Sons, 1978.

Dicks, Henry. *Licensed Mass Murder.* New York: Basic Books, 1972.

Elliott, B.J. *Hitler and Germany.* New York: McGraw-Hill, 1968.

Fest, Joachim. *Hitler.* New York: Harcourt, Brace, Jovanovich, 1974.

Gellately, Robert. *The Gestapo and German Society: Enforcing Racial Policy.* New York: Oxford University Press, 1992.

Gervasi, Frank. *Adolf Hitler,* Volumes I and II. New York: Hawthorn, 1974.

Goldston, Robert. *The Life and Death of Nazi Germany.* New York: Bobbs-Merrill, 1967.

Grunberger, Richard. *Hitler's SS*. New York: Delacourt Press, 1971.

Hitler, Adolf. *Mein Kampf*. Boston: Houghton Mifflin, 1943.

Klein, Mina C., and Arthur. *Hitler's Hang-ups*. New York: E.P. Dutton, 1976.

Langer, Walter. *The Mind of Adolf Hitler*. New York: Basic Books, 1972.

Mosse, George. *The Crisis of German Ideology*. New York: Grosset & Dunlap, 1964.

_____. *Nazi Culture*. New York: Grosset & Dunlap, 1966.

Noakes, J., and G. Prodham, eds. *Nazism: A History in Documents and Eyewitness Accounts, 1919–1945* (2 vols.). New York: Schocken, 1990.

Pinson, Koppel S. *Modern Germany: Its History and Civilization*. New York: Macmillan, 1966.

Procktor, Richard. *Nazi Germany*. New York: Holt, Rinehart & Winston, 1970.

Raab, Earl. *The Anatomy of Nazism* (pamphlet). New York: Anti-Defamation League of B'nai B'rith, 1961.

Shirer, William. *The Rise and Fall of the Third Reich*. New York: Simon & Schuster, 1960.

Snyder, Louis. *Hitler and Nazism*. New York: Bantam, 1967.

Smith, Gene. *The Horns of the Moon*. New York: Charterhouse, 1973.

Spielvogel, Jackson J. *Hitler and Nazi Germany: A History*. Englewood Cliffs, NJ: Prentice Hall, 1988.

Thalmann, Rita, and Emmanuel Feinermann. *Crystal Night*. New York: Coward, McCann & Geoghegan, 1974.

Trevor-Roper, H.R. *The Last Days of Hitler*. London: Collier, 1962.

Waite, Robert, ed. *Hitler and Nazi Germany* (pamphlet). Hinsdale: Dryden Press, 1969.

JEWISH HISTORY

Barnavi, Eli, ed. *A Historical Atlas of the Jewish People: From the Time of the Patriarchs to the Present.* New York: Knopf, 1992.

Baron, Salo W. *A Social and Religious History of the Jews.* New York: Columbia University Press, 1993.

Eban, Abba, and David Bamberger. *My People: Abba Eban's History of the Jewish People.* New York: Behrman, 1979.

Gilbert, Martin. *The Atlas of Jewish History.* New York: Morrow, 1993.

Goldston, Robert. *Next Year in Jerusalem; A Short History of Zionism.* Boston: The Atlantic Monthly Press, 1978.

Johnson, Paul. *A History of the Jews.* New York: HarperCollins, 1988.

Keller, Werner. *Diaspora.* New York: Harcourt, Brace, Jovanovich, 1971.

Mosse, George. *Jews and Non-Jews in Eastern Europe, 1918–1945.* New York: John Wiley & Sons, 1974.

_____. *German Jews.* New York: Fertig, 1970.

Roth, Cecil. *A History of the Jews.* New York: Schocken, 1961.

Sachar, Howard. *The Course of Modern Jewish History.* New York: Dell, 1958.

Schweitzer, Frederick. *The History of the Jews Since the First Century* A.D. New York: Macmillan, 1971.

Shapiro, Harry L. *The Jewish People, A Biological Survey.* Westport: Greenwood Press, 1960.

Trepp, Leo. *A History of the Jewish Experience.* New York: Behrman, 1962.

ANTI-SEMITISM

Abel, Ernest. *The Roots of Anti-Semitism.* London: Associated University Presses, 1975.

Abram, Leon. *The Jewish Question.* New York: Pathfinder Press, 1970.

Allport, Gordon. *Some Roots of Prejudice.* New York: American Jewish Congress, 1946.

Arendt, Hanna. *Anti-Semitism.* New York: Harcourt Brace, 1968.

Bankier, David. *The Germans and the Final Solution: Public Opinion under Nazism.* Cambridge, MA: Blackwell Publishers, 1992.

Blitz, Samuel. *Nationalism and Anti-Semitism in Modern Europe.* Pittsburgh: University of Pittsburgh Press, 1927.

Cohn, Norman. *Warrant for Genocide, The Myth of the Jewish World Conspiracy and* Protocols of the Elders of Zion. New York: Harper & Row, 1967.

Cuperman, Pedro. *Argentina; The Genesis of a Prejudice.* New York: New York University Press, 1977.

Flannery, Edward. *The Anguish of the Jews.* New York: Macmillan, 1965.

Forster, Arnold, and Benjamin Epstein. *The New Anti-Semitism.* New York: McGraw-Hill, 1974.

Gilman, Sander L., ed. *Anti-Semitism in Times of Crisis.* New York: New York University Press, 1991.

Gordon, Sarah. *Hitler, Germans, and the "Jewish Question."* Princeton, NJ: Princeton University Press, 1984.

Grosser, Paul, and Edwin Halperin. *The Causes and Effects of Anti-Semitism.* New York: Philosophical Library, 1978.

Hay, Malcolm. *The Foot of Pride.* Boston: Beacon Press, 1951.

Korey, William. *The Soviet Cage; Anti-Semitism in Russia.* New York: Viking Press, 1973.

Long, Emil. *2000 Years.* New York: Exposition Press, 1953.

Massing, Paul. *Rehearsal for Destruction: A Study of Political Anti-Semitism in Imperial Germany.* New York: Harper & Row, 1949.

Morais, Vamberto. *A Short History of Anti-Semitism.* New York: W.W. Norton, 1976.

Mosse, George. *Germans and Jews.* New York: Fertig, 1970.

Parks, James. *Anti-Semitism: A Concise World History.* Chicago Quadrangle, 1964.

Pinson, K.S., ed. *Essays on Anti-Semitism.* New York: Conference on Jewish Relations, 1946.

Poliakow, Leon. *The History of Anti-Semitism,* Volumes I and II. New York: Vanguard Press, 1965.

Pulzer, P.G.J. *The Rise of Political Anti-Semitism in Germany and Austria.* New York: John Wiley & Sons, 1964.

Sartre, Jean-Paul. *Anti-Semite and Jew.* New York: Schocken, 1948.

Schorach, Ismar. *Jewish Reactions to German Anti-Semitism 1870–1914.* New York: Columbia University Press, 1972.

Tal, Uriel. *Christians and Jews in Germany.* Ithaca: Cornell University Press, 1975.

Trachtenberg, Joshua. *The Devil and the Jews: Medieval Conception of the Jew.* New Haven: Yale University Press, 1943.

Valentin, Hugo. *Anti-Semitism Historically and Critically Examined.* London: Gollancz, 1936.

Voronel, Aleksander, and Vicktor Yakhot, eds. *I Am a Jew: Essays on Jewish Identity in the Soviet Union* (pamphlet). Moscow: Academic Committee on Soviet Jewry and the Anti-Defamation League, 1974.

_____. *Jewishness Rediscovered* (pamphlet). Moscow: Academic Committee on Soviet Jewry and the Anti-Defamation League, 1974.

HISTORY OF WORLD WAR I AND WORLD WAR II

Black, Cyril E. *Our World History.* Boston: Ginn, 1965.

Dupuy, Trevor N. *European Resistance Movements.* New York: Franklin Watts, 1965.

Feder, Bernard. *Viewpoints in World History.* New York: American Book Company, 1968.

Leckie, Robert. *Delivered from Evil: The Saga of World War II—The First Complete One-Volume History.* New York: HarperCollins, 1988.

_____. *The Story of World War II.* New York: Random House, 1964.

Roselle, Daniel. *A World History.* Boston: Ginn, 1969.

Sears, Stephen W., ed. *World War II: The Best of American Heritage* (American Heritage Library). Boston: Houghton Mifflin, 1993.

Index

A

abstract art, Hitler and, 80
Adenauer, Konrad, 196
agriculture, slavery and, 3
Albania
    Italian occupation of, 146
    Jews in, 111
    Nazi resistance in, 145–146
Alexander II, Czar, 112
Alexander III, Czar, 112
allegiance, oath of, 69
Allied Control Commission, 175, 195
Allies, 52, 55
    Antonescu bows to, 147
    blockade of, 182, 184
    espionage of, 179
    hope for victory of, 160
    Jewish soldiers as members of, 166
    liberation of Nazi camps and, 176
    Normandy landing of, 175
    warnings of punishment by, 146, 182, 195
Alsace-Lorraine, 52, 82
America
    declares war on Japan, 140
    discovery of, 9
    Nazi war criminals in, 197
    supplies war planes to Israel, 212
American Civil Liberties Union (ACLU), 202
American Joint Distribution Committee (JDC), 83, 184
Amsterdam, 200
ancestry, Jewish, 95
Anielewicz, Mordechai, 163, 164
annexation, 82
anti-Jewish
    feelings, 211
        Greek and Roman, 1
    laws, 2, 3, 93–94, 125
        enforcement of, 180
        in Poland, 114
    resentment, 5
anti-Semitism, 3, 6, 23, 66, 211
    American, 100, 217

assimilation and, 114
Catholic Church tries to erase religious, 196
in Cuba, 101
European, 179
in former Soviet Union, 213
German, 48–49
    as political movement, 49
    in schools, 81
    today, 216
Herzl's theory on, 193
Jewish optimism regarding, 48
of Martin Luther, 10
new wave of, 51
in pamphlets, 24
partisans and, during World War II, 165
in Poland, 112
pressure groups and, 183
racist, 12
religious
    death of, 12
    in Poland, 114–115
resistance to, in Western Europe, 125
in Russia, 215
    outlawed, 138
    violent, 214
waning of, 9
in Western Europe, 161
Antonescu, Ion, 147
Arab(s), 193
    birth of Israel and, 211
    citizens of Israel, 212
    community in Argentina, 215
    embargo, 217
    hostility, 194
    Jewish refugees and, 101
    oil, 213
    terrorists, 202
Arafat, Yasir, 212
archive, 121
Argentina, 199
    anti-Semitism in, 215
armaments, Jewish lack of, 159, 163
armistice, 51, 52